W9-CUA-338

A
writer's
guide to
literature

A writer's guide to literature

WALTER J. De MORDAUNT
California State College at Los Angeles

McGraw-Hill Book Company

NEW YORK   ST. LOUIS   SAN FRANCISCO   TORONTO   LONDON   SYDNEY

To Jane and Michael

Library of Congress Catalog Card Number 64–8273

Preface

THIS BOOK is designed to guide the college student through some of his problems in literary analysis and critical writing. More specifically, the text relates the techniques of literary investigation to the practical problems of organizing and developing a critical essay. Both beginning and advanced students in composition and literature should find aid and advice here. The emphasis is first upon the simpler forms of interpretative writing, then upon deeper analysis and the writing of various kinds of literary critiques, and finally upon background and evaluative studies. The order is not fixed, and since the chapters are self-contained, the instructor may skip around in the book at will.

Each of the four parts of the book is intended to do a different job of instruction. Part One, written directly to the student, focuses upon planning and writing interpretative, analytical, and critical compositions. Part Two, "A Checklist of Grammar and Mechanics," with its correction key, provides the symbols and references needed for marking and correcting errors. Part Three, "A Glossary of

655880

Literary Terms," is also written with the student writer in mind. Here, the working tools for literary analysis are set forth in definitions and discussions which often include suggestions for writing papers. Part Four, "Points of Departure," is composed of five groups of statements by well-known literary critics and commentators. Separate sections are devoted to the definition and discussion of poetry, the drama, novel, short story, and essay. The student writer is thus provided with a background in basic literary theory for the particular genre of literature he is studying.

In all, the book aims to be the only companion text needed for a course in composition or literature in which papers or examinations are important teaching devices. For the literature itself, the instructor may draw upon the vast range of inexpensive paperbacks; he need not concern himself that these are not always college or textbook editions with extensive editorial apparatus.

The book does not attempt to instruct the student in the writing of poems, short stories, or other literary forms exclusive of the essay; rather, it attempts to lead him into an appreciation of literature and to a capability of expressing that appreciation, mainly in expository prose.

For the beginning freshman, several writing projects are described (in the first part of Chapter 5) in which the student may use literary models for papers about his personal experiences. The instructor who wishes to ignore this section, however, may do so without damage to the main plan of the book. Thus, in the second semester freshman course, for instance, the instructor may wish to begin with other writing projects.

As far as possible, the book is arranged in an order of increasing difficulty. In support of this arrangement, the various exercises in the separate chapters provide material for class discussion, for in-class writing projects, for themes written out of class, and for self-help. In composition, instructions for personal-experience themes and early interpretative themes (both in Chapter 5) are followed by writing projects in literary analysis (Chapter 8); background studies and evaluative critiques (Chapter 9); self-help and class projects like the précis, the literary report, and the paraphrase of a poem (Chapter 10); and finally a discussion of the techniques of writing essay examinations (Chapter 11). These sections are interspersed with exercises and discussions of methods of analysis and writing. Notable here are the analyses of hypothetical student themes at the end of Chapter 3, the strategies for writing literary critiques in Chapter 6, and the sample student analysis and explication in Chapter 8.

Discussions of pitfalls constitute part of the instructions, and the student is shown why some kinds of writing about literature are more successful than others. The main approach is to help him gain the literary skills needed for mature discussion of literature. With these skills, he should be enabled to write the papers that his instructor can read, if not always with pleasure, then at least with sympathy and interest.

It is impossible to name all those who in one way or another have contributed to the making of this book. Where specific ideas of literary critics have been used, particular credit is given.

Though the author has attempted to avoid a limited rationale, the groundwork of particular critics has necessarily prepared the way for the advice and suggestions here. The reader will be aware that an emphasis is placed upon the techniques of close reading and analysis of the details of literature. This emphasis is derived from the teachings of critics like Cleanth Brooks and Robert Penn Warren, in *Understanding Poetry;* I. A. Richards, in *Principles of Literary Criticism* and *Practical Criticism;* William Empson, in *Some Versions of Pastoral* and *Seven Types of Ambiguity;* Richard Blackmur, in *Language as Gesture;* John Crowe Ransom, in *The World's Body;* Yvor Winters, in *In Defense of Reason;* Kenneth Burke, in works like *A Grammar of Motives* and *The Philosophy of Literary Form;* and William K. Wimsatt and Monroe

Beardsley, in *The Verbal Icon*. These critics have fostered a general philosophy of literature exemplified in textbooks like Laurence Perrine's *Sound and Sense* and John Ciardi's *How Does a Poem Mean?*, whose kinship to the present book may be felt. In the "Glossary of Literary Terms," the influence of the Thrall-Hibbard-Holman *Handbook to Literature* is to be found occasionally.

It is the author's intention, however, for his book to perform a service that is distinct from those in all these sources. In general, the author believes it would be a mistake, in a book on the basic skills of literary interpretation, to send freshmen and sophomores to difficult works of literary criticism; yet many of these books have much to offer when applied practically.

Although specific citation of indebtedness is made whenever possible in the text, the author wishes to acknowledge a debt of gratitude to all his teachers, both those he has known personally and those he has only studied in books.

Walter J. De Mordaunt

Contents

four   Points of departure

part one

Writing literary essays and examinations

one

Reading and analyzing works of literature

THIS IS a guidebook to help you write about literature. Though the book is centered on your writing problems, this introductory chapter is devoted mainly to showing you how to read and analyze specific works of literature. Early in your college career—the earlier the better—you will begin to realize that serious reading must precede your other efforts. Your chances of producing a college-level composition would be limited drastically if you wrote from vague, sketchy, or incomplete knowledge of the subject matter. Your best discussion of literature should grow from your best reading, just as a plant grows vigorously from fertile soil. To cultivate this soil for your writing is the main function of this book. To keep many kinds of weeds out of your written composition— for example, irrelevancy, oversimplification, vagueness—requires first some specific guidelines and suggestions for reading. You may find some of these helps in the following sample analysis.

ANALYZING A SAMPLE PIECE OF LITERATURE:
BROWNING'S "MY LAST DUCHESS"

To understand some typical problems in studying a work of literature, read over the following poem by Robert Browning in two ways. First, skim the poem for its story and for what you can discover about the speaker. Second, read it again—several times—for details.

MY LAST DUCHESS

Ferrara

That's my last Duchess painted on the wall,   1
Looking as if she were alive. I call
That piece a wonder, now: Frà Pandolf's hands
Worked busily a day, and there she stands.
Will 't please you sit and look at her? I said   5
"Frà Pandolf" by design, for never read
Strangers like you that pictured countenance,
The depth and passion of its earnest glance,
But to myself they turned (since none puts by
The curtain I have drawn for you, but I)   10
And seemed as they would ask me, if they durst,— *arrogancy*
How such a glance came there; so, not the first
Are you to turn and ask thus. Sir, 'twas not
Her husband's presence only, called that spot
Of joy into the Duchess' cheek: perhaps   15
Frà Pandolf chanced to say "Her mantle laps
Over my lady's wrist too much," or "Paint
Must never hope to reproduce the faint
Half-flush that dies along her throat." Such stuff
Was courtesy, she thought, and cause enough   20
For calling up that spot of joy. She had
A heart—how shall I say?—too soon made glad,
Too easily impressed; she liked whate'er
She looked on, and her looks went everywhere.
Sir, 'twas all one! My favor at her breast,   25
The dropping of the daylight in the West,

"IN–READING" AND SUPERFICIAL READING

At this point, you should be warned of two serious pitfalls in the way you proceed with your reading. First, you should at all costs avoid reading into the literature ideas that the author did not put there. No matter what kind of subject matter you read, you will find need for this caution at one time or another. Especially when you have to write about your reading you may often be tempted into such irrelevancies, in order to support the points in your essay. In this poem, for instance, you could err by making up a story about the Duke's domestic life that is not necessarily expressed or implied in the poem itself. You might commit this fault more or less unconsciously in order to illustrate, for instance, that the Duke could not abide his last Duchess.

For example, you might say that the Duke murdered the Duchess because she did not obey his commands. It is true that such a reading is left open by the lines:

> . . . I gave commands;
> Then all smiles stopped together. There she stands
> As if alive . . . .

Nowhere, however, does the Duke confess himself a murderer. Thus, you would be unconsciously falsifying the Duke's character if you said that the poem states unequivocally that the Duke murdered his Duchess. Also, you would be losing sight of one of the most interesting subtleties in the poem: the idea that the Duke is arrogant enough not to be afraid to imply to the envoy that he has killed his last wife. This more adequate reading permits you to observe both that the Duke *may be* (not simply "is") a murderer and that his future wife had best heed his commands, lest her end be as disastrous as that of the lady pictured on the wall.

The other pitfall besides fallacious in-reading is to fail to read deeply enough. This flaw results from getting the general idea of the literature but neglecting the details. In committing this error

[handwritten margin note: no evidence true duke killed duchess]

you would both oversimplify the literature and fail to understand and appreciate the relationships between its parts. To avoid this superficiality is as much a matter of the care you take in reading as of your native intelligence. In the Browning poem, for instance, you would notice even on first reading that the first and the last of the poem are devoted to descriptions of a painting and a sculpture. But in your later study, unless you ponder these parts carefully, you may fail to see their full bearing on the rest of the poem. Certainly, you would see the Duke's arrogant, contemptuous nature, as well as his pride in fancying himself a connoisseur of art. Unless you perceived some of the spirit of this poem, however, you might miss one of Browning's central points: *the Duke is totally absorbed —for the first twenty lines of the poem—in enjoying the picture of a person whom he despised, in whose death he felt no regret.* Certainly, this adds a hard, inhuman touch to the Duke's character. And when you put this selfish enjoyment together with the Duke's distaste for the dead woman's cheerful lightness of heart (for instance, in accepting favors with natural graciousness), you begin to see rather deeply into his corrupt and degraded personality. The Duke's final comment about the sculpture helps to reinforce this impression. The lesson about reading here is not to rush through your study of the literature, not to assume, when you have the gist of the assignment, that you can safely neglect its details.

INTERPRETING THE DETAILS

Noticing details in proper perspective, then, is what distinguishes a good reader from a poor one. Moreover, in your writing, the difference between a good composition and a mediocre one— though both papers may be grammatically correct—is also likely to be determined by the thoroughness of your grasp of the details in your reading. Solving this problem does not require an ability to recall long lists of disconnected facts. Though you should use your memory to the fullest, especially in examinations, you will need to develop a more truly intellectual ability than simple memory. This is the faculty of synthesis, the skill of seeing the connections between facts and ideas. In your reading, you will use this skill to interpret details in the light of the general sense, the context, and the overall form of the literature.

For instance, by line 3 of Browning's poem, you should see that the Duke is extremely proud of the portrait. At line 5, the presence of a listener (who you later find is the envoy) should be clear to you; and in lines 6, 7, and 8, you should realize that the Duke is flattering the listener. The Duke assumes that the envoy appreciates "the depth and passion" in the portrait and wants to know who the artist is. At lines 9 and 10, the parenthetical remark is another clue to the Duke's habit of autocratic authority. By line 15, you should begin to see something of the Duchess's temperament; it is obvious by now, also, that the Duke and Duchess were not on the best of terms. We could continue in this way through the whole poem, adding more and more details.

Observe now how easy it would be to become lost in a forest of such details, which become thicker and thicker as the poem progresses. Within only fifteen lines, we have noted six or seven details, and it would be possible to multiply these according to the depth of the literature and the reader's perceptions of what is on the page. What is needed, then, is a principle of organization, a center of gravity whereby all these details would assume order and relative importance. For this poem and for most of your other reading assignments, you can find such a principle by stepping back from the literature and seeing some of the problems that were solved by the author. The procedure is simple, though the task itself may be difficult: what you do is to study the details in the light of the problems faced by the author. Here, you should recall your first reading of the literature and observe how the details fit into its overall structure.

STUDYING LITERARY STYLE

At some stage in nearly every reading assignment, you should take account of the style of the literature, the author's *modus operandi*. With poetry, this work should be more painstaking than with any other kind of literature. Certain essays, novels, and plays should also receive your careful and detailed scrutiny, depending upon their excellence as literature and the degree of your ability in stylistic analysis. One basic reason to be concerned with literary style is that you are learning to be a writer yourself.

Though your problems of writing may often be different from those of a literary author, your best practical study sessions—aside from the hours you spend actually writing—should be devoted to noting compositional problems and solutions in the works you read. In Chapter 10 of this book, you will find some exercises to help improve your style and to help develop your analytical abilities. For these exercises, as well as for the present section, you should make frequent use of the Glossary in Part Three. Study such terms as *Point of View, Ambiguity, Figurative Language, Structure, Texture, Form, Genre,* and the title term (*Essay, Poetry, Tragedy, Novel,* etc.) for the kind of literature you are reading. For poetry, also, be sure to study *Prosody:* because in poetry the sound may be as important as the meaning, it is a good practice to make a special metrical analysis of every poem you write about, whether in your paper you refer to metrics or not.

The poem above by Browning presents some particularly instructive problems of composition, especially as related to time and point of view. Consider, for instance, that Browning, himself a Victorian who died in 1889, is presenting a scene in an Italian city during the Renaissance, probably the sixteenth century. Also, he is telling separate stories about three people: the Duke, his last Duchess, and the proposed new Duchess. Though he himself is removed 300 years from the scene, Browning describes the stories as occurring in the present (the Duke is now bargaining with the envoy); in the past (the Duke tells of his troubles with his last wife); and in the future (the bargaining involves the future new Duchess, the Count's daughter). All these problems of time must be solved so gracefully that the reader is scarcely aware of them. The emphasis in the foreground is a drama of character, which is not weakened but made more intense by the perspectives of time.

Browning's problems in point of view are even more interesting and challenging. Notice that all the reader knows about the Duchess is what he learns from the Duke, whose contempt for her is obvious; yet the poem succeeds in presenting an extremely sympathetic picture of her. Conversely, though the Duke himself is revealed only through his own words, the reader sees him as grasping and depraved. Indeed, on close inspection of the Duke's references to gifts and favors, his "nine-hundred-years-old name," his *objets d'art,* and especially the dowry, this abnormal emphasis on material possessions is seen to be one of the main elements in the reader's unsympathetic disposal toward the Duke. What Browning accomplishes here is the more impressive when you realize that though the Duke himself is superficial, Browning manages to make his words do duty for the envoy's reactions, as well as for the feelings of his dead wife. Thus, even though the narrator has no real strength or depth of character, his statements imply a great range of behavior in the other characters, both of those present dramatically in the poem and of those absent.

In brief: the problems faced by an author help to determine his way of writing. In the Browning poem, the very multiplicity of compositional problems enables the poet to achieve a rich, poetic effect. In your analysis of the styles of other works of literature, you should always be alert to such conciseness and economy of expression. You should also try to discover the reasons for its excellence—or for its failings. Usually, if you can discover the central difficulties of the author in writing the literature (here, time and point-of-view problems), you can begin to understand some of the details of its style.

DENOTATION AND CONNOTATION

A good literary author has at his command many methods by which he can vary the depth and breadth of his style. Several of these devices are explained in the Glossary. As a student of literature you should study such articles as those on *Ambiguity, Analogy, Figurative Language, Metaphor, Prosody, Style,* and *Texture,* in order to master some of the terms involved in stylistic analysis. The terms *denotation* and *connotation,* however, are so important as to warrant a separate discussion here.

If you look up the word *mother* in a recent, fairly complete dictionary, you will find a total of thirteen accepted meanings. Some typical definitions are: "a female who has borne offspring; female parent"; "holding a material relation: the *mother* church"; "to bring forth as a *mother;* produce; create."[1] All thirteen meanings are *denotations* of the word *mother,* since the dictionary is concerned with the things, the actions, and the qualities that words *directly point toward.* What the dictionary tells you are the facts— the directly stated, impersonal, verifiable, universally agreed-upon phenomena signified by each word. Therefore, after the word *mother,* you do not find such definitions as "loving care, knitting by the fireside"; "warmth and safety when you are good, tears and punishment when you are bad"; "the one who bandages your hurt knee; the one who kisses Father when he comes home"—and so on. This second type of meaning involves not only what the word points to, but also what it suggests, and is called *connotation.* The connotation is the more indirectly stated, personal, emotional, suggestive meaning. For *mother,* "loving care, knitting by the fire-

---

[1] By permission from *Funk & Wagnalls Standard® College Dictionary.* Copyright 1963 by Funk & Wagnalls Company, Inc.

side" is a distinctly connotative definition, whereas "female parent" is a denotative definition, a dictionary definition. Even though you find few connotative meanings in the dictionary, they are just as valid and important as denotative meanings.

The connotations of some types of words are much more numerous than their denotations. Depending upon the amount and kind of ideas, emotions, and feelings that cluster around a word, its suggestive value may be either great or small. Words denoting members of the family usually fall within the class of expressions that are highly charged with connotative meaning. *Sister, brother, son, daughter, father, mother*—even *uncle* and *aunt, grandmother* and *grandfather*—are words with extreme connotative power simply because of the universal human condition. Presumably, everyone has or has had most of the relations named above, and has a great many feelings about them. Therefore, while there are possibly only a score or so of possible denotations for the word *mother,* there are hundreds of connotations.

In the study of literature, this double power of words to point out and to suggest has some obvious applications. For instance, an author like Shakespeare, who can control his connotative meanings, is able to suggest his ideas to the reader, rather than merely state them literally. Macbeth's

Tomorrow, and tomorrow, and tomorrow
Creeps in this petty pace from day to day
To the last syllable of recorded time. . . .

could of course be said denotatively in fewer words—perhaps something like: "Boring little duties will always occupy human life." But Shakespeare's lines, as they are written, *mean* more because in their repetition and rhythm and metaphoric rightness, they *connote* more.

In the Browning poem, let us investigate a key word in a key phrase to see how its connotations function. Consider the phrase, "Her husband's presence" in lines 13, 14, and 15:

> . . . Sir, 'twas not
> Her husband's presence only, called that spot
> Of joy into the Duchess' cheek. . . .

Here, the word *husband* is important in the Duke's complaint about the Duchess. Probably it would be more natural to express this idea by saying, "It was not *my* presence only . . . ." The Duke, however, wishes to use the connotations of the word *husband* at this point in the poem, and the word *my* would not carry these meanings. He wants to suggest that he had rights of possession over the Duchess, so that she would be in the wrong if she allowed herself to be pleased by anyone else. He feels that she was guilty, not because she was unfaithful, but because he could not dominate her every mood. Later in the poem, the reader sees that the Duke treated his wife only as a wayward possession. His use of the word *husband,* with its connotation of rights to bestow happiness, is one of his attempts to justify his attitude—and one of the ways he blinds himself to his own evil. Moreover, the Duke has smuggled into his remarks not just the idea that a husband has the right to please his wife, but also that she has no right to receive even the smallest favor from another. The word *husband* alone, it is true, does not accomplish all this suggestion; but used as it is, this word adds its part to the total impression.

Taken together, denotation and connotation constitute the whole broad field of communicative meaning. In literature, the term *connotation* usually implies the suggestive power of individual expressions; as such, it is one important branch of indirect statement generally. It is in poetry, where sound joins meaning most profoundly, that controlled use of suggestive meaning can be the author's greatest triumph. In Browning's poem, when the Duke attempts to suggest that his late wife was unworthy of his own greatness, he paradoxically "gives away" his own mean and degraded character. Thus, the suggestion hidden behind the Duke's statements is more powerful and operates in different ways than he realizes. Obviously, other kinds of literature besides poetry employ connotations also. To the degree that a work is imaginative, not merely factual, it may use many of the devices of linguistic suggestion.

TECHNIQUES OF STUDY

A variety of writings can be included under the general heading of "literature," and in most cases a given type of material demands its own particular kind of study. There are, however, some general techniques of reading that you may apply to any assignment in literature. From your study of Browning's poem, you may have observed two methods of reading: reading for the overall form of the literature, and reading for the details that make up that form. You should do these readings at two different times, or at least in two different frames of mind. For your first reading, note that the terrain you pass through may include guide marks to help the reader find his way. For instance, in some novels and in most works of nonfiction, the table of contents, often neglected by beginners, can show you quickly, and with no troublesome leafing through the book, its general plan. In short stories and poems, subdivisions are often marked by section numbers or stanza breaks. In essays and other nonfiction, topic sentences are important; these are usually the sentences that begin the paragraphs. If the assignment is a whole book, notice chapter headings and subdivisions with titles in large print. Notice extremely short paragraphs, since the author may be using them to emphasize an important point or to sum up his material thus far. All these suggestions urge you to get a preliminary view, a general idea of the assignment, before you begin a detailed study. At the end of your first reading, therefore, step back mentally to take in the whole work in a single glance.

With the structure of the work in mind, your second reading

(and, for poetry, many more readings) should be very slow and detailed. Go slowly enough to absorb qualifications, illustrations, shifts in thought from one subdivision to the next. During this study, read as slowly as you can without allowing your mind to wander. As in driving, speed can kill—in reading, it kills depth of comprehension—but you can read so slowly that your mind bumps you off the track into irrelevancies. The most skillful reader is thus not the fastest reader, contrary to a widespread belief. If he is studying literary structure and style, the best reader is the slowest reader whose mind stays on the book. Reading so slowly means that you learn to see everything on the page, including the inter-relationships between the elements of the literature. Punctuation, word choice, placement of phrases and clauses, length and variety of sentences and paragraphs—all help to indicate *style*. These elements are not irrelevant to the subject matter. Part of your job may be to see *how* the author uses these devices, *why* he makes the stylistic choices he does, as well as simply *what* he says.

This second reading should take up all the time you can allot; and as long as you are seeing new things each time, third, fourth, and fifth readings will not waste your time. Students too often say of an assignment, "I've read it," and then proceed to put the book out of sight and mind. The reading experience therefore fades into a pale memory, and in minutes the student may be able to recall only superficial subject matter. Vaguely and with much effort he may tack on one or two details. To test your reading, ask yourself whether it has formed the ground of some of your own independent thoughts, both about subject matter and about style of writing. Decide whether the book has meant something to you after you have closed its covers.

The meanings you get should be active, not passive. That is, the ideas you gain from the book should be worked into your mind, not simply placed there lightly, for the first fair breeze to blow away. For example, suppose you are reading Newman's *Idea of a*

University, illustrated in the passage on pages 113 to 114. An active reading would enable you to accomplish not only the structural analysis of the paragraph suggested in the exercises following this passage. It would include this work and more, since Newman would be saying something to you, personally. He would be providing you with material to take apart analytically, and to put back together again, in the context of your own thinking. Thus, your own ideas about what constitutes a university would not be simply displaced by those of Newman. Rather, what you thought before you read the essay would be enriched, qualified, mingled with what you thought after you read it. The active reading could have added a new element to your personality, because you were able to absorb new meaning. To accomplish such absorption from reading takes practice, in which you can become more and more proficient as you achieve the ability to integrate your reading with the other aspects of your experience.

ATTITUDES TOWARD LITERATURE AND WRITING

You may find that you have a great variety of literary types to read and to write about in this course. Therefore, to make precise distinctions, it is a good idea to look up such terms as *genre, novel, poetry,* and *essay* in the Glossary. If your reading assignments are mostly essays, you may wish to get a bird's-eye view of the history of the literary *essay* by reading the Glossary entry for this term, and to read the section on the essay in Part Four, "Points of Departure." If you are reading a *novel,* a *comedy,* a *tragedy,* an *epic,* or a *lyric* poem, it is a good idea to study the appropriate term in the Glossary, so that you can place the book you are reading in a context of other works of the same kind. Part Four can help you with these genres of literature also. Though admittedly the types are not always clear-cut, still the essential nature of each type of literature is relatively simple to learn.

One common misconception about literature is that it is useless, because it is "only fiction." Another is the prejudice (now apparently going out of fashion even with the unlettered) that literature, being "only poetry," is merely for the effete and sophisticated. Another is that literature is just too boring to bother with, when so many other exciting things are going on. These opinions about literature may result from an anxious ambition to get ahead in one's own special nonliterary field; from a failure to see what is on the page, even when looking at it; and from a typically modern impatience with anything that does not give satisfaction quickly, easily—and superficially. It is true that you cannot gain a sound literary education with great speed and much facility; but it is also true that a good background in literature cannot be superficial, and that your literary training should serve you well your whole life through. Literature is fiction and nonfiction; it is poetry and nonpoetry. It is not only for a few but for everyone who can master it. Basically, it is the knowledge and culture you can get from books. One way to avoid falling into a prejudice against reading is to take pleasure in your literary studies and approach them with an eagerness to learn.

In this course, your outlook toward writing is nearly as important as your attitude toward reading. To write with depth and perception is likely to be hard work, and to write well about literature is especially difficult. Moreover, writing is something you do alone. The quality of your composition can reveal the stuff you are made of; especially with papers that are difficult to write, you can and should take satisfaction in doing a good job on your own. Most college students have taken courses in English and in composition all through their grammar school and high school years, and many have built up a distaste for writing that is hard to overcome. You can avoid being a victim of such feelings if you recognize frankly that writing is both difficult and rewarding. Indeed, the more difficult it is, the more satisfaction you can take in doing it well. Your inner glow of accomplishment should be even more important to you than the grades you make on your papers and in the course itself.

Because writing is such a personal matter, you should learn to be a good judge of your own progress and achievement. For this purpose, beginning with your first paper, you should keep a record of the errors you make and the ways in which you correct them. Since many instructors keep the papers after the class has corrected them, it is best to make copies of everything you write for the course. When you study your own work for self-improvement, these copies, if you have made them carefully and neatly, will come in handy.

Your first few papers will be important indicators. You should begin early to make a study of your own writing, regardless of whether your instructor puts many or few red marks on your papers. It should not be *his* job to proofread your work: *you should proofread,* and correct all the errors you can find before you hand in your papers. If you discover either by your instructor's comments or, much better, by your own study that you have problems of grammar, wordiness, or awkwardness, work on these by yourself. Do not expect a great deal of class time to be devoted to such matters. For your own errors of punctuation and sentence structure, check your papers carefully against the correction symbols in the "Checklist of Grammar and Mechanics." (See Part Two.) If you eliminate these flaws early in the course, you will have a much better chance for success. Next, work on problems of paragraph structure and wordiness. Get a thick notebook and fill it with the exercises in Chapter 10. The best way to improve your writing is to read and write, read and write, read and write—again and again.

AN OUTLINE–GUIDE TO LITERARY STUDY

The following list of questions is divided into four sections to provide study aids for fiction, nonfiction, poetry, and drama. When you have read a work of literature and wish to analyze it, turn to the appropriate section of this guide and answer some of the questions. Often you can base your papers on your answers. Sometimes answering only a single question thoroughly will suffice for a brief paper; at other times, you may use a section of the following questions as the basis for an outline of your paper. You may find further help in Parts Three and Four, "A Glossary of Literary Terms" and "Points of Departure," which define most of the terms and describe the different kinds of literature. The terms printed in italics here are defined in the Glossary. For other terms, consult your dictionary.

I. Questions to be applied to *short stories* and *novels:*

 A. *Plot and structure*
   1. Is there an introduction? If so, what is its purpose and how does it lead the reader into the story?
   2. Are there *flashbacks,* or is there a story within the story? If so, explain how the author has shifted from one to the other, or how they fit together.
   3. Explain the generating circumstance—the key event or situation that starts off the plot and helps to keep it going.
   4. How does the author secure *suspense*—mainly through devices of plot, or mainly through his *style?*
   5. What is the most crucial *scene?*—the turning point?
   6. Explain what forces are in conflict and show how the author embodies these forces in the *characterization.*

B. *Point of view*
   1. Show the relationships between the point of view and the plot.
   2. Is the story told from the point of view of the first person? If so, what part does the narrator play in the central action of the story?

    3. Is the limited third person used? What difficulties does this point of view offer to the author? How does he overcome them? (See Chapter 5.)

    4. Is an *omniscient observer* telling the story? Can this observer be characterized specifically? If so, describe him.

    5. Is the *stream-of-consciousness* technique used? If so, explain the purposes for which the author uses this technique.

C. *Theme and purpose*

    1. Explain and make specific the underlying human experience in the story, and show how the central characters confront a problem of life.

    2. Is the theme presented explicitly or implicitly?

    3. Explain how the author expresses a *purpose,* a message, a philosophy, or an attitude toward life.

D. *Characterization*

    1. Which character most fully exemplifies, illustrates, or embodies the theme? Explain his relationship to the theme. How is the *audience* supposed to regard him?

    2. Are the characters highly individualized or are they generalized? Are they used as *symbols* for a class of people? If so, explain the distinctions between their individualities and their more general characteristics.

    3. What is the decisive trait of the *protagonist* that helps to determine the climax of the story?

    4. Describe some of the more significant interrelationships between the characters. Explain their personalities and their dispositions toward one another.

    5. Describe the protagonist and explain why the reader should care enough about him for his story to be suspenseful.

E. *Motivation*

    1. Do the characters act in the crisis according to previously given traits, or is their behavior illogical? Explain whether

you think any illogical behavior is or is not a flaw in the story.

2. Are there marking incidents or clues—devices used by the author to anticipate or give warning of the climax? If so, explain them.

3. How basic are the motives? Do the characters fight for their lives? Is the motivation flippant or poignant?

4. If there is dialect, identify it, and show how the locale helps to determine the motives of the characters.

F. *Scene*

1. In how many places does the story occur? How does the variety of scenes affect the forward movement of the plot?

2. How clearly and by what details are the settings revealed?

3. Illustrate some of the transitional devices by which the author indicates a change of time, place, or action.

4. If there are flashbacks in the story, show how they are dove-tailed into the plot. Identify the flashback as either dramatic or generalized *narration*. Show how the flashback technique either does or does not function in conjunction with the stream-of-consciousness technique.

II. Questions to be applied to *essays* and books of nonfiction:

A. *Theme*

1. What is the central topic?

2. Find the author's own best statement of his thesis idea.

3. Write an epitome (see Chapter 10) of the literature in two or three sentences using only your own words.

B. *Structure*

1. Make an outline showing the main divisions of the literature with enough subheadings to indicate relative emphasis.

2. Show how the separate sections or paragraphs are linked together. Quote examples of effective transitions.

3. Describe in detail the structural devices of the literature. Is the literature dramatic? If so, explain the forces in conflict.

C. *Style*
   1. Does the author use *irony* or *satire?* If so, make clear what he is satirizing and what he is in favor of.
   2. Is the style humorous? What are the devices the author uses for *humor?* How are these to be distinguished from satirical devices?
   3. Point out and explain the uses of several interesting examples of *figurative language,* of unusual sentence or paragraph structure (see Chapter 7).
   4. In the midst of his *exposition,* does the author use *narration* for an example? If so, point out the devices of writing that enable the writer to shift from one type of composition to another.

D. *Point of view*
   1. What is the author's relationship to his audience? How and when does the author address the reader directly? Does he offer advice?
   2. Explain the author's attitude toward his topic and show how this attitude affects the point of view of the literature.
   3. Contrast the point of view of one section with that in another section of the literature.

E. *Purpose*
   1. Is the author's purpose basically to entertain?—to influence? —to inform?—or a combination of these purposes?
   2. Write a clear explanation of what the author is trying to accomplish.
   3. Specify the area of behavior or of character that the author is especially concerned with and show how the author wishes the reader to regard this area.

III. Questions to be applied to *lyric* and *epic* poems:

A. *Theme*
1. What is the real subject of the poem? Does it differ from the apparent subject? If so, point out the basic contrasts.
2. Show how the apparently irrelevant details in the poem help to give substance and meaning to the theme. (See *Texture*.)

B. *Style and tone*
1. How does the attitude of the narrator affect the tone of the poem?
2. Does the attitude of the poet affect his style? If so, how?
3. Is the poem humorous or satirical on one level and serious on another? Explain these levels and show how the poet makes them part of a single, unified effect.
4. Point out examples of *irony, paradox, simile, metaphor,* or other important figures of speech.

C. *Point of view*
1. Is the poet speaking in his own person?
2. Does the poet use a fictional narrator? Distinguish the poet from the narrator.
3. Describe the set of attitudes from which the poem was written.

D. *Structure and prosody*
1. Scan the poem and describe the devices of meter, rhyme, and stanzaic, or paragraph, structure. (See *Stanza* in the Glossary.)
2. Explain the mechanical structure of the poem, including its sound effects, and show how this structure fits with its intellectual content—the meanings and ideas in the poem.
3. Write a brief paraphrase of the content of the poem. (See Chapter 10.) Reflect the ideas so as to clarify the more difficult parts of the poem.

4. Describe the interlocking of the parts of the poem. Point out transitions and show how the poet moves from one point to the next.
5. Make clear any hidden principles of organization, such as a complex of symbols used to parallel or to echo one another.

IV. Questions to be applied to the *drama:*

A. *Structure and plot*
   1. Can the play be classified according to the definitions in the Glossary of *tragedy* or *comedy?* If so, identify the elements that enable you to make this classification.
   2. Is the play classifiable according to subject matter as well as according to *genre*—tragedy of revenge, comedy of manners, etc. If so, explain the particular genre and show why the play represents it.
   3. State briefly the central action around which the play revolves.
   4. Is the play divided into acts and scenes? If so, indicate the reasons for the divisions and subdivisions.

B. *Style*
   1. Are figures of speech, rhymed poetry, or *blank verse* used? If so, specify the *figurative language* and verse form and the kinds of subject matter so treated.
   2. Identify the dramatist's devices of dialogue (for example, his different uses of the *soliloquy*), and show how these devices are used for characterization.
   3. Is there dramatic irony? If so, explain the pattern of ironic events or characteristics.

C. *Characterization*
   1. Is there a central character? If so, is he or she basically

heroic or unheroic, sympathetic or unsympathetic? (See *Identification.*)

2. Identify the sympathetic and unsympathetic traits in the central character and show how the audience is supposed to feel towards these traits.

3. Explain how the dramatist uses basic character contrasts.

4. Are the minor characters grouped in interesting ways in factions of two or three or more? Do these factions in the play add to or detract from the major tension and suspense?

5. Show the relationships between the central character(s) and the minor characters.

D. *Setting*

1. Are there shifts in scene? If so, do these shifts detract from the unified dramatic effect? If not, does the play lose interest because of the sameness of the setting?

2. Are many scenic props required for stage presentation? Describe these props and indicate whether or not their use would improve the play.

3. Describe the most appropriate costuming for the chief characters in the play and relate this costuming to the actions and prestige level of the characters.

4. Describe the theater and the stage to be used.

E. *Purpose*

1. Is there a moral to the play? If so, is this moral hidden or is it easy to detect? How does the author wish to influence his audience?

2. In what light does the author present evil and vice?— punishment for crime? How does this treatment indicate purposefulness or lack of purpose on the part of the playwright?

3. What characters carry the burden of guilt and how are these characters to be regarded by the audience?

two

Choosing a literary topic

BEFORE YOU discuss a work of literature on paper, it is usually a good idea to step back and review your experience with the book, to get an overall view of your subject matter. In the early stages, your preparations to write a paper and to take an essay examination should be identical. To decide upon how you will write your paper or exam, you should think systematically about your reading assignment, so that all its parts assume a clear relationship with the whole. In this background thinking, you should try to see your reading both as a collection of different ideas and as a single, unified composition.

For example, let us assume that you have read the selection from Wordsworth in Part Four and that you expect to write a paper about this passage. Before you decide on a topic, you should try to gain some clear ideas of what Wordsworth is saying, because the emphasis in your paper will be derived from Wordsworth's statement, both in general and in detail. Therefore you would note that approximately the first one-third of his comments are distinctions between the emotions of poetry and those of real life; that a second, smaller part of the passage distinguishes between the pleasures of the poet and those of the scientist; and that the final part focuses upon the kind of knowledge that is the special province of poetry. In all, you would see that Wordsworth is attempting to define poetry by a process of elimination and refinement. It is this attempt at definition that gives the selection its unity.

To write well about such a piece of literature, however, you need to discover a manageable topic. You should not present your reader with a tissue of summaries that merely generalize Wordsworth's ideas, or that wander aimlessly. Even while you are reading, therefore, it is a good idea to plan your writing project so that it will have both direction and interest. Your own specific statements about the selection, not vague generalities, will hold your reader's attention. If you plan your paper without thinking of the details you will need to fill it out, your writing job will be difficult, and you will have to generate each new idea as you go.

A basic flaw in many student papers about literature is that the writer has not decided on his purpose. Your purpose should determine the form and content of what you write—what you say and how you say it. If, while you are reading, you have an eye to the writing you may do later, your chances of deciding upon an effective purpose will be greater. In general, your overall writing purposes will be to help you understand the literature and to improve your own composition.

In writing an essay about the differences between science and literature, for instance, you would focus upon the second part of the passage from Wordsworth. You would have much more of value to say, and Wordsworth's comments would mean more to you, if you reread them with your own proposed composition in mind. Setting down your thoughts about such a work helps to impress it on your mind and enables you to discuss it more intelligently in class and with friends. Also, writing about such literature is the closest you can come to an ideal situation—a conversation with the author himself. In some ways your writing can even surpass this experience, since for your own comments, you have commonly had the leisure to reread the book and to revise your ideas.

SEVEN STEPS TOWARD WRITING

You may observe each of the following steps more or less thoroughly, according to your needs. If you have trouble understanding the literature, you should take more time on the early steps.

1. Reading notes and notes for writing

While you read, you should stop and think occasionally about the paper you may write or the exam you may take, and you should allow some tentative plans for your writing project to germinate in your mind. A good idea is to use two notebooks, or two sections of one notebook, for this work—one for outlining the literature itself and the other for ideas and suggestions for your paper. In the notes for writing, never miss a chance to jot down good ideas. These ideas should stem from your reading but should be essentially your own thoughts and interpretations. Keep your notebook for these jottings accessible; the notes you make may be as random and disconnected as you like.

Your reading notebook, however, will be neater; it will contain the essential points of the book in your own words, and will be in essence an outline of the literature itself. It is a good idea, when you have finished making this outline, to sum up your reading in a single short paragraph, so that you can see the unity of the work at a glance. To do this part well, you should read over the section in this book on the epitome. (See Chapter 10.)

Some students find it worth the expense to make preliminary notes in the margins of their books. If you do this, you may use such notes as sources which you may expand in both your reading and writing notebooks. Preliminary marginal notes, if carefully made, are especially valuable with rather difficult reading material. The following paragraph from Wordsworth has already been referred to; the marginal notes are like warning signs to slow down and to analyze meanings in the text:

1. Pleasure of poetry goes deep, helps bring meaning and value to life.

1. Nor let this necessity of producing immediate pleasure be considered as a degradation of the Poet's art. It is far otherwise. It is an acknowledgement of the beauty of the universe, an acknowledgement the more sincere, because not formal, but indirect; it is a task light and easy to him who looks at the world in the spirit of love: further, it is a homage paid to the native and naked dignity of man, to the grand elementary principle of pleasure, by which he knows, and feels, and lives, and moves.

2. Poetic pleasure is not to be condemned; it is the source of human sympathy—even with pain.

2. We have no sympathy but what is propagated by pleasure: I would not be misunderstood; but wherever we sympathize with pain, it will be found that the sympathy is produced and carried on by subtle combinations with pleasure. We have no knowledge, that is, no gen-

eral principles drawn from the contemplation of particular facts, but what has been built up by pleasure, and exists in us by pleasure alone.

3. *Even scientific knowledge springs from pleasure* (which may exist as satisfaction of scientist's curiosity).

3. The Man of science, the Chemist and Mathematician, whatever difficulties and disgusts they may have had to struggle with, know and feel this. However painful may be the objects with which the Anatomist's knowledge is connected, he feels that his knowledge is pleasure; and where he has no pleasure he has no knowledge. What then does the Poet? He considers man and the objects that surround him as acting and reacting upon each other, so as to produce an infinite complexity of pain and pleasure; he considers man

4. *Poet deals with the grand plan, with man's place in nature.*

4.

5. *Poet sees all the qualities of man—especially his intuitive nature.*

5. in his own nature and in his ordinary life as contemplating this with a certain quantity of immediate knowledge, with certain convictions, intuitions, and deductions, which from habit acquire the quality of intuitions; he considers him as looking upon this complex scene of ideas and sensations, and finding everywhere objects that immediately excite in him sympathies which, from the necessities of his nature, are accompanied by an overbalance of enjoyment.

6. *Poet understands that man must enjoy in order to sympathize.*

6.

When you have transferred such marginalia to your notebook, you may find that some of them suggest whole sections of essays that you could write. For instance, consider the third note above. The parenthesized item here is an original thought on the part of the student. It is only suggested, not stated, by Wordsworth. Thinking hard about how such an idea works in with what Wordsworth *does* say could yield an excellent paragraph for your own paper.

The notes you have made from your reading, with an epitome, should help to give you ideas to write about. As you progress you will be working more and more with your notes for your paper. Your basic goals now are to select a controlling idea and to decide upon a principle of organization for your paper. In choosing a controlling idea, you will have to weed out unsuitable ideas. When you come to impose an order upon the parts of your paper or examination, your writing should have the classical virtues of unity, emphasis, and coherence. You should have these goals in mind through the following steps.

2. *A list of ideas to defend or explain*

One of the best ways to learn about a subject is to argue for your ideas in writing. When you write about your reading—a little defensively, just as you would defend your statements in conversing with a friend—you are forcing yourself to think as deeply as you can about your topic. In this thinking, you necessarily come across ideas that stir your enthusiasm; you wish to express them, to stand up for them. This enthusiasm should cause you to discover both new ideas and more effective ways to express your old ideas.

Consider the following two lists of topics for brief papers about Homer's *Iliad*. Notice that the items in the list on the left are either too vague and general or that they would lead the reader of your paper away from a deeper consideration of the book. Then observe that the titles on the right are good topics for short papers and that they are modified from the corresponding inferior topics. What makes them better is that they are broken down, reduced in scope, or changed from irrelevance to relevance.

VAGUE	SPECIFIC
Trophies of War	Chryseis and Briseis—Their Parts in the *Iliad*
Men vs. Men	Achilles vs. Agamemnon
	Hector vs. Aeneas
Gods vs. Men	Gods against Hector
	Gods against Diomedes
Brutality	Trojans at the Mercy of Achilles
	Greeks at the Mercy of Hector
Gods vs. Gods	Xanthus vs. Hephaestus
	Aphrodite vs. Hera and Athena
Friendship	Achilles and Patroclus
	Odysseus and Diomedes
The Structure of the *Iliad*	Achilles as Tragic Hero
	Zeus and Athena as Determiners of the Plot
Miracles	How the Gods Save Their Favorites
	Miraculous Omens
Armor	Hephaestus' Magic
	Variety and Composition of Weapons
	The Ships as Fortress
The Epic Simile	Classification of Types of Epic Similes
Greek Architecture	The Effect of the Greek Wall
Greek Seamanship	The Ships as Line of Defense

3. Choice of the best idea

Your enthusiasm for your topic, which makes your writing vital, is easier to maintain if you focus on a relatively specific idea. It may be a new idea or one that you have often thought of before; but if it is new to you, try to be sure that it is not trite to others and that you understand its ramifications. Your overall controlling idea should be more general than your supporting details, but more specific than the controlling idea of the book you are writing about.

It may be like a subtitle of the book, which identifies some pervasive aspect of the whole topic. Or it may be like a chapter heading, which focuses upon a limited segment of the topic. Instructors usually prefer student papers about the topics that show a wide range of reading. What you should realize is that a good idea for an essay may pervade every part of a literary work and still be a specific idea.

4. Tailoring your idea

Most early student essays about literature turn out to be shorter than they seem, in the planning stage. It may be helpful if you start out by writing a general statement like the following: "In *Walden,* Thoreau advised man to imitate the simplicity of nature." You could then try a few sentences in support of this statement, to discover the drift of your own ideas and interests. It would be a mistake to write a whole paper on the very general and vague topic of simplicity in nature. Moreover, the idea does not suggest much of a principle of organization for your paper. Though the specifics that you could use in the body of the paper would be almost limitless, they would also be disconnected and lacking in unity.

Therefore, as you write, try out some specific ideas in a rough draft. Before you decide on a final topic for your paper, you should not discard your original concept. Even when you begin to see its flaws, consider your proposed topic from several different angles: "Thoreau's own occupations were often as simple as those of birds and animals." Or: "Thoreau saw the railroad as a symbol both of needless complexity and of man's godlike ingenuity." Or: "Thoreau's trips to Concord allowed him to compare human society with nature." Having thought of these more usable ideas, which are narrowed down from the general statement about "simplicity of nature," you should be reminded of the details you would need to write good essays about Thoreau's *Walden.* If you see fit to do so, your final version could eliminate the original vague and general statement entirely.

5. Allowing for comparison and contrast

Possibly your most valuable devices in writing about literature are *comparison* and *contrast*. Even in papers not devoted to measuring one thing against another, you can use these forms as two good ways to clarify your ideas and to control the pace and movement of your composition. Once you gain some practice in comparing and contrasting literary topics and ideas, you may wish to use these forms as the overall structures of many of your papers and examinations.

The examples below and on pages 80 to 84 should give you some idea of the range and possibilities of comparison and contrast. They are structural miniatures of longer papers—just as a paragraph is often a structural miniature of a whole composition. Comparison and contrast are two sides of the same coin, but each device does have its own emphasis:

COMPARISON

In Thackeray's *Vanity Fair*, Becky Sharp and Amelia Sedley, two products of Miss Pinkerton's school, together capture the hearts of all the important male characters in the book. Though Amelia seems unselfish at first, the reader often finds her treatment of the faithful Dobbin cruel and ruthless. In these episodes, at least, she is not superior to the selfish and scheming Becky.

CONTRAST

As she constantly reminds her victims, Becky Sharp, the chief character in *Vanity Fair*, must shift for herself. Therefore, she controls nearly all the male characters in the book to serve her purposes. In contrast, Amelia Sedley dominates only one poor soul, the faithful, doglike Dobbin, and she can use Dobbin only because he truly loves her. Moreover, Becky uses her social prestige, her brains, and her money, when she has it, and these are advantages that Amelia often lacks.

Note that comparison implies some basic differences, while emphasizing similarities. Contrast, on the other hand, implies some basic similarities, while emphasizing differences. If there were no differences at all, you would not have two separate ideas to compare. If there were no similarities at all, your contrasts would lack a single basis of meaning.

6. Using quotations for topic ideas

When scarcity of good ideas to write about is your problem, write down a brief quotation that appeals to you and consider its relevance to other parts of the book. If you choose your quotation carefully, it can steer your thinking into clusters of interesting relationships that you may explain and illustrate. Although nearly any work of literature will do, Shakespeare's plays are excellent hunting grounds for such quotations, and the speeches of his characters often reveal relationships and involvements that offer much to write about. Consider Othello's repeated use of the word "honest" to characterize Iago, or Rosalind's baiting of Touchstone and Jaques in *As You Like It,* or nearly any famous quotation from *Hamlet;* and observe how, the more you analyze the dramatic implications of these passages, the more far-reaching they are. Of course, you do not always have to use a quotation—a single scene or even part of a scene may suffice. Note also that the work of essayists like Emerson, Pascal, Montaigne, and Bacon invite such consideration of interrelationships.

Several hints can help in planning such a paper. First, do not choose your quotation or passage haphazardly, but preferably from a list that you jot down as you reread the book. Second, settle on a single passage and keep returning to it, as a guide for your thinking and as a unifying element for the writing you will do. Finally, be sure the idea you choose allows you to give clear evidence that the relationships you specify do, in fact, exist. Most likely, you will need to cite, economically and with correct emphasis, other parts of the book besides the passage that embodies your topic idea.

7. Using the Outline-Guide, the Glossary, and "Points of Departure"

When you have read the literature and have decided on a topic or a set of topics to write about, you should try to see your proposed writing project in proper perspective. For this purpose, the outline questions provided at the end of Chapter 1 should be useful. Also, many topics for papers are discussed in the articles in the Glossary and in the five sections of Part Four of this book, "Points of Departure." When you have finished your reading assignment, you may choose an idea from the Glossary or from Part Four.

Then find the section of the outline that bears most closely on the idea you have decided on for your paper. Be sure that you can answer these questions and even ask and answer more like them. It is this section of the outline that you will try to make yourself an authority on, and your answers to the questions could comprise the plan you use for your essay. Your goal in this analysis is to understand even the parts of the literature that did not interest you upon first reading, and that did not at first seem to be related to your writing project.

EXERCISES: *As background study for these exercises, it should be helpful to read the Glossary article on the* essay. *The passages from Thoreau (pages 115 to 116), Emerson (page 105), and Newman (pages 113 to 114) illustrate the formal essay; the selection from Joseph Wood Krutch (pages 379 to 386) illustrates the informal essay. For further preparation, read the section on "The Essay" in Part Four, "Points of Departure."*

A. Arrange the following topics from the most general to the most specific:

1. The Essay in Nineteenth-century England
2. The Prose Style of Charles Lamb
3. The Familiar Letter as a Forerunner of the Literary Essay
4. The Bible as a Forerunner of the Literary Essay
5. The History of Periodical Literature
6. Thoreau's Use of Metaphor in *Walden*
7. Fictional Devices in Thoreau's *Walden*

  8. Is the Essay a Forgotten Art?
  9. The Essay and the Lyric: Birds of a Feather

B. Assign one of the above topics to each of the following lengths: 300 words; 400 words; 500 words; 750 words; 1,500 words; 2,500 words; 5,000 words; 25,000 words; book length (over 100,000 words).

C. For the four longest student papers and for the book-length topic, explain some possible subtopics and some sample chapter headings.

D. Given as much class instruction and study time as you needed, which of the topics above do you believe you could make into the most interesting essays? That is, if you had to investigate one of these topics and write a paper on it, which one would you choose *and why? Explain your answer in detail.*

E. Assuming that you were assigned to write an in-class theme of 500 words on one of the above topics, *with only your present knowledge of the literary essay as a genre,* which of the topics would you choose? Explain some of the ideas you would put into your theme. Explain why you would not use each of the other eight topics; give three or four reasons for rejecting each topic.

three

Planning for literary relevance

ONCE YOU have chosen a topic and have decided on some of its main aspects to write about, you should try to envision an over-all pattern for your essay. This will not be a final outline of the complete paper, because it is both confusing and undesirable to try to think out all the details and how they will fit together before you start writing. Indeed, the spontaneity of your essay should be part of its attractiveness; your writing would be dull or awkward if you tried constantly to limit your statements to an extremely rigid, preconceived plan. But a rough blueprint of how you will proceed can be very helpful. It can even encourage your spontaneity and help your style to sparkle with original phrases. Such a flexible plan would improve your style by freeing your mind from the worry and bother of plotting out, as you write, the kind of material that comes next. It is annoying and frustrating to think of an important idea too late when writing a paper. What you must do in such a case is to rewrite the deficient passage and build in the omitted idea. The job is somewhat comparable to breaking down a brick wall to build in a forgotten and needed window or door.

A PLAN FOR DIRECTION

You should be aware of two closely related overall plans that you may use together in many of your papers. The first of these plans illustrates several important principles. First, you should give your reader a clear idea of the topic of the paper in your introduction. Second, your writing should have a direction, a progress toward a conclusion. Third, the details should support your essential conclusions. Thus, your overall plan may be like an inverted triangle:

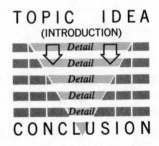

The "point" of the paper, as of the triangle, is at the conclusion, and you go through the steps of reaching this point by arranging the parts of the general topic in an order of increasing interest, specificity, or relevance. As indicated by the outlines of the rectangle, the actual paragraphs or sections of the paper may not become shorter as the paper progresses. Indeed, some of the later aspects of your topic may require more lengthy treatment than the early parts. But just as the horizontal lines of the triangle become shorter, the details of the subject become more cogent and seem more forcibly to imply the conclusion, the goal toward which all the preceding parts of the essay have been directed.

A special plan for papers about literature

For papers about your reading assignments, it is also helpful to keep the above diagram in mind. Since any good essay has its own integrity, regardless of its subject matter, your own writing should never wander outside the general idea stated or clearly implied in your introduction. In the diagram above, the horizontal lines of the rectangle indicate this integrity, since they are of the same length as the line denoting the general idea. If these lines were longer, they would run past the limits of the rectangle into another, irrelevant idea. Thus, especially in a paper on literature, you must be careful both to keep the details relevant to the general topic (broken lines) and to arrange these details according to a principle of increasing interest (solid lines).

In writing about literature, you may find an added diagram helpful. Your main problem, especially in your early literary papers, may be to keep your details relevant to the reading assignment, without merely summarizing it or retelling it. Except when you are expressly assigned to write such a summary, you must make your own ideas the central focus of your papers. *At the same time, you must write about the literature itself—not some other, unrelated topic.* The wheel diagram admonishes you to be both original and relevant to the literature:

The hub of the wheel is the concept you have decided to defend or assert. (How to choose this idea is explained in Chapter 2; how to make it into an assertion is described in Chapter 4.) The spokes of the wheel are the separate aspects of your own idea. (How to select and arrange these parts is explained in Chapter 4.) The rim of the wheel is the self-contained nature of the literature itself. Notice that the details of your own topic idea touch the literary work at several points, and that your details are not merely reproductions of those of the work of literature. Your essay may be arranged like the triangle, working from the general background to the crucial point at the last; but it is also like the wheel, with your own original idea as its center.

WHEN TO USE THE PLANS

For most students, these general plans should serve at the beginning and at the end of the writing process. Once you have a good idea, do not wait too long before you start to write. The longer you put off the first sentence, the harder the whole paper will be to write. Therefore, get to work as early as you can: have an idea and a plan in mind, but do not allow your plan to sap the vitality from your idea. This can happen if you try to work out all the structural solutions to your problems before you do any writing. If you find that your first few sentences are weak and unsuitable for the paper, you can cut them out later.

In short, this advice means that you should use a general outline both as a stimulus for writing and as a guide—not as an excuse for needless delay. If you can see, roughly, how your idea could be fitted into such a plan as that described above, and if you feel eager to write, go ahead. See how the first few sentences go. Do not stop even for spelling and minor mechanical problems, but try a rough draft just to test whether your idea is really as good as you thought it would be.

BALANCING YOUR IDEAS ABOUT LITERATURE

Each of your papers about literature presents its own special problems of planning. Your best general guidelines, however, are the goals of your composition. Usually, for instance, you wish to offer evidence that you have devoted some real study to your reading assignments. The best way to render this evidence is not to try to reproduce the literature itself. You cannot do this, because however expert you are as a writer, you do not have the point of view of the original author. Your attempts to rewrite the literature would therefore merely water it down, and you could give yourself little opportunity for showing the reader—who is usually your instructor —not only that you have read the assignment but that you have thought about what it means. Thus, nearly every paper with a literary topic that you hand in to your instructor should reflect both the content of your assignments and your own commentary about this content. One of your main problems in planning may therefore be to allow for the right amount of emphasis on the literature itself and on your own ideas about it.

If this problem gives you much trouble, you should work on it by yourself without expecting extra help from your instructor. For this purpose, the variety of exercises in Chapter 10 should help you improve your ability to disentangle your own ideas from those of the author whose work you are writing about. To this end, some of the self-help exercises direct you to summarize or to replicate the literature and to avoid making any comments about it. Being thus able to isolate the ideas of the original piece of literature, you should find yourself more capable of doing the writing in which you are asked to express more of your own ideas. As a student you should realize why these self-help exercises are to be distinguished from class papers and examinations.

In elementary school, and even in high school, one frequent test of your reading ability may have been to review, in class discussion and on paper, some of the ideas taken from your assignments. In college, you are asked to do this and more—to order and to unify your literary experiences by writing about them. The best way to accomplish this order and unity is not just to use your mind as a reflector that bounces off your reading experience and remains unchanged by it. Rather, you must learn to give your mind more scope and depth by a close familiarity with the content of your reading materials. Writing down your own ideas, distinct from those in the literature but clearly relevant to them, is an important part—the part you contribute—of the building of your mental equipment. The class papers and examinations you write should thus be good indications to your instructor, not just of whether you have read your assignments, but of whether you have studied them and thought about them.

PLANNING FOR READER INTEREST

Another guiding principle in planning your composition is to consider the reader of your papers—usually your instructor. A frequent and serious mistake made sometimes even by advanced students in composition and literature is to regard the instructor's primary function and duty as one of checking up on the student's reading—merely to see whether he is doing his homework or not. This limited and rather mechanical idea of the purpose of his instructor may often be the cause of the anxious scribbling out of anything and everything that the student can remember from his reading assignments. The same cause may be responsible for papers that are merely watered-down summaries, containing little thought or comment that originated with the student himself. To avoid these flaws in your own papers, you should realize that your instructor is always within his rights when he questions you about your assignments, but that also he wishes to help you get the most value from your reading and writing activities. When he does give writing assignments and examinations, his purpose is thus often much broader than it may seem to be. When you fulfill his assignments, therefore, you should keep in mind this broader purpose. The point of these comments is that in college your writing should be an enrichment of your literary study and experience, not merely an attempt to show that you have spent a certain number of hours with a book.

REVISION: A CAUTION

Before you hand in any paper, you must be extremely careful to polish away the minor errors that you may have made in your early, hasty versions. Because many students fail to follow through at this point, a special caution is in order: *Do not throw away all your hard study by failing to revise and correct your paper. Proofread, especially for comma splices, for fragments, for omissions of the apostrophe, and for spelling.*

The final version of the paper should also be checked against the overall plan. Remember that the point of all your planning is to produce a good essay—one that interests your reader, one that says something original in a graceful, sensible way. The outline can be thrown away once this objective is achieved. Thus, it would show lack of understanding of the writing process if you were to set down an outline and follow it slavishly into blind alleys, pointlessly overemphasized transitions, irrelevancies, and awkward phrases. The plan must therefore be flexible. You may find that parts of your essay have followed the principles of good composition without an extreme amount of detail in your planning. Conversely, your final check for overall form may indicate many lapses, even where you worked hardest. If so, you may need to revise both your plan and the details of the paper itself. In such a revision you may have to polish your sentences to make them relevant.

Before you make your final draft, in a fair hand or in clear typing, read your paper over with an objective eye. *Your attempt here is to see your writing from your reader's point of view.* He will approach your essay with no special eagerness to read, no ready-made knowledge of your attitudes and beliefs. Therefore, revise your paper to make your ideas vital and interesting. Here again, many students fail to follow through. Your first concerns should be the clarity of your statement and its interest value. No one cares to read flat expressions, common ideas, superficial comments without vigor or depth. To include them in your paper just to meet the length requirement is padding. It is all right to be awkward and wordy in a rough draft, but the paper you hand in should be graceful, economical, and pleasant to read. To achieve these goals, the overall structure should be evident and clear, so that your reader follows each stage of your discussion. Style and structure should work together to engage the best attention of your reader.

A WORD ABOUT IN–CLASS WRITING

Most teachers grade in-class themes and examinations with the realization that it takes time to revise your writing. Nevertheless, you should learn your own best speed and quality of composition, so that you can produce your best work in the time allowed. You will have to do most of your written college classwork under time pressure, and it would therefore be meaningless to complain that your English teacher assigns you too many in-class themes.

If you have trouble writing acceptable quality and quantity in the time allowed, two suggestions may help. First, have your reading assignments more clearly in mind, so that you can write more readily about them. This means to study harder and longer and to come to class with a clear idea of the structure and details of your assignment. Second, practice writing on your own, so that you gain a facility of expression, an ability to say things directly and gracefully. This practice will help you see what structured, consecutive writing really is. Moreover, it should eliminate the feeling that your own written words are strange and foreign to you. With practice in writing, you should be able, increasingly, to pin down your best ideas by means of your most effective expressions placed accurately in a coherent overall structure.

EXERCISES: *Study the following Shakespearean sonnet and the four hypothetical student critiques. The papers were written to illustrate some serious errors in overall structure and style, as well as some of the possibilities for writing offered by such a poem.*

Your analysis of the themes should teach you (1) that, with good literature as subject matter, there is a great deal you can say in your papers; (2) that you can study and know your topic well and still fail to follow through in your written work; and (3) that your writing should center on your clearest ideas, not your vague imaginings, about the literature itself. None of the essays is perfect. Some sentences and paragraphs are under- or overdeveloped, some are awkward and wordy, and some reveal a basic, underlying structural flaw. In each paper, spot the passages that seem to have been most hastily or inadequately thought out, and explain how these parts should have been revised. Mark the specific mistakes with the symbols of the correction chart for the "Checklist of Grammar and Mechanics." Then, for each paper, assign a grade.

Finally, write a paragraph or two of commentary, in a total of about 200 to 300 words. In cases where you think the papers should receive failing or nearly failing grades, your comments should explain what is wrong; but even in the inferior papers, you should point out passages that show some depth of insight, some originality of expression.

You may be asked to analyze these papers in class; consequently, though you may not have to hand in your written comments, you should have them before you in your notebook during the class discussions. Remember to refer to the line numbers of the sonnet and of the essays whenever possible.

SONNET LXXIII

That time of year thou mayst in me behold 1
When yellow leaves, nor none, nor few, do hang
Upon those boughs which shake against the cold,
Bare ruin'd choirs, where late the sweet birds sang.
In me thou see'st the twilight of such day 5
As after sunset fadeth in the west;
Which by and by black night doth take away,
Death's second self, that seals up all in rest.
In me thou see'st the glowing of such fire,
That on the ashes of his youth doth lie, 10
As the death-bed whereon it must expire,
Consum'd with that which it was nourish'd by.
 This thou perceiv'st, which makes thy love more strong,
 To love that well which thou must leave ere long.

SHAKESPEARE'S DEATH SONNET

In the four parts of Shakespeare's Sonnet LXXIII the reader 1
discovers three metaphors of four lines each in the first twelve
lines and a couplet that presents the point of the whole sonnet
at the end. The most difficult line is line 4, but when the reader
sees that the words "bare ruin'd choirs" mean "limbs of a 5
tree in winter," even this difficult line is clear and he also sees
that there is very much richness in line 4, especially in the
word "late." "Late" means that the birds sang on the tree
limbs recently (in the autumn), and that they sang until "late"
in the season. The word "late" also is used to foreshadow 10
death, just as a dead person may be spoken of as "the late
Mr. Jones."

The tree is the idea around which the first four lines is
written, and the poet tells his beloved that she sees him as an
old man, like a tree in winter. The second four lines talk about 15
sunset. They tell his lady that he is like a fading day. Night is
also in the second quatrain. Like the bare tree branches, night
also represents approaching death. That is what death's second
self is—night. All this is connected to the last two lines because the poet says his lady sees he is old and loves him 20
anyway.

The third quatrain presents a fire that like the tree and the fading day represents approaching death. Because the fire is lying on its ashes of youth and is in its last glowing, as is stated in lines 9 and 10. And so the sonnet shows three dying things—a tree, a day, and a fire, it compares these with the poet himself, who is also dying. The last couplet ties it all up. He says she sees he is old and it makes her love him more because he will probably die before she does. This idea is in the poem and is not just one I made up, because the last line clearly says she knows she will "leave" him before long, but she still loves him well anyway.

The poem is written in old language, which makes it have more charm. The three metaphors don't have to be just about a tree and a day and a fire, they could be about any dying things, but Shakespeare makes them fit well together by the rhyme scheme and by the feeling of bleakness they all have in common.

LOVE CONQUERS ALL

Sonnet LXXIII is not what it seems on the surface. It tells a story that is masked by references to the cold of winter, twilightime, and the dying embers of a fire. It is a sad story, since at the end, the poet and his beloved must part. The main three sections of the sonnet, with four lines each, progress from the yellow leaves of autumn, to the ending of a day, to the fire that dies out in line 12. This progression is like the sadness of life, as one grows older he uses up the fuel of life just as a fire burns out from using up the fuel that kept it alive.

The final couplet, however, gives us the clue that this is a love story. If one reads the sonnet over again after reading this couplet you can see what Shakespeare is saying. He says that in the saddest times of life, like in the winter when the trees are bare and the birds no longer sing, at the end of the day when everything is gloomy, and even when the fire burns out at night. During all these times, he has one cheerful thought that keeps him going.

This thought is his love. It is a beautiful idea, because his lady returns his love, and because she feels just exactly as he does even though they must part very soon. Shakespeare says

that because these two people feel the same way in the gloom-
iest times of life, this fact makes her love him more in line 13.
It is very easy to feel the way other people do during happy
times. For instance, when someone else laughs, you may tend
to laugh, too, but in the sad times, it takes a soul-mate to feel   25
just the same way you do. So Shakespeare says that the lady
in this sonnet perceives how he feels, and because she sym-
pathizes with him she loves him more.

In conclusion, Shakespeare has chosen the best things possible to show the sadness and to contrast it with his love.   30
There is nothing more dismal than a tree with only a few leaves
hanging on it. Everyone has observed how the somber part of
the day is at twilightime. And although a fire at night is always
cheerful, it is very gloomy when all that is left are ashes. In
each of these things Shakespeare has given a tinge of happi-   35
ness that reminds him of his love. Birds singing, the beauty of
the sunset, and the happy fire.

UNITY IN SHAKESPEARE'S SONNET LXXIII

The three quatrains of Shakespeare's Sonnet LXXIII achieve   1
unity and continuity by the skillful portrayal of an over-all
dramatic situation and by effective words and phrases. The
dominating images in the quatrains are winter time, twilight
time and the last glow of the fire. Without the artistic handling   5
of ambiguities and connotations, these images would tend to
break into three separate parts. The most obvious device for
continuity is the repetition, in lines 1, 5 and 9 of "thou mayest
in me behold," "In me thou see'st" and "In me thou see'st."
These phrases introducing each quatrain remind the reader that   10
the poet is comparing himself with things old and dying, for
the benefit of his beloved. In the final couplet, the phrase "This
thou perceiv'st" repeats this idea for the fourth, most emphatic
time.

Hence, even on the surface of the poem there is a dramatic   15
situation—the poet confessing his weaknesses to his lady—
that helps to unify the three quatrains and the couplet into a
single unit. If the reader remembers the tradition in the Elizabethan amatory sonnet that the beloved is to be praised or

chided in the final two lines, he can see that the unifying situa- 20
tion goes deep into this poem. In this sonnet, Shakespeare
compliments the lady for two qualities: her perceptiveness in
understanding his weakness, and her generosity in loving what
is both infirm and transitory. The compliment to the lady's
understanding (to her head) is made obvious by the repeated 25
phrasings "In me thou see'st," etc. The praise of her generosity (of her heart) is implied subtlely but effectively in the
final couplet.

The linguistic devices for unity and transition spring from
this situation and from the images themselves. There is only a 30
little mechanical logic behind these images but there is a good
deal of esthetic rightness. The logical progression is from the
dying year, to the dying day, to the dying evening, in the
embers of the fire. The esthetic rightness, however, pervades
the whole poem, and one may discover it in any single line. 35
The words and phrases referred to in the introduction to this
paper may be typified by line 4. As William Empson has noted,[1]
"Bare ruin'd choirs" suggests the tree alluded to in lines 2
and 3: "choirs" in Shakespeare's day were wooden lofts in a
church, the benches as well as the singers themselves. Also, 40
the "sweet birds" help to link the church loft with the tree and
with the expression of emotion needed in this part of the
sonnet.

In this way, the phrases throughout the poem involve one
another by the interlocking of their double and triple meanings. 45
Other examples could be cited, but in a short paper probably
the Empson citation will serve adequately to illustrate Shakespeare's linguistic artistry.

TIME IN SONNET LXXIII

Shakespeare's Sonnet LXXIII presents three manifestations of 1
the effect of time, and a final defiance of time. We know the
poem is to be about time from the opening phrase, "That time
of year . . ." and as the poem goes on, we realize that Shakespeare constructs each of his first three ideas around two 5

---

[1] In a citation from the *Oxford English Dictionary* (in *Seven Types of Ambiguity,* New Directions, 1940).

parts. First, he presents an object—a tree, a day, and a fire. Next, he shows the effect of advancing time upon that object. Hence, the winter makes the tree bare of leaves, the night takes the sun away from the day, and ashes of age and death rob the fire of its glow. The final couplet rises above these effects of time; it even contradicts them.   10

Within each of the first three parts is at least one complication of this simple idea. These complications usually come from the words being used symbolically. For instance, the leaves in line 2 and the choirs in line 4 symbolize youth and   15 happiness because everyone associates leaves with springtime and choirs with singing. But these leaves and choirs are yellow, and ruined because of the effects of time, symbolized here by winter. In the second part, the night symbolizes death, the effect of time on the day, which symbolizes life; and the sunset   20 again symbolizes youth and happiness. The sunset has faded away because of the effect of night on day. In the third part we see a feeble fire, which symbolizes both life and youth, like the sunset and the leaves and the choirs in the lines above.

Through all of the poem, the poet has also been referring to   25 himself as growing old. Therefore, when the reader reaches the fire idea, he can see that the "death-bed" of the fire symbolizes also the death-bed of the poet. Of course, the poet is not literally on his death-bed, any more than he is literally shaking like the leaves were shaking against the cold that also symbol-   30 ized death—in line 3 above. But all these symbols do make the poem gloomy, and this is what Shakespeare wants. As was said in the introduction, the last couplet contradicts the effects of time that have been expressed throughout the sonnet. Time has ruined the tree and the day and the fire, but it does not   35 ruin the poet's beloved's love but makes her love stronger. So the effect of time is the opposite in the last two lines from what it was in the preceding parts of the poem. This reversal of the effect of time helps give the end of the sonnet its power.

four

Beginning, middle, and end

IT IS ASSUMED in this chapter that you have analyzed your reading assignment according to the outline questions at the end of Chapter 1, have decided on several ideas to write about, and have a general plan in mind.

Reduced to its utmost simplicity, a master plan might be stated as follows: Assert your controlling idea; support your ideas with details.

SUGGESTIONS ON HOW TO BEGIN

Beginning a paper is easiest when you start out with an idea and a plan like those described in Chapters 2 and 3. In writing, you always have one saving advantage: you can throw out or revise your early paragraphs if you see later that they do not do their job well. Most professionals scrutinize their introductions very carefully. Knowing how important first impressions are, the careful writer works hard on his introductory phrasings to achieve a high polish, a clear air of authority, a pleasant or even exciting invitation to read on.

In life, when you meet a person, you know that his first impression of you may last through the whole acquaintance. Therefore, you try especially hard not to be dull and awkward in your greeting and early remarks. Similarly in your writing, if you blur or mar your introduction, you give your reader every reason to expect that dullness, awkwardness, or superficiality will follow. Each paper you write must recommend itself to your reader on the merits of your treatment of its topic; it must offer him an interesting idea expressed in an individual, personable way. Occasionally, it may be helpful to think of your topic as having character and personality, much like a human being. Thus, to write a good introduction may involve tact and a kind of social grace, as well as skill in phrasing. Also, it is better to begin a paper with a topic you know well, just as you may do a better job introducing a friend than a stranger.

The following checklist of suggestions is concerned not only to help you write a good introduction but also to illustrate several ways of making your central concepts interesting to your reader.

The literary topic assertion

The *topic assertion* is the main idea of your paper, the thesis that you have decided to defend or explain. Your topic assertion should give your writing its unity, its emphasis, its coherence—three classical virtues that even the best literature can rarely do without. Ordinarily, the topic assertion is suggested in the title and is fully stated in the first paragraph:

HOTSPUR AND FALSTAFF: TEMPERAMENTAL OPPOSITES

In *Henry IV*, Shakespeare presents two contrasting personalities and illustrates their diametrically opposed attitudes on every important issue in the play. In alternating scenes, Falstaff, the gay, fat fellow of the tavern, discourses with good-natured bluster on subjects like honor, personal property, kingship, the booty of a robbery, sack, women, and song. Dovetailed between these scenes, Hotspur rants about honor and kingly gratitude, consoles and chides his Kate about the dangers of war, and cavils "on the tenth part of a hair" concerning his portion of the proposed booty of war. The parallelism is not so exact as to intrude on the attention of the audience. But once the audience has seen Falstaff's attitude, they are stimulated to want to see Hotspur's, as well as Prince Hal's reactions to them both. Indeed, without Prince Hal, the contrasts would be pointless.

Such an introduction not only sets forth the main subject of the essay—the contrast between Hotspur and Falstaff—but also points toward the middle parts of the paper. The introduction accomplishes this preparation by listing several topics that can be dealt with in detail, and by showing how a discussion of Prince Hal's reactions will help to support the topic assertion.

Making your assertion clear

In the example above a good many details could readily choke out the clarity of the main idea. What saves the introduction from obscurity is the writer's insistence, in the title and throughout the paragraph, on the contrast between the two characters. If, later in the paper, the reader were to discover more ideas about Prince Hal than about Hotspur and Falstaff, the introduction would not have done its job. In that case either the first paragraph or the whole paper would have to be rewritten.

Details are nearly always needed in the early parts of your papers. As long as they clarify your meaning and do not slow down the pace of your discussion, you should use them. In the following examples, note that the introduction on the left seems rather cluttered with one or two too many details. In contrast, the example on the right tends to overgeneralize the subject, and the reader wishes to see at least one specific example.

A HUMORIST ON MODERN ABUSE OF NATURE	E. B. WHITE AND THOREAU
In his essay on *Walden*, E. B. White accuses the twentieth century of trampling upon Thoreau's most cherished values about nature. In this "letter" to Thoreau, White pretends a friendly attitude. Using barbed humor about beer bottles in the picnic grounds and a faded shirt in the pond, he builds a serious indictment of the values of modern society. His contrast is all the more powerful because it is implied, not stated. . . .	E. B. White wrote a "letter" to Thoreau that makes fun of modern society. White shows how people today do not follow Thoreau's values and how modern society is not as good as life in the nineteenth century. White makes fun of people today for not caring about nature. . . .

The introduction at the left above is best, since the reader has a fair idea of what the subject of the paper is. Nevertheless, because the paragraph is excessively compressed, and because the details are not well ordered and connected, the reader may expect a rather slow, plodding time of it. In contrast, the paragraph at the right above wastes words on vague, repetitious statements: ". . . makes fun of modern society . . ."; ". . . modern society is not as good as . . ."; ". . . makes fun of people today. . . ." Here, the reader would begin to resent having to read so many words for so few ideas. Your introduction should neither bury your topic assertion in a welter of details nor spread it too thin.

Avoiding apology, irrelevance, and postponement

Especially in essay examinations, students tend to hem and haw in their opening sentences: "Although I feel better prepared to discuss *Huckleberry Finn* than *Tom Sawyer,* I shall attempt to write about the latter." Such an introductory sentence commits all three errors described in this rule. It damages the reader's confidence in the writer's knowledge of the subject; it wastes twenty words on an immaterial comment; and it needlessly delays the main discussion itself.

Similar errors occur even in more thoughtful introductions. For instance, consider the failings in the following opening sentences: "This paper will be concerned with the stylistic relationship between *Huckleberry Finn* and *Tom Sawyer*," or: "In matters of style, *Huckleberry Finn* and *Tom Sawyer* include some similarities and some differences," or: "I intend to write about several points of style in *Huckleberry Finn* and *Tom Sawyer*." In each case the reader senses the postponing tactics of the writer. The first and third examples tell the reader what the subject will be; once he really gets into the paper, the reader may observe that these first sentences are too obvious to need saying at all. The second example is likewise redundant. If there are only some similarities, there are also only some differences between the books.

Avoiding generality and the overobvious

Especially for short essays and for papers written in class, the suggestion to avoid generality and the overobvious can save both you and your reader much needless labor and confusion. After reading a long book, you may be tempted to ignore this rule, and try to write down all your ideas at once. The result of this attempt would be a jumbled, incoherent mass of retellings and critical fragments. You do not have to rewrite a whole book or essay to show your instructor that you have done a thorough reading. Neither can you prove such a reading if you describe a single chapter or section of a book, ignoring the rest. In your topic assertion, do not bite off more than you can chew, and do not set out to prove the obvious.

TOPIC ASSERTION IS TOO BROAD
Plato's *Republic* is an example of many philosophical ideas about reality, politics, ethics, and art.

TOPIC ASSERTION IS TOO OBVIOUS
In Plato's *Republic*, Socrates attempts to define the nature of justice.

These assertions invite you to a boring recital of what Plato has already said. You should try for ideas that allow you to be interesting, that make your paper vital because you wrote it. While you must therefore shun the obvious, you must also eschew the obscure and outlandish. Do not devote your paper to a strained attempt at entertaining your reader, but select an idea that offers chances to express your own mind. This is not so difficult to do as it may sound. The lesson is simply to focus your thinking on whatever aspect of your reading materials interests you the most. To know where these interests lie always requires a thorough perusal of the book, and when you express these interests in a paper you nearly always reveal the extent and quality of the reading you have done.

Leading into the literature

The ideas you decide to uphold should take you straight into the literature, not away from it, and your paper should be neither oblique nor evasive. Even with a cogent idea to defend, you have to face the pitfall of digressing into areas that get you nowhere. For instance, such an assertion as "Lucretius' *On the Nature of the Universe* is a primitive example of twentieth-century ideas about physics" may stimulate a paper that is either relevant or irrelevant to Lucretius' book. The wrong way to write this paper would be like painting a room from the door inward. You would write yourself into a corner if you immediately began trying to give a full explanation of modern physics and ignored Lucretius. The right approach would be to assume that your reader has common knowledge about modern physics—simple ideas about molecules, atoms, and electrons—and to illustrate how accurately Lucretius has anticipated these ideas. You would waste no words explaining this common knowledge, but would devote your paper to a discussion of how Lucretius anticipates the nuclear age.

You should be aware of two basic reasons that underlie the frequent violation of this rule in student papers. The writer may wish (consciously or not) to avoid discussing the book because he may not have read it carefully, or because he feels intimidated by his instructor's greater knowledge of the subject. The remedy for the first mistake is simply to study the assignment, but the cure for the second is just as simple. Since learning is a cooperative endeavor, more than merely a conflict of minds, no student is expected to compete with his instructor. Therefore, if your instructor knows a great deal about his subject, you should be grateful; when you write about this subject, allow your respect for scholarship to enrich, not to impoverish, what you say. Of course, this does not mean that you should parrot the teacher or slavishly agree with him on every point.

Allowing for reference to many points in the literature

You may validly center your remarks on a single passage, scene, or episode; but usually, you should also explain how this part of the literature bears on the other parts. The point is that you should not treat a part of a work as if it were a whole. This rule can pose a stimulating challenge, one that may give you some good ideas for subject matter. Since a work of art must contain no irrelevancies, you could show how some apparently unrelated aspect of the literature is really essential to its overall unity and integrity, as in the following topic assertion: "The episode of the Old Man of the Hill in Fielding's *Tom Jones* seems to be a pointless digression—a detraction from the main plot—but this episode is a statement in miniature of the philosophy behind the whole book."

SUGGESTIONS FOR THE BODY OF THE PAPER

Since the topic assertion can be expressed in only a paragraph or two, the bulk of your paper will be composed of defense and support. If the assertion has been well considered, clearly and cogently stated, the largest part of your paper should be relatively easy to write. But, in the midst of your paper, if you have to expend part of your mental energy thinking up new ideas to support, you will have to work without the help of a generating principle. In general, you should remember the need to make your reader see the good sense of the basic ideas behind your essay. Understanding all aspects of your assertion, therefore, is not all there is to your writing job. You must also realize that your reader is constantly in the dark, requiring you to shed new light on his path at every step.

Relevance of support

In your essay or examination you have a chance to put to use the long hours you have spent in your reading. Do not throw this work away by devoting many words to irrelevant ideas. Surprisingly enough, when they have to write about their reading, some students seem bent on using any pretext to discount their own hard efforts. One reason you may be subject to this failure to follow through is the labor of writing itself. It is difficult first to restrict your thinking to a work of literature and then to write about only a single aspect of that literature. When you put pen to paper, you are therefore liable to follow the easy path, to write whatever comes into your mind, even irrelevant ideas.

The way to avoid this error is to permeate your mind with the literature, as well as to choose a propitious topic assertion to defend. You should read with your fullest attention on the book, so that you can write with your best recollection of what it says. Read slowly enough for the atmosphere of the literature to absorb you, and fast enough to avoid allowing your mind to wander. Ideally, you should live through the episodes in your reading while you also stand aloof, maintaining your own critical faculties intact. When you write, this double task of creative and critical reading, if well done, will help you to recall the literature and to analyze it with greater understanding.

Stating key assumptions clearly

In stating key assumptions, you will need to understand them thoroughly, to make them fully, and to express them explicitly. An assertion like "Ibsen's *Enemy of the People* shows how political power, if unchecked by conscience, corrupts both government and governed" assumes that there is a broader issue—political power versus conscience—behind the corrupt actions of Mayor Stockmann and the attempt at reform by his brother, Dr. Stockmann. In your paper you should clearly indicate—though not waste words upon—this underlying assumption.

Many assertions about literature will probably rest upon assumptions concerning the purposes or the goals of the author. The question, "What were the intentions of the author?" may therefore underlie many of your comments about your reading. Logically this question cannot be answered fully since a reader of literature can say validly, "We do not know what the author *intended;* we only know what he *achieved,* and intention and achievement are often two different things." In many instances the author is dead and cannot be questioned about his intentions. In other cases, the author's intentions were partly subconscious and therefore inaccessible even to his own conscious mind. You do have the literature to consult, however, and you can—and should—make inferences about the author's intentions and how well he fulfilled them. The lesson you should learn from this logical dilemma is always to label your guesswork as guesswork, never to be dogmatic.

Using effective transitions

A transition is a device for showing the reader that the composition is moving forward. The most obvious connective devices are usually employed to link together the larger sections and paragraphs. For this purpose, and occasionally to connect the smaller ideas within a paragraph, you may use words and phrases like *moreover, however, nevertheless, therefore, thus, hence, because, since.* To see how such expressions are used, read almost any page in a book of nonfiction, spot the connective expression, and note how it joins ideas together. Sometimes the ideas will be consecutive, with the transition merely helping the style to flow more smoothly. At other times, however, the connected ideas will be widely spaced or so diverse as to need obvious transitional devices.

Transitions are difficult when your composition is forced and halting. If you are advancing smoothly toward a clear goal, each new idea will normally contribute to the progress and your style will flow naturally; without a goal, every new sentence seems to the reader like a fresh beginning. What goes first should therefore contain a hint of what follows, and this hint is clarified as the reader advances. It is not that your early ideas should be vague and your later ones clear. The point is, rather, that every statement joins hands with at least two of its neighbors—the one before it, and the one after. Occasionally, also, you will need to tie a passage together by connecting an opening comment with a closing one, or two other statements that are not consecutive. The best transitions for all these purposes are linkages in thought. In the following paragraph from Coleridge's "On Shakespeare as Poet and Dramatist," the ideas are particularly well connected.

> In judging of different poets, we ought to inquire what authors have brought into fullest play our imagination and our reason, or have created the greatest excitements and produced the completest harmony. Considering only great exquisiteness of language and sweetness of metre, it is impossible to deny to Pope the title of a delightful writer; whether he be a poet must be determined as we define the word: doubtless if everything that pleases be poetry, Pope's satires and epistles must be poetry. Poetry, as distinguished from general modes of composition, does not rest in metre; it is not poetry if it makes no appeal to our imagination, our passions and our sympathy. One character attaches to all true poets: they write from a principle within, independent of everything without. The work of a true poet, in its form, its shapings and modifications, is distinguished from all other works that assume to belong to the

class of poetry, as a natural from an artificial flower, or as the mimic garden of a child from an enamelled meadow. In the former the flowers are broken from their stems and stuck in the ground; they are beautiful to the eye and fragrant to the sense, but their colours soon fade, and their odour is transient as the smile of the planter; while the meadow may be visited again and again with renewed delight; its beauty is innate in the soil, and its bloom is of the freshness of nature.

Note how the third and fourth sentences above connect with the first. A simplified paraphrase may explain this linkage. Sentence one: Poetry exercises our faculties completely. Sentence two: Pope, though pleasing, does not yield this complete exercise. Sentences three and four: Poetry appeals to the whole personality because it is written "from a principle within." Although Coleridge has repeated his topic idea in the third sentence, he also advances the paragraph toward the fourth sentence. The way Coleridge explains the inward principle—using the analogy of a meadow in nature and a fabricated garden—is especially appropriate to the idea of naturalness expressed in the fourth sentence. The conclusion of the paragraph thus flows easily from this middle. Moreover, in the most suggestive way, the final statements harken back to the introductory ideas about imagination and harmony.

Defending your assertion adequately

In defending your assertion do not ignore evidence that tends to disprove it. Like a good lawyer, you should readily admit the facts that are available to your opponent, and you should neither falsify them nor minimize their importance. In supporting your own assertion these facts should clarify, not weaken, your position. For example, consider how the disclaimers in italics in the following paragraph help to draw the limits of the assumption stated in the first sentence.

In Joyce's *Portrait of the Artist as a Young Man,* the family dinner is a recurrent scene that helps to trace the development of

Stephen's personality. In this book the reader observes the young man as he grows up, returning repeatedly to the family group. *Stephen's artistic sensibilities need, for their growth, a great variety of other settings, and many of these are unique, never to be repeated.* But at the dinner table, Stephen can be observed at different periods in his life—his own changing character silhouetted against the relatively constant characters of his family. *Certainly, one sees the family in a variety of circumstances, and his father, mother, brothers and sisters change their attitudes toward Stephen.* Nevertheless, for this contrast, Joyce does show a constancy in these characters, as well as in the setting itself.

This paragraph calls for many details to fill out the remaining parts of the paper. The emphasis in these details would fall first on the several dinner scenes, and the writer would show, in the middle of the paper, how Stephen is presented in each of them. Other details would illustrate the consistency of some of the chief characters besides Stephen, and how he is set off against them. The disclaimers themselves would also receive attention in the body of the paper. The writer would indicate in passing some of the variety of unique scenes in Stephen's life and the differing circumstances of his family, referred to in italics above.

Avoiding digressions
An outline can nearly always help you avoid sidetracking your paper into byways that lead nowhere. Therefore, you should ordinarily construct a framework for your essay—even if this is only an unwritten mental plan—before you write. Your outline may be one of the general types illustrated in this book in Chapter 3. Whatever kind of overall structure you employ, it should serve as a guide to remind you of the limits of your topic, to help you make your writing move in a progression toward your conclusion, and to show you where to put up signposts so that your reader will more readily follow the stages of your essay.

Using a proper tone

In an argument, employ a tone of respect both toward the book and toward your imaginary opponent. A critical argument is not merely a squabble; it consists of more than deprecation and name-calling. Especially when you feel strongly about an issue, you may unwittingly allow your emotions to spoil your ideas. Moreover, you may sincerely believe that you have squelched an opponent when in reality your own comments could be reduced to little better than mudslinging.

You are not admonished here to make your writing flat and dull, but to observe the difference between interest and distortion. Thus, when a writer cools down a heated argument, he also makes his statements more effective. It is true that your reader must either take or leave what you say, but it is also true that while he is reading, he cannot ask you questions or reply to your comments. If he disagrees with what you say, therefore, he is helpless to express his own arguments to you. If you antagonize him, he has only one immediate recourse—a fatal one to your arguments—to stop reading your paper.

Two good checks against allowing emotionalism to damage your writing are always available to you. First, you should allow any emotional comments to cool off before you write them in a final draft. With papers written in class, you do not have time for many drafts, and so you should guard against excessive or unwarranted feeling in the first place. Papers written out of class may be revised on successive days, as your ideas become clearer to you.

If possible, you should prepare several versions of the most debatable parts of your paper. From these versions you would choose the best for your final draft. The other way to guard against emotionalism is to be sure that you are getting to the core of the issue. If basic issues, rather than irrelevancies, are the points that you discuss, your argument will be both clearer and more thoughtful. Also, your paper will be less likely to go wrong in its tone.

SUGGESTIONS FOR THE CONCLUSION

The end of your essay may sometimes require as much attention as its beginning. Here, you should leave your reader with the emphatic thought of your paper, an idea that does more than merely restate the topic assertion of the introduction. Certainly, by the end of the paper, the reader should know what the writer is trying to illustrate or prove. For longer essays, a final summing up of the main points is helpful, but for short papers of only two or three pages, such summaries may weaken your effect, rather than strengthen it. For everything you write, the conclusion should be slightly different in style, in tone, and in content from the preceding parts of the paper. The following suggestions should help you make your concluding paragraphs distinctive.

The concluding summary

The summarizing conclusion should usually be reserved for papers of over three pages, when the reader may tend to forget the main points. For instance, consider a five-page essay in which the topic assertion is: "Mark Twain achieved unity of effect in *Life on the Mississippi* by overcoming a serious obstacle." The middle of the paper would explain what this obstacle was—variety of type of composition. The summarizing conclusion would help to show how the middle of the essay is connected with the topic assertion:

> *Life on the Mississippi*, then, is a vast compendium of moods and styles that reinforce Twain's practice in the four classical types of composition. It represents Twain's narrative virtuosity in the frontier tall tale, as in "The Professor's Yarn"; it reveals his skill at complex exposition, as in the intricate chapters on sounding and piloting; it illustrates splendid artistry in description, especially in the passages on steamboat racing and on the unpredictable appearance of the river; and it presents an ability in rhetoric and argumentative writing, as exemplified in his suggestions for a pilots' trade union. In short, the book achieves unity in spite of its lack of restriction to any one kind of writing, while demonstrating a certain roughshod excellence in them all.

Even though it is a summary, such a conclusion should not ordinarily repeat any phrases from the body of the paper. The four sections of the above paragraph attempt both to remind the reader of what was said in the four parts of the middle of the essay and to illustrate how these parts are tied in with the main idea.

Conclusions of brief papers

There is no reason for an elaborate concluding summary of short themes written in class. Moreover, a final paragraph beginning with a phrase like "In conclusion," or "To sum it all up," may seem pompous or wordy, especially in a paper of only two or three pages. Nevertheless, even in your brief papers, you should plan for the main emphasis to come last, as the parting comment with which you leave the reader. Even though you have put your topic assertion early, all parts of your essay should move toward this parting comment. It should not be possible to cut off either the head or the tail of your essay and still keep the animal alive. Thus, one test of the conclusion, as well as of the other parts of the essay, is whether or not you would sacrifice any important meaning by eliminating it.

The following conclusion might culminate a short paper titled "A Message in 'The Catbird Seat,'" in which the assertion is that in one of James Thurber's funniest stories, there is an admixture of soberness:

> . . . But the most serious aspect of this very humorous story is Thurber's insistence upon the dignity of even a file clerk's job. Mrs. Barrows's flippant use of trite jokes has so roused Mr. Martin's righteous indignation that, by the use of stream-of-conscious technique described above, Thurber almost condones his chief character's thoughts of murder.

This type of conclusion also harkens back to the middle of the essay and to the topic assertion. Though this is not the only way of ending a paper, it performs the service of reminding the reader of the support that has already been offered for the final point. It does not, however, drag the reader through a needless repetition of what has just been said.

Making the conclusion emphatic

It is best to be definite, not vague, in your final sentences. A conclusion that drivels off into irrelevancy or generality leaves a bad taste in the reader's mouth: "More can be said about symbolism in Hawthorne's short stories than we have space for in such a brief paper." This is as though the writer were apologizing to the reader for not having treated the topic fully. When you feel that such an apology is needed, inspect your topic idea again, to see if it needs to be more severely limited. If it does not, simply drop the apology and brighten up your last sentences with accurate diction. If your main idea does need limiting, you may need to rewrite the essay, or to cut out the generality in your topic assertion.

Harmony between conclusion and assertion

The single requirement of all conclusions is a sense of finality in style and in content. In both long and short essays, your best method of achieving this tone is to reinforce your support for what you have been asserting throughout the paper. One method to achieve this reinforcement is to treat your topic assertion as if it were a question; in your conclusion, you may give the final answer: ". . . Thus, if it were asked whether Dreiser's style has any literary merit, one should answer: 'Only if one interprets "literary merit" to mean journalistic accuracy.'" This device may work more smoothly and effectively if you frame the question as a hypothesis and avoid the question mark. Even here, the quotation marks and the colloquial use of the fragment are not virtues of style; they are merely unusual devices to heighten the reader's awareness of the final point.

Avoiding the tacked-on conclusion

Most weak conclusions result from poor planning. Often the writer has forgotten some qualification or relatively minor idea in the body of the paper and so tacks it on at the end. Thus out of place, the idea may be overemphasized or misconstrued by the reader: ". . . Thus, Dryden does not represent a simple, classical position on the unities. It is true, however, that he stresses unity of action, which makes him seem very classical indeed." This conclusion shows that an adequate discussion of the qualifying idea should have been planned for the body of the paper.

EXERCISES: *Study the following list of topics as possible writing assignments:*

1. It is as important (or more important, or less important) for the average student to study literature in college as it is to study science.
2. Since poetry and fiction deal mainly with things that never happened, the most important part of literature is nonfiction.
3. The study of philosophy should (or must, or should not) be included in a literature course.
4. It is more valuable to study fiction than nonfiction.
5. Communication is more worthwhile and complete in speaking than in writing (or vice versa).
6. In learning to think logically, the reading of books is greatly overrated (or underrated) by the general public.

A. From the above list of topics, point out which ones would require the most argumentative support: facts or logical ideas marshaled to prove a topic assertion or to illustrate the solidity of an opinion. Choose two or three of the topics and describe in general terms the beginning, the middle, and the end of essays you might write using each of these topics.

B. For homework, write a general description of a sample paper on one of the above topics. In this description, specify the probable length in the number of words, and include a list of ten or fifteen possible ideas for the paper, in sentence form, like the list above. Divide your list into two or three ideas for the introduction, ten or twelve for the body, and two or three for the conclusion. Be ready to explain in class some of the statements you would need to include in the paper. If requested to do so by your instructor, write your list on the blackboard and explain to the class how you would progress from each one of your ideas to the next.

five

Writing the essay: experience and interpretation

IN THIS CHAPTER, two kinds of essays are related to your reading materials. Your instructor may refer you to one of the projects here when a paper is due. In any specific writing project, the nature of your composition may be determined by (1) the kind of literary study your instructor wishes you to do, and (2) the nature of the literature you will write about. Ordinarily your instructor will specify the literature; and using these assignments for suggestions, he may tell you more or less specifically the type of composition you are to produce. Even so, you should not slight the problem of relevance. You should know that, especially early in the course, it is surprising how many papers finally arrive on the instructor's desk that have little or no bearing on the assignment. Though the irrelevant work may not always fail, it can hardly achieve real success, simply because it is not what was asked for.

71

Indeed, the instructor may validly judge the papers according to directness and relevance in fulfilling his assignments, as well as according to how well they are written.

The kinds of papers you write may be determined also by the nature of the literature itself. That is, besides your writing assignment, the classification of the literature, its subject matter, and even its style, can help you decide what to say.

One kind of paper might be suggested by a drama, another kind by a novel, still other kinds by a philosophical essay or a lyric poem. Though you have no hard and fast rules to follow, you would probably write differently about a short story based primarily on plot development, as opposed to one based primarily on character development. Similarly, a serious literary essay on the hydrogen bomb would call for a different kind of writing than would a humorous essay on Christmas presents. Thus, depending on the emphasis that seems most appropriate for your paper, you can shape your ideas and comments in accordance with the literary classification, the subject matter, and the style of your reading assignments. You should consider these aspects of the literature when your instructor makes a writing assignment.

LITERATURE AND EXPERIENCE: FOUR WRITING PROJECTS

In the first four writing projects described in this chapter, you have some freedom to discuss your own experience. In each case, however, you are asked to use examples from literature as models and guides for your writing, and your compositions should not leave your reading assignments behind. One important goal here is a more thorough understanding of the literature and its details of style and structure; another is the practice you get in writing under controlled conditions. The basic rationale of the four projects in this section is to provide some groundwork in writing the kind of expository essays that center more directly on the literature itself.

If you have already had such a background, your instructor may give you a choice of only one or two of these essays, or he may decide to skip this section and to begin with the second section of this chapter, "Writing Literary Interpretations."

Description of a scene like that in a reading assignment
Before you write this theme, study a piece of literature in which the point is to make the reader experience a scene or an atmosphere. Then choose a topic for your paper that is similar to the description in the literature. Try to select your subject matter with an eye to using some of the feelings, attitudes, or stylistic devices in the text. An overhasty decision on your topic would make the paper difficult to write; a thoughtful decision may yield satisfaction both to you and to your reader.

For example, suppose that in class you are studying Francis Parkman's *The Oregon Trail* (a passage from this book is quoted on pages 103 to 104). The author describes his experiences during a journey in 1846, from the Mississippi westward to Oregon. While the class is reading the book, suppose further that your instructor asks you to write a theme describing briefly a scene from your own experience like one of those in Parkman's book. One specification in this assignment might be that your writing is to mingle scenic matter with action. A problem you should solve early is to fit your topic to the needed length of the paper. For a short essay, the aspects of the scene you will cover must be limited and the actions must be brief. If you tried to describe a trip to Europe in a three- or four-page theme, obviously you would have to ignore vast tracts of ocean and land; likewise, your essay would have to omit many of your most important experiences. Therefore, for this paper, you could settle on a small area and an unpretentious segment of time and action.

Your instructor may ask you to specify the part of the literature you are using as a model. Let us say that you choose a short passage in *The Oregon Trail* that describes the confusion and bustle of the town of Independence, Missouri, where Parkman shows all kinds of frontier emigrants gathering provisions for the long journey to Oregon. Though you have probably had no experience with frontier emigrants, you may finally decide to describe the activity in a busy variety store that reminds you of Parkman's scene. Your theme might include some comments like the following:

> In the excitement of Saturday morning, a father and his twelve-year-old son tinkered at the electrical counter, selecting materials for a doorbell; two small girls gravely inspected new outfits for their doll; an escaped toddler with a forgotten tear drying on his cheek gaped wonderingly at a large tank of varicolored tropical fish; a harassed mother deftly thumbed through a pile of children's garments for the required size. Everywhere the vital quest for merchandise was infused with a kind of cheerful hurry and a fascination—almost a hypnotic trance—at the plenitude and readiness of the available satisfactions.

Besides your topic, another important matter is the style you employ. You may succeed with a topic that at first seems unrelated to the assigned literature if you can show, through a fitting style, how your idea is really relevant when it is more deeply considered. Using different styles is one of the skills you should learn in the course, and if they are not forced or unnatural, your phrasing and syntax can help you to be more accurate in fulfilling your assignments. Even the exact topic treated in the literature can result in a failing paper if when you are asked for an original composition, you simply rewrite or loosely summarize the literature, or if your style places your composition outside the area of your assignment.

A character sketch of a person similar to a literary character
Your best decision for this paper may be to write a character sketch of someone you know. Since the first essay assigned in this group described a place, this one may properly focus upon an indi-

vidual in your experience. Moreover, nearly every literary work includes some illustration or discussion of human traits, and it should therefore be easy to tie this theme in with your classwork in literature. Suppose you are reading James Hilton's *Goodbye, Mr. Chips* or Dorothy Canfield Fisher's *Seasoned Timber,* both of which describe selfless, inspired schoolteachers, devoted to their students and struggling with the problems of life. Or you may be reading the popular *Catcher in the Rye,* by J. D. Salinger, which in one part describes a schoolteacher from the point of view of a sensitive, flippant adolescent. It would be appropriate if your sketch employed an approach similar to that of the literature (without, of course, violating good taste, or the needed formality of a college essay, as Salinger's style of vulgate conversation may occasionally do). Let us assume that you decide to describe a teacher like Mr. Chips in your own past in a reminiscence like the following:

> Mr. Thompkins—"Tommy" in our parlance—really cared whether his students learned algebra. With his glasses perched dangerously over his eyebrows, his bald spot shining in a ray of the afternoon sun, he would write a formula on the board. When the squeaking chalk stopped, there would be a long, intense pause, while the class tried to absorb the mathematical relationship. A smile of joy would come over Tommy's face during the silence, a smile of delight at the precision, the lovely balance and symmetry, he had just symbolized. It was this genuine worship for order and exactness that was Tommy Thompkins' quality that his most devoted students always spotted and tried to imitate.

One goal of this assignment is for you to study the literature as a type of composition and then to try your hand at producing an example of this type. Another is to study human nature, in both literature and life, deeply enough so that your writing about individuals is rich and thoughtful. It would be a mistake to let these two goals conflict; therefore, do not follow your literary model so slavishly as to belie the true facts and shadings of the personality you are describing.

An expression of your own opinion
on a subject treated in a reading assignment

In this theme, which may be more original than derivative, your literary model should provide only hints on what to say. The literature itself does not need to be a statement of opinion, but your own essay should treat the subject to reveal your point of view and attitudes. Your early problems of choosing a topic should be largely solved, since you will be writing in the general area covered by the literature. You may find that your most difficult preliminary task is to center on a special aspect of the topic that is limited enough for adequate treatment in a brief paper. Second, when you have found this aspect, you may not be quite positive what your real opinions about it are; therefore, you may have the somewhat puzzling job of discovering a part of yourself anew. That is, a clear point of view for your paper may demand that you commit yourself to a stand, a definite position, in respect to the issues you write about. Achieving such a point of view always involves a certain amount of skill in self-analysis, which may become a valuable writing asset: If you know what you think and how you feel about your topics, you can write more acceptably about them.

Let us take the example of your outlook toward college education. Suppose you have been reading Newman's nineteenth-century essays on what a university should be. (One of these essays is illustrated in the passage on pages 113 to 114.) Suppose further that you decide to write your theme for this assignment explaining your ideas on the most desirable approach toward learning in the schools of today. With this general idea, let us say that you finally narrow your subject down to a specific debate, which you entitle, "Modern Education—Service or Opportunity?" Some of your remarks in such a paper might go as follows:

> Through my schooling I have watched some of the less desirable consequences of treating education as a service rather than an opportunity. When service is the goal, a specific limited area of

knowledge is to be learned in a definite length of time. For instance, addition, subtraction, and some rudiments of multiplication must be mastered by the second grade; algebra and plane geometry by the junior year of high school. With such a schedule, the dullest students must either fail and drop out or cause the whole class to slow down until virtually everyone has learned the required subject matter. Too often, the schools follow the latter course; as a result, the bright students find no challenge, no opportunity to stretch their minds. In such a system, "comfortable mediocrity" prevails— comfortable, that is, to the larger middle sections of the student body, but conducive of restlessness and unexercised ability in those higher levels that should receive the most attention.

Such a theme should move toward an ending that clinches the point. Certainly, as above, much of the essay may be comprised of explanation of what is meant by the key terms. Here, the writer is working toward adequate definitions of "service" and "opportunity." Nevertheless, there should also be plenty of examples in such a paper. These you should glean from episodes, scenes, and personalities in your own experience that tend to illustrate directly the validity and good sense of your expressed opinion. These illustrative parts of your essay may offer some difficulty, chiefly in emphasis and economy; you should select and handle the examples carefully, lest they become the main burden of your essay, or sidetrack your thought, or require excessive wordage. In short, this assignment should exercise your best powers of rhetoric; in fulfilling it, you may demonstrate both originality and ingenuity of expression.

A humorous essay or a satire on the subject matter
or in the style of a reading assignment

If you decide on the humorous essay, it is probably best to use a humorous text as the basis of your work for this assignment. To hit your mark in this theme, you may need to observe some practical distinctions; for these, read the definitions of *Humor, Irony,* and *Satire* in the Glossary. Notice that humor says directly what it means, usually in light touches of banter or fun. There need be no labored attempt to provoke laughter in this composition; rather, you may be successful enough if there is simply a suggestion of a smile or a chuckle in your essay:

> As a child, I was like many boys who live near a river or stream, and who have read *Tom Sawyer*. One of my early thrills was catching my first fish. I had never dreamed that my stick-and-string outfit would catch anything. Hence, when I actually pulled the flopping thing to shore, had captured it, and made sure it was mine, I was excited beyond measure. One of the illustrations in my copy of Twain's book was of Huckleberry Finn, strolling down the street past the post-office loafers, with a string of fish dangling from his line. Thinking I would imitate this bravado, I tried to string my catch: I didn't know about the spaces in the gills and I nearly ruined the fish. Finally, I simply carried it home, in my two smelly hands—jubilant and proud.

One pitfall in compositions of this kind is the lapse into overeasy and rather shallow narrative. Also, the paper may break into separate parts, so that the essay lacks unity and singleness of effect. Both difficulties can be avoided by having a clear topic assertion that your examples tend to prove or illustrate.

Satire, a different kind of writing, usually has its thesis idea built into the style itself. If you write a satirical essay for this assignment, you may need to say the opposite of what you mean—but say it in such a bold-faced way that your reader cannot miss the point. Your literary text here might be a political work like Swift's *A Modest Proposal,* or *Gulliver's Travels,* or Aldous Huxley's *Brave New World.* Consider the following paragraph from a satirical essay.

> Our society is so devoted to its gadgets, machines, and bomb threats that life may yet become pleasant in spite of itself. The only trouble is that we lose track of reality. Jonathan Swift's solution was to float a society on a synthetic cloud, and to wake people

up with professional ear-flappers. Aldous Huxley's answers were
the Big Brother, the psychiatrist, and the happiness pill. I suggest
a different way out: Since we are mad, let us be governed by those
who are truly in the know about madness—not psychiatrists, but
madmen themselves. Let us move our government to the mad-
houses, which are larger than government buildings and more
populous. For our greatest leader we should naturally elect the
greatest madman. . . .
This system would have many advantages. For instance . . . .

As you see, writing of this kind may challenge your wit and your
sense of fun; once you get started, however, you may tend to let
your composition become uncontrolled. This problem nearly always occurs when the writer laughs so heartily that he fails to see
the possible reactions of his reader. Unaware of what is happening,
the writer thus ignominiously loses the effect he has aimed at.
Therefore, if you write a satire, you should do your best to see
your material objectively. If your essay does what you want it to
do in the cold light of the morning after—instead of merely in the
heat of writing—your wit and humor may shine also for your
reader.

WRITING LITERARY INTERPRETATIONS: FOUR WRITING PROJECTS

This section attempts to show you how to write more directly
about your reading. Here, your goal will be to record your impressions of specific literary works. Thus, because your writing will be
interpretative and explanatory, the emphasis will be on *exposition*
rather than on *narration, description,* or *argumentation.* (See these
terms in the Glossary). In your efforts to explain the meanings of
your reading assignments, you can begin to make use of the tools
and devices in the Outline-Guide on pages 19 to 27, the terms
listed in the Glossary, and the theories discussed in Part Four,
"Points of Departure." When you begin to write the literary interpretations described here, refer to the relevant passages in these
sections. (The terms printed in italics are treated in the Glossary.)

A literary comparison

In this kind of paper, you should emphasize the similarities between two works or two parts of the same work. In most cases you will use two pieces of literature by different authors, although if you have read two similar works by the same author, you may think of an especially good idea for a paper. Short stories, novels, and lyric poems are particularly well suited for projects like this one. Your instructor may choose the works to be compared, or he may ask you to make this choice. If the decision is up to you, remember that the subjects you choose do not need to be alike in all respects. In fact, you may write a more successful essay if they seem to be rather different. Your composition would then achieve the interest that attaches to overcoming an obstacle: in spite of apparent differences between your subjects, you would be showing their similarities.

It is important, however, that you have a common basis of comparison. For instance, except in rare examples, you should not try to compare a *plot* with a *scene* or a *characterization* with a *style.* In most cases, neither should you compare a *novel* with an *essay,* or a *short story* with a *lyric* poem. Though it may be acceptable to treat a novel and a short story in the same paper, or even a novel and a *tragedy* or *comedy,* it is wise always to be clear about these distinctions in *genre.* The main reason for this caution is logical enough: Literary similarities tend to lose their meaning when the works compared are different in genre. Usually, also, it is best to compare works that are similar in length. In this matter, however, you have some leeway.

For instance, let us assume that you are to compare two of Tolstoy's novels, *War and Peace* and *Anna Karenina.* In the introduction, you would note that many differences in *structure* between these books are caused by the discrepancy in length. After observing this distinction, you could illustrate some of the similarities in which length does not play an important part.

Incidentally, you should remember that to compare long and complicated works like these may entail a great deal of wasted work unless you settle upon a very specific idea for your paper. If you were to launch a general comparison upon general ideas, your paper would wander like a rudderless ship. Therefore, the longer the works you compare, the clearer your plan for writing should be. The plans described in the preceding chapters should be especially helpful here. With long works of fiction, your best comparisons may focus upon specific details of *characterization*.

In this example, suppose you compare two central characters: Anna Karenina and Natasha Rostov in *War and Peace*. A general comparison, relating each character to all the events of the plot, would yield only vagueness, or an endless recital of details. A more effective treatment might be a comparison of the characters of the two women at the moment that each one decides to elope with her lover. One of your paragraphs might run as follows:

> Because Anna is married and Natasha is not, one must expect great differences between them, especially at such a crucial junction in their lives. But beneath these differences runs a strain of similarity: both women are swept off their feet by the same kind of gallant, selfish young men who are out for a lark. More important, Anna and Natasha both realize that they are taking an irrevocable step, a step that will obliterate their former lives completely. The ultimate consequence to Anna, of course, is suicide; to Natasha, for a long time, the result of her mistake is tantamount to suicide. . . .

Many of your literary comparisons may be somewhat like this brief, hypothetical passage. That is, you will not attempt to prove similarities that are complete in every respect. Rather, you will be pointing out likenesses that you must qualify and explain by referring to specific events or situations. Also, you may find that practice in writing such comparisons is a valuable aid to you, and to your reader, in gaining a perspective on the works you compare. When you study two works from such a definite vantage point, they should tend to clarify each other in your mind. This clarification should be reflected in the sharpness of your interpretative commentary.

A literary contrast

Since contrast is the obverse of comparison, much of the advice in the foregoing discussion applies in this one also. Thus, your contrasts will be more valid and effective if the works or subjects you choose to write about are of the same *genre* or type and of similar importance and length. In fact, it is even more important here that your essay be unified than in a comparison. Moreover, the writing of a contrast entails deciding whether to mingle your discussions or to keep them separate, and you may encounter the same problem in writing comparisons. Finally, the purpose of a contrast usually differs: To envision a subject more clearly, you place it against a contrasting background or set it side by side with a contrasting subject.

When you choose your two subjects, consider the matter from your reader's standpoint. For example, suppose you are studying Shakespeare's *Hamlet* in class. Ask yourself what your own preferences would be from a list of subjects (see also Chapter 2 for suggestions about such lists, kinds of subjects, and starting points). Would you rather read a paper that contrasts Laertes with his father Polonius; or Ophelia with Queen Gertrude; or Hamlet with Horatio; or Rosencrantz with Guildenstern; or Hamlet's father (as the Ghost) with the new King Claudius? Some of these subjects you might eliminate because the papers would be too long; others because the compositions could involve a dull process of hairsplitting; still others because the elements do not appear similar enough to yield valid contrasts.

Let us assume that you decide to contrast the old king with the new king—Hamlet the elder with King Claudius. For an early part of your essay you could plan to describe some fundamental distinctions. For instance, though Hamlet the elder appears only as the Ghost, he is clearly as important a character as King Claudius but in a different way. After the ghost appears to Hamlet and urges revenge, the old king is important as a motive for Prince Hamlet's wild, indecisive behavior. King Claudius, of course, is important as the object of the revenge.

In writing your contrast, you would have to solve some typical problems of writing. First, you would need to make it clear on what basis you intend to contrast the two kings. One possible point of contrast is Hamlet's proposed revenge. Second, you would have to avoid irrelevant digressions. In this case, you may be tempted to give excessively long descriptions of Prince Hamlet's behavior, or the other motives and possible objectives (like the Queen), of his revenge. Your best guidance here would be to remind yourself of your subject matter: a *contrast between the kings.*

For the central, focusing part of your paper, let us say that you decide to interpret the scene in which Prince Hamlet reproaches his mother for marrying Claudius, whom he suspects of murdering his father; in this scene, also, the ghost appears before them both. Particularly relevant is the speech in which Hamlet shows his mother pictures of the two kings:

> Look here, upon this picture and upon this,
> The counterfeit presentment of two brothers . . .

The problem in writing an essay of this type is how to use such a scene and such a passage. Obviously the passage would be directly relevant to your writing project. But should you merely quote it, or should you analyze what it means to the Queen and to Hamlet himself, or should you avoid all reference to any characters except the two kings? Specific answers to these questions depend on the kind of essay you wish to write, but one general answer may be given: Direct reference to the literature—especially for important parts of your essay—should be for the purpose of adding support or evidence to your topic assertion. (The topic assertion is explained in detail in the first part of Chapter 4.) To illustrate one possible answer to this typical problem, we shall assume that you have decided to defend the following assertion: "Hamlet the elder represents the code of honor whereby a son must avenge his father's death; King Claudius, in contrast, represents the forces against this code of honor." One of the paragraphs in support of this assertion might use the scene in question as follows:

> When Hamlet reproaches his mother for marrying King Claudius, he shows her two pictures of the brothers and contrasts them. Here, he compares his father with Hyperion, Jove, Mars, and Mercury; and his uncle with "a mildew'd ear," and he calls him "a murderer and villain," "a king of shreds and patches." Yet in the middle of this scene, the ghost of his father appears dramatically with the words,
>
> Do not forget: this visitation
> Is but to whet thy almost blunted purpose.
> But, look, amazement on thy mother sits.
> O, step between her and her fighting soul . . .
>
> This appearance is another example of the elder Hamlet's function in the play—to keep his son on the track of justice and honor, to keep the Prince from getting embroiled in other matters. . . .

Interpretation of a literary structure

In this project you may use some of the skills of comparison and contrast gained in writing previous essays. Also, if you have written one or two essays using the literary models mentioned earlier in this chapter, the practice in close observation of the text should serve you well. You should not, of course, duplicate the kinds of paper you have written before. The main idea of your essay here might be to explain your impressions of the different parts of a literary work, to describe how they affect you as a reader. The essay may thus be a mingling of comparison and contrast, since you may need to single out the parts of the work and to show both their similarities and differences. To record the reasons for your impressions, you may wish to refer closely to the text, and possibly even to illustrate its style with brief quotations.

Depending on your instructor's specifications, you may use any genre of literature for your structural commentary. The reason for this wide field of subject matter is that every kind of literature makes use of obvious divisions between its parts: *lyric* poems and *essays* are divided into *stanzas; short stories* into sections, or at least paragraphs; *novels* and general nonfiction into chapters; and *epic* poems into books. When you have settled on a piece of literature to write about, your best plan for this paper is to observe and mark out these divisions. Then, when you begin to describe its structure, it will be easy to refer to the parts.

Let us take Steinbeck's short story, "Flight," as an example. This is the story of a Mexican boy who idles away much of his time at home throwing a knife at a tree. When he suddenly gets into an argument, almost as a reflex, he kills a man with the knife. The last half of the story concerns his flight; as he runs away, his condition becomes progressively more hopeless. His horse is killed; he struggles with hunger; he leaves his hat and his gun behind; and when his pursuers shoot at him, his hand is pierced by a rock fragment. To write about the structure of this story, distinguish first its basic mechanical divisions. An early pitfall to avoid is merely to start retelling the details of the story. You may have to write small summaries of the separate parts, but you are not bound to keep your reader in the suspense of the fiction itself. As long as your discussion is clear, it may shift from part to part as you illustrate similarities and differences. Here you are not trying to duplicate your author's *narration;* instead, your writing is *exposition*—an explanation of the story, not a retelling.

Using Steinbeck's story as an example, a hypothetical paragraph may illustrate some of the procedures and methods of writing available to you:

A surprising fact about Steinbeck's "Flight" is that its two main parts are about equal in length. Though the story receives its title from the second half, when Pepé runs from his pursuers, the first half—showing him at home with his mother and his brothers and sisters—achieves a great deal of important interest. It is here that the reader begins to care about Pepé, even to pity him and his family, isolated as they are, living in the dust. But it is here also that Steinbeck shows Pepé as a boy, preparing to be a man but not yet needing to be one. When Mama Torres says that a boy does not become a man until a man is needed, the reader begins to wonder what challenge Pepé will have to face. In his flight, Pepé meets this challenge. . . .

One way to continue would be to contrast the two parts of the story, and to illustrate how its tone differs because of Pepé's altered circumstances. In this contrast you could show how Steinbeck's characterization of the boy contrasts, and yet blends into, the author's treatment of him as a man. A unifying principle behind the paper could be Mama Torres's statement that maturity results from a need, not from simple growth. In writing this kind of essay, such a principle of unity can help you avoid writing two disconnected parts instead of a single, integrated essay.

Explanation of a literary point of view

With this kind of essay, you can make a special study of the way an author handles his materials. At least four articles in the Glossary may give you some help here, and it would be wise to study them before you proceed. Read the definitions under *Omniscient observer, Point of view, Flashback,* and *Stream of consciousness,* as well as the title term for the kind of literature you plan to write about. In your preliminary reading note that *point of view* may mean three things. First, point of view is attitude or position, as when one says, "From my point of view, reading is a greater pleasure than watching television." Second, the term may refer to style of writing: Thus, a story beginning, "I entered the house with trepidation . . ." is told from the point of view of the first person, because the narrator refers to himself as "I," and because he plays an active part in the story. In third-person and omniscient points of view, third-person pronouns are used for all the characters. Finally, point of view may refer to time sequence or setting, as when an author writes in the present tense or shifts from scene to scene.

The *short story* and the *novel* are used most frequently for papers on this topic because point of view always presents a challenge to the author of fiction. The essayist and the poet, however, may experiment with varying points of view; and when they do, their works make excellent subject matter. The key to the problem of what would make a good subject for this type of study is the frequency and kind of changes or shifts in the literature itself. For instance, if an author shifts from first to third person, or from the omniscient observer to the stream-of-consciousness technique, you could write an interesting explanation of the reasons for these shifts. Or if an author shifts the time sequences from the present to the past, and perhaps also changes the *tone* and the settings of his story, you may find these shifts relevant to a discussion of point of view. Whatever your topic, it is wise to be clear about the purposes your paper is to serve. The best essays of this kind are studies of the reasons for shifts in point of view.

Ordinarily, such shifts are evidence of the author's skill and smoothness of style; rarely are they flaws or artistic inconsistencies. For instance, in fiction, there is rarely a shift from one narrator to another narrator. In many cases, the shifts are slight and barely noticeable, but they are almost always marked by new sections or chapter headings or at least by a stanza or paragraph indention. These divisions constitute the jointures that help to define literary *structure*. Thus, if you have written a structural commentary like that described in the preceding section, you have had good practice for this paper.

Some shifts in point of view should be identified, so that you may better understand them. The dream stanzas in Blake's "The Chimney Sweeper" (page 91) are an example of a story within a story. The poem begins to tell the narrator's story; but in the third, fourth, and fifth stanzas, the narrator shifts from telling his own story (in the first person) to that of little Tom Dacre (in the third person). Tom's story also changes in scene, from the reality on earth to a setting in heaven. Together with these relatively mechanical shifts is a shift in attitude or position, from resigned misery to happiness. In *Hamlet* is a more pronounced example: Prince Hamlet contrives to have a little play, *The Murder of Gonzago,* presented before the court. Thus, on the stage at this time, there are two sets of actors and props, and the shift in point of view is extremely abrupt. Yet in an emphatic way it illustrates a device used by most writers of fiction who have more than one aspect of a story to tell and who must shift from one aspect to another.

The following anonymous poem may provide an example for a paragraph describing a shift in point of view:

> In the garden there strayed
> A beautiful maid
> As fair as the flowers of the morn:
> The first hour of her life
> She was made a man's wife,
> And was buried before she was born.

The paragraph might run as follows:

> This little poem presents a lovely scene in the first three lines, together with a riddle in the last three. What makes the shift from the tiny story to the tiny riddle artistic is that the paradoxes at the end are solved by the story at the beginning. The miniature structure of the poem reflects the subject in a mirror image: just as the birth of the beautiful maid is also her death, so the beginning of the poem is also its end. Thus, the shift from one kind of composition in the first three lines (narration) to another kind in the last three lines (exposition) is justified by the interlinking of the riddle and its solution.

six

*Problems in writing the
literary critique*

The first section of this chapter illustrates three writing strategies that you may apply both in essay examinations and in critical papers.

Writing about literary types

For the first strategy, we shall see how an objection to a topic idea can actually stimulate the writing of a paper. Let us suppose that the emphasis of your composition is simply a classification of the assigned reading matter, with the bulk of your paper supplying evidence. Some works of literature are classic examples of types (see *Genre* in the Glossary). *Oedipus Rex* is a tragedy; the *Odyssey* is an epic poem. But is a modern television play like Rod Serling's *Patterns* a tragedy? (See *Tragedy* in the Glossary.) If you think so, you could write a paper to defend your classification. Having done the background work suggested in the preceding chapter, you would note a basic objection to your topic idea. This objection—that the central character of the play is not a tragic hero—could help you compose an introduction for your paper:

> *Patterns* appears to violate one of Aristotle's requirements of tragedy but in reality does not. Aristotle says that the tragic hero, because of his tragic flaw, must be defeated by his problem. In Serling's play, the central character, Fred Staples, is not a tragic hero; indeed, he even wins a kind of success against the forces that would destroy him. However, Andy Sloane, Fred's best friend, is defeated by these forces in the classic way. If *Patterns* is a tragedy, then, Andy Sloan, or the forces he represents and symbolizes, must be the central issue of the play. What happens is that Fred Staples and Andy Sloane are fused into one image; Andy represents Fred's tragic flaw, and when Andy dies, part of Fred dies also. . . .

An important part of such a paper would show, by citing evidence from the play, that Andy and Fred are to be considered by the audience as a single unit, and that Andy does, in fact, represent Fred's tragic flaw.

A paper of this kind might employ the following basic framework:

> *Topic Idea:*   Classification of a work of literature.
> *Introduction:* Statement of the case against the classification proposed by the topic idea.
> *Main Body:*   Evidence from the literature itself that objections to this classification are not valid.
> *Conclusion:*   Statement, or restatement in a new way, of the reasons why the classification proposed in the paper is valid.

Any work of literature, on a scale from the most classic examples of literary types to those works that seem to defy classification, can serve as subject matter for a paper written on this general plan. Also, the plan might be modified to suit different subjects.

According to the nature of the literature that you discuss, your topic idea can affirm or deny any given classification. The paper on Serling's *Patterns* could deny that the play is a tragedy by supporting the objection about the lack of unity in the tragic hero. As a third possibility, the paper could assert that the play both is and is not a tragedy. As long as you make your thesis clear and support it with good evidence, you are free to adopt any position that seems valid to you.

Distinguishing between levels of meaning

The second sample strategy shows how deeper levels of meaning in the literature can stimulate ideas to write about. William Blake's "The Chimney Sweeper" suggests a good subject for such a paper.

THE CHIMNEY SWEEPER

When my mother died I was very young,   1
And my father sold me while yet my tongue
Could scarcely cry " 'weep! 'weep! 'weep 'weep!"
So your chimneys I sweep, and in soot I sleep.

There's little Tom Dacre, who cried when his head,   5
That curled like a lamb's back, was shaved; so I said
"Hush, Tom! never mind it, for, when your head's bare,
You know that the soot cannot spoil your white hair."

And so he was quiet, and that very night,
As Tom was asleeping, he had such a sight!   10
That thousands of sweepers, Dick, Joe, Ned, and Jack,
Were all of them locked up in coffins of black.

And by came an Angel who had a bright key,
And he opened the coffins and set them all free;
Then down a green plain leaping, laughing, they run,   15
And wash in a river, and shine in the sun.

Then naked and white, all their bags left behind,
They rise upon clouds and sport in the wind;
And the Angel told Tom, if he'd be a good boy,
He'd have God for his father, and never want joy.   20

> And so Tom awoke, and we rose in the dark,
> And got with our bags and our brushes to work.
> Though the morning was cold, Tom was happy and warm;
> So if all do their duty they need not fear harm.

This poem represents the kind of literature that has more than one level of meaning. Since nearly all good fiction and much non-fiction falls in one way or another into this multileveled class, it would be wrong to assert that only poetry can say more than one thing at a time. Blake's poem is used as an example because it illustrates, in brief compass, a certain cluster of literary characteristics.

Your background thinking for an essay about a selection from this kind of literature may have several aspects. But your whole approach may be governed by two key procedures: first, to distinguish the levels of meaning for your reader, and, second, to point out how these levels are interrelated. An important subsidiary task may be to show the reader why the literature is written as it is. For example, you may need to explain why it would damage the poem to omit a line or a phrase, or to change the order of the stanzas.

Before continuing, read the poem again to see whether you can discover more than a simple, surface story. In this reading, some clues may help. In the eighteenth century, when this poem was written, small boys were sold as workers; the little apprentice sweepers climbed up inside chimneys and cleaned out the soot, which they collected in bags. The boys were often mistreated by their masters, and like Tom Dacre in this poem, many had their heads shaved. Children generally and orphans in particular were exploited mercilessly and often suffered neglect and disease. As you read for deeper meaning, observe that this situation offers Blake a fine opportunity for some trenchant commentary upon the guilt involved in commercial exploitation of children.

If you have studied the poem with these hints in mind, the outlines of the two main levels of meaning should be clear to you. One involves the story told by the boy who narrates the poem. The other level of meaning, hidden beneath this little story, involves the author's condemnation of adults who mistreat children. A brief 500- to 600-word paper about this poem could be shaped, then, around your perceptions and interpretations of these two meanings. Much of the substance of your paper would be devoted to showing that the deeper level of meaning exists. Thus, you would be arguing against an unseen opponent—a hypothetical reader who can perceive only the surface meaning, and who must be presented in a forceful way with facts and quotations that indicate some poetic depth. If you can begin to show him the ways in which this depth is achieved, you may have a better chance to bring him around to your side of the argument.

Before writing such a paper, you would need to read the poem several more times, to arm yourself with enough evidence to make your case valid and to persuade your opponent. Also, you would need to be convinced yourself before you could hope to convince anyone else. To begin with, it would be obviously useful to explain the needed facts from outside the poem, like those about the chimney sweepers' trade. But you would need more immediate evidence than this if your essay is really to make its point: that Blake is not just telling a children's story but is protesting against an evil of his time. Your best evidence, clearly, should come frome somewhere within the poem itself. And the more places you can refer to in the poem, the better.

One good approach in gathering such evidence is to take note of what goes with what. Thus, every part of the poem is linked with some other part. The following comments on the surface story are alternated with comments in italics on the deeper level of meaning. Reading for all that is on the page, you should see that the first stanza sets a pitiable scene: a very young, motherless boy is sold (*What kind of a father would sell his son?*) before he can pronounce the word "sweep." "Weep!" is repeated four times. *Is there not a chance, in this repetition, that the author is telling his reader to weep for the child, who is obviously advertising his trade by calling out the word?* The reader may feel that the child is pitying himself, but the second stanza shows that he has enough fortitude to console his friend, and undue self-pity would not be consistent here. *Does not the author imply cruelty, or at least exploitation, by all that has occurred up to now: the child selling, the chimney sweeping itself, sleeping in soot, and the head shaving?*

In the dream stanzas of the poem (stanzas 3, 4, and 5) a little drama is played within the poem. *In its general outline, the dream is clearly an escape from the black, sooty world of coffins and death, to a clean, shining one of playful sport and joy. In this contrast is a potent accusation of society, since the author is effectively showing the children as society has made them, as against what children should be.* An Angel with a bright key rescues thousands of children, who first wash themselves and then rise on clouds to play. *The Angel, the key, the green, the river, the clouds—all are symbols of a qualified optimism in Blake. When put together, they indicate the poet's faith in the human spirit, and the invulnerability of real innocence. Obviously, the newly washed—innocent— children in the dream have the most powerful ally of all: God Himself. At least in heaven, good children may be truly happy.*

The reader is shocked back to earth in the final stanza. The children, however, awake and go bravely to work; in the cold darkness one of them (*warmed by his dream*) is happy. The last line draws a moral: doing one's duty will yield safety, or at least freedom from harm. *The last stanza and especially the last line constitute a most powerfully ironic statement. Blake cynically states the watchword that all overlords, despots, and exploiters preach to those they hold in subjection: do your "duty"—that is, do the work or serve the purpose that is demanded of you—and you will be safe. Here, as Tom Dacre happily contemplates the message of the Angel—an overlord higher than any master of chimney sweepers—Blake shows that in this higher sense, the saying is true.*

This example of the thinking that goes into a paper illustrates one way to keep your ideas original and to avoid digressing into irrelevancies. The pattern of thinking behind this project would definitely apply in writing the same kind of paper about a novel, a play, or a short story; and you could also use it to discuss many essays. First, determine whether there is a deeper level of significance than that on the surface; second, collect all the explicit and implicit occurrences and illustrations of that aspect of the literature; third, describe their relationships; fourth, form a conclusion about the general meaning of these relationships, not forgetting that if the literary work is a work of art, the ultimate meaning is a unified one.

Writing the literary character sketch

For another kind of paper, let us suppose that you are asked to write a literary character sketch. Your main problem in writing a sketch of a fictional personality is to avoid retelling the story. You face this problem because every character in a fictional work of art is involved in some way with the events of the plot. The temptation is to let the author do your thinking for you by allowing yourself to slip into a chronicle of the actions that your character performs or that he is involved with. This error would place the emphasis of your paper on events, instead of on characteristics, as in the following example about Sophocles's *Oedipus Rex:*

> After Oedipus unwittingly kills his father, he solves the riddle of the Sphinx and frees Thebes of the plague. He is then drawn into the trap set by the Oracle when he marries the Queen—who turns out to be his mother. Finally, his remorse causes him to blind himself with his mother's broaches.

To avoid thus slipping into summary, you should assume that your reader has also read the literature. In writing your paper, you should extract from the literature not a chain of events but the characteristics of the personality you wish to describe. It will require your best efforts to make the actions in the plot constitute only minor parts of your paper, and still to be specific and interesting. The technique you should learn is to show how what your fictional character does helps to reveal what he is. Study the use of action in the following example:

> Throughout the play—in accusing Creon and Tiresias of plotting to overthrow him, in accepting as coincidence Jocasta's story of the crossroads murder—Oedipus seems to have been willfully blind to his crimes. Blinding himself literally therefore seems to him and to the audience just punishment, appropriate to his character.

Not only the actions of your topic character but the reactions of other characters to him can help you to display his traits. Such actions and reactions, of course, also help your author to delineate the character. The difference between your own writing and that of the author, however, is that your purpose is to explain the character—first to isolate him and second to analyze his traits. The point of view of your paper, therefore, should be objective. In an essay that is nonfiction, and that is as factual as you can make it, tell your reader directly what personality traits are implied by the behavior of the character and his effects on others:

> That Oedipus is sincere, at least in the beginning, is shown by his sending for Tiresias and the shepherds; that he loses his temper easily, by his rage at Tiresias and at Creon, both of whom show signs of fear when they confront him with the simple truth.

Contrast this kind of writing with the way the playwright handles these episodes. The author shows the character in action; in this case, he presents Oedipus, Tiresias, Creon, and the shepherds in heated conversation on the stage. From this live action the spectator, or the reader, must deduce the personalities of Oedipus and the other characters. What your paper accomplishes, its purpose and its goal, is just this deduction of traits from your own reading experience. You engage in the same kind of analysis when you talk objectively, without malice or praise, about one of your own acquaintances. As long as you do not write fiction, and as long as you avoid changing or adding to the story, this approach can give you a clear vantage point from which to write.

Other aids to your description are the relevant aspects of your character's status and importance in relation to the other characters in the story. Also, his parentage, his childhood background, or the story of how he came to be what he is—if you use them without waste of words and with proper emphasis—can help you draw your word picture of him. In each of these subsidiary items, you should keep your writing specific and avoid long digressions. Your reader already knows the self-evident facts, and each reference you make to them should be brief and to the point. Items that a reader remembers only with some difficulty—like Oedipus's double relationship to persons like Creon, who is both uncle and brother-in-law—are not self-evident facts.

USING SECONDARY SOURCES

A secondary source may be defined as writing by professional critics that takes literature for its subject matter. Examples of one kind of secondary source are the commentaries in Part Four of this book; these selections attempt to define different kinds of literature and to show their functions. If you read them as class assignments, they may stimulate a good deal of controversial discussion —mainly because they are theoretical and because they explain causes with which you may disagree. For instance, Eric Bentley's "Broadway—and the Alternative" explains some possible reasons for the low quality of contemporary theater. One of these reasons, he claims, is that the modern-day appetite for cheap entertainment excludes any chance that the drama may express deeper human values.

Such assertions may stimulate arguments about the drama of today, and these discussions could even include comments on the movies and television. Description and interpretation of specific contemporary works of literature—like Rod Serling's *Patterns,* discussed earlier in this chapter, or the work of Arthur Miller or Tennessee Williams—would be used to support one side or the other in the arguments. Certainly, the writing of student papers on these topics could become a vital adjunct of the discussions. Thus, an important aspect of secondary sources for your papers is the stimulus to writing and the variety of ideas they can contribute to your own composition.

QUOTING AND PARAPHRASING

In the papers you write, you may often wish to make paraphrases of and take extracts from the literature itself and from a secondary source or sources. The mechanics involved here are important, and each example presents its own problems. The most important counsel about using secondary sources is to be honest. When you quote, you must use quotation marks or indentions and give the precise source in a footnote, including edition and page number(s). Footnotes and bibliographies are really minor items in short papers, except for this necessity to avoid the relatively infrequent cases of conscious theft—for that is what plagiarism really is—or to avoid the more common cases of unconscious omission of credit. It is often better to paraphrase than to quote. But when you draw upon someone else's work, *regardless of what form you put it into, you must give proper credit*.

To distinguish between a direct quotation and a paraphrase is not difficult. Suppose, for instance, that you were writing an essay entitled "Dryden's Definition of a Play." In your introduction you may decide to quote Dryden's "An Essay of Dramatic Poesy" (see pages 308 to 311). Your paper might begin:

> After only a small quibble, the characters in Dryden's "Essay of Dramatic Poesy" all agree on the precise wording of a definition of

> a play: "a just and lively image of human nature, representing its passions and humors, and the changes of fortune to which it is subject, for the delight and instruction of mankind" . . .

Because this quotation is rather long, you may need to use indention instead of quotation marks. Your instructor may specify that a quotation of more than one sentence or more than three lines should be indented.

To illustrate the paraphrase, let us assume that you do not wish to quote directly. Your paper might be entitled "Dryden on the Unities." In this case you are not concerned with the exact wording of the definition of a play. In the body of your paper, however, you may need to paraphrase as follows:

> . . . Dryden's Neander, however, gives the dramatist more leeway in observing the unities because he understands the definition of a play more thoroughly than the others. He sees that this definition is a policy, not a rule, to the effect that *drama should reflect the spirit of life, so that the audience may enjoy the play and learn from it.*

The definition that is quoted in the first example is paraphrased in the second. Note that in the paraphrase the student uses only his own words. Especially in key passages, this is important: even if you use only one or two words of your author, if these are crucial words, you must use quotation marks. Note also that for both quotations and paraphrases, footnoting problems are alike. See *Footnote* in the "Checklist of Grammar and Mechanics."

For problems like whether or not to place commas, periods, and question marks inside or outside quotation marks, consult the Checklist. A brief, systematic study of punctuation in and out of quotations should be well worth your time; in this study, you may often refer to *Quotation Marks* in the Checklist. Moreover, the entries under *Bibliography* and *Footnote* may be very useful here, and you may also need the information under *Brackets, Ellipses,* and *Underlining.* To observe some of the chief applications of using direct quotations, read the sample passages and essays in

Chapters 5 and 8. With these studies as background, your writing about literature should assume grace and authority.

SUMMARY OF THE DO'S AND DON'T'S
OF QUOTING AND PARAPHRASING

A brief summary of the do's and don't's of quoting and paraphrasing may be helpful. First, always be sure your reader knows what material is being quoted. This means that you must check your source carefully to put all the quoted material between quotes or within indented matter. Second, be sure that the reader knows whom you are quoting. Instead of footnotes, or in addition to them, you may introduce many of your quotations by phrases that indicate the sources; sometimes more than one source must be shown, as in the following example:

> Dryden's Neander goes on to quote and to translate a French parable: *"Il est facile aux speculatifs d'etres severes, etc. ' 'Tis easy for speculative persons to judge severely . . .' "*

Third, be sure your reader knows why you include any given quotation. Sometimes a brief explanatory passage of the quotation is needed. A common failing, however, is to repeat a comment twice, once in the paper, and again in a quotation. In a great many cases, either one comment or the other should be dropped, to avoid needless repetition, as in the following:

> As Crites says, the unity of time is observed by portraying the events of one day: "The unity of time they comprehend in twenty-four hours, the compass of a natural day. . . ."

A final suggestion is to work your quotations into your essays so that your style flows smoothly. Quotations that are not complete sentences may be used without *ellipses* (see this term in the Checklist) if the omitted material is irrelevant. In any case, the part of the sentence that is your own should flow smoothly to or from the quoted part:

> Regarding the unity of place, Crites says he agrees with the ancients that "the scene ought to be continued through the play in the same place where it was laid in the beginning. . . ."

The rules and suggestions for paraphrases are similar to those for quotations. It is often true, however, that in a paraphrase you must be careful to avoid quoting unconsciously. Moreover, you must be meticulous to indicate that you are using not your own idea but a paraphrase of someone else's; for this purpose, often a brief introductory phrase will suffice:

> *Dryden's Crites interprets the unity of action to mean* a single event of the plot, around which the whole play revolves. . . .[1]

Footnotes are even more valuable for paraphrases than for quotations, because your reader may wish to compare your paraphrase with the original material itself. Your best policy here is to point out clearly, in the footnote, the passage you are paraphrasing.

[1] The paraphrased material is in lines 23 to 29 on page 310 of this book.

seven

Types of paragraphs

AS A WRITER, you should observe that the best examples of composition are found in good literature. Therefore, in your reading, it is wise to take note of the different compositional structures. Just as a student of architecture studies the work of Michaelangelo, so a student of writing should have an eye for the architectonics—the structure and technique—of his reading materials. A convenient unit for such a study is the paragraph, and you should be alert to the variety and versatility of paragraph forms. It is best to use various kinds of subject matter in this study. The following examples from literature and from criticism illustrate only a sampling of the kinds of paragraph development. You should realize, in studying them, that nearly every writer makes up many of his own paragraph structures just as nearly every architect makes up many of his own basic floor plans. Nevertheless, because their purposes for writing are often similar, different writers may employ the same kinds of paragraphs. The examples in this chapter illustrate a few of these common types.

ENUMERATION

One of the best ways to develop a paragraph is to present a list of items that help to illustrate or qualify a topic idea. To be sure that your paragraph is solidly constructed, it is usually best to write your topic idea first. The order of your examples themselves may pose some problem, but if you try to see your subject matter through your reader's eyes, you can usually think of an effective progression. Also, you must be careful to avoid monotony, especially if your list is long. As you read the following paragraph from Francis Parkman's *The Oregon Trail,* try to discover: (1) several guiding principles of organization and (2) a single, coherent over-all plan that orders the description.

But in the meantime my ride had been by no means a solitary one. The face of the country was dotted far and wide with countless hundreds of buffalo. They trooped along in files and columns, bulls, cows, and calves, on the green faces of the declivities in front. They scrambled away over the hills to the right and left; and far off, the pale blue swells in the extreme distance were dotted with innumerable specks. Sometimes I surprised shaggy old bulls grazing alone, or sleeping behind the ridges I ascended. They would leap up at my approach, stare stupidly at me through their tangled manes, and then gallop heavily away. The antelope were very numerous; and as they are always bold when in the neighborhood of buffalo, they would approach to look at me, gaze intently with their great round eyes, then suddenly leap aside, and stretch lightly away over the prairie, as swiftly as a race horse. Squalid, ruffianlike wolves sneaked through the hollows and sandy ravines. Several times I passed through villages of prairie dogs, who sat, each at the mouth of his burrow, holding his paws before him in a supplicating attitude, and yelping away most vehemently, whisking his little tail with every squeaking cry he uttered. Prairie dogs are not fastidious in their choice of companions; various long checkered snakes were sunning themselves in the midst of the village, and demure little gray owls, with a large white ring around each eye, were perched side by side with the rightful inhabitants. The prairie teemed with

> life. Again and again I looked toward the crowded hillsides, and was sure I saw horsemen; and riding near, with a mixture of hope and dread, for Indians were abroad, I found them transformed into a group of buffalo. There was nothing in human shape amid all this vast congregation of brute forms.

Often an author's purposes allow him to adopt several plans at once. For instance, in the above paragraph, Parkman wants to illustrate that he rode among a surprising number of different kinds of animals. Therefore, although he does have a coherent over-all plan, he also gives his scene the same kind of haphazard and casual appearance that it had to him as he encountered it. Another goal of his writing here is to comment upon the more interesting items in his list, for instance, to explain how the buffalo looked at him and to show some of the remarkable features of the prairie-dog village. In all, Parkman wants to be accurate, vivid, and interesting, to give his reader the chance not merely to observe the animals themselves but also their separate idiosyncrasies and the broader scene to which each part of the paragraph contributes its own effect.

EXERCISES:

A. How many animals does Parkman describe in the paragraph? What is the significance of your answer here?

B. Read again the parts describing the buffalo; explain the separate orders in time and space of the items about the buffalo. Why does Parkman return to the description of the buffalo at the end?

C. Specify four or five words in each of the following classes that seem to you to help bring the prairie to life for the reader. For each word, explain how and why the word is vivid or appropriate: verbs, nouns, participles, and simple adjectives.

D. Read again the description of the prairie-dog villages beginning, "Several times I passed . . ." Explain in detail Parkman's description of the villages. Did he have a plan for this part of his paragraph? If so, what is it? If not, why not? How does the prairie-dog village fit in with the larger elements in the scene?

E. Explain the over-all structure in several different ways. For instance, show how point of view and pace of movement from beginning to end affect the style and the compression of the details.

F. Vocabulary: *declivities, supplicating, vehemently, fastidious, demure, congregation.*

ABSTRACTION

To write a paragraph filled with abstract statements is very easy when you do not think very deeply about your topic. But to make your abstractions really say something is difficult. Things you cannot put your finger on—like truth, democracy, totalitarianism, religion, character, love, hate—are often elusive and vague in themselves. And when you try to write about them, they may seem to evaporate, like a morning fog. Therefore, it takes observation, intelligence, and even intuition to write a truly valuable paragraph of abstractions. Those three qualities of mind, plus a knowledge of life, enabled Ralph Waldo Emerson to write the following series of abstractions with some real insight into human nature.

> God offers to every mind its choice between truth and repose. Take which you please,—you can never have both. Between these, as a pendulum, man oscillates. He in whom the love of repose predominates will accept the first creed, the first philosophy, the first political party he meets,—most likely his father's. He gets rest, commodity, and reputation; but he shuts the door of truth. He in whom the love of truth predominates will keep himself aloof from all moorings, and afloat. He will abstain from dogmatism, and recognize the opposite negations, between which, as walls, his being is swung. He submits to the inconvenience of suspense and imperfect opinion, but he is a candidate for truth, as the other is not, and respects the highest law of his being.

In some ways, analyzing such a paragraph is like inspecting the structure of a single room in a building. You cannot understand the architecture of a whole book by studying one paragraph, but you can see some important strengths and weaknesses of the over-all structure. A paragraph is a miniature composition to about the same degree as a room is a minature building—both paragraph and room are designed to fulfill their specific functions. Therefore, the rule is: Different functions yield different paragraph structures. For one reason you may need to write a generalized paragraph; for another, you may wish to use an abstract paragraph; for a third, a paragraph of examples, and so on. There is no perfect type of paragraph structure, just as there is no perfect room, but only one that serves its purpose well—or not so well.

EXERCISES:

A. In Emerson's paragraph, define the word *repose,* as fully as you can.

B. Define *commodity* and *dogmatism* without using the dictionary; then look them up and redefine them.

C. Identify two figures of speech; and show, in detail, the functions of each.

D. Why does Emerson say that one who loves truth keeps himself aloof?

E. Explain the meaning of the sentence: "He will abstain . . ."

F. Identify "the other" in the next to last line.

G. Vocabulary: *oscillate, commodity, abstain, dogmatism.*

ELABORATION

This rather unorthodox term refers to a special technique of composition that you may develop in your own writing. In studying paragraph structure, it is important to realize that methods of development may be mixed. In any given example you may discover elements of two or three kinds of paragraph. The following two paragraphs from Walter Pater's "Criticism and Personality" combine the techniques of enumeration and abstraction in order to explain the process of criticism. When you read the first paragraph, observe that one of Pater's purposes is to contrast one kind of inquiry, illustrated by the series of questions, with another, illustrated by the statements concerning truth, experience, and beauty. In the second paragraph, note how Pater picks up and elaborates the main idea that he has hinted at, the idea that the critic's business is analysis of the specific effects of works of art.

"To see the object as in itself it really is," has been justly said to be the aim of all true criticism whatever; and in aesthetic criticism the first step towards seeing one's object as it really is, is to know one's own impression as it really is, to discriminate it, to realise it distinctly. The objects with which aesthetic criticism deals—music, poetry, artistic and accomplished forms of human life—are indeed receptacles of so many powers or forces: they possess, like the products of nature, so many virtues or qualities. What is this song or picture, this engaging personality presented in life or in a book, to *me?* What effect does it really produce on me? Does it give me pleasure? and if so, what sort or degree of pleasure? How is my nature modified by its presence, and under its influence? The answers to these questions are the original facts with which the aesthetic critic has to do; and, as in the study of light, of morals, of number, one must realise such primary data for one's self, or not at all. And he who experiences these impressions strongly, and drives directly at the discrimination and analysis of them, has no need to trouble himself with the abstract question what beauty is in itself, or what its exact relation to truth or experience—metaphysical questions, as unprofitable as metaphysical questions elsewhere. He may pass them all by as being, answerable or not, of no interest to him.

The aesthetic critic, then, regards all the objects with which he has to do, all works of art, and the fairer forms of nature and human life, as powers or forces producing pleasurable sensations, each of a more or less peculiar or unique kind. This influence he feels, and wishes to explain, by analysing and reducing it to its elements. To him, the picture, the landscape, the engaging personality in life or in a book, *La Gioconda*, the hills of Carrara, Pico of Mirandola, are valuable for their virtues, as we say, in speaking of an herb, a wine, a gem; for the property each has of affecting one with a special, a unique, impression of pleasure. Our education becomes complete in proportion as our susceptibility to these impressions increases in depth and variety. And the function of the aesthetic critic is to distinguish, to analyse, and separate from its adjuncts, the virtue by which a picture, a landscape, a fair personality in life or in a book, produces this special impression of beauty or pleasure, to indicate what the source of that impression is, and under what conditions it is experienced. His end is reached when he has disengaged that virtue, and noted it, as a chemist notes some natural element, for himself and others.

A writer of lesser skill and experience than Pater might consider that the first of these paragraphs says all that needs to be said on the subject. After all, Pater has explained what esthetic criticism is; though he has not used a formal definition, the writer may be sure that the reader understands the general idea. But in this case, as possibly also in examples from your own composition, the general idea is not enough. Therefore, Pater adds a short elaboration. The second paragraph, it is true, partially repeats what has been said, but the repetition adds a required emphasis and focus. When this focus has been achieved, Pater then satisfies the reader's need for details by reference to special aspects of art. Finally, he advances his discussion one step further by connecting the process of criticism with that of education.

EXERCISES:

A. In this passage, Pater offers some valuable suggestions as to how you may proceed in writing a literary interpretation. Of what pitfall does Pater warn a prospective critic of the arts?

B. According to Pater, what specific qualifications of personality should a critic of the arts possess?

C. What does Pater say, or clearly imply, is valuable about "music, poetry, artistic and accomplished forms of human life"?

D. Exactly in what passages of the second paragraph does Pater clarify his earlier discussion of the "powers and forces" of art?

E. Pater opens the paragraph with a quotation from Matthew Arnold. Explain in the order of their appearance how the details of both paragraphs are related to this quotation.

F. Vocabulary: *esthetic, metaphysical, disengage.*

DISTINCTION

To develop a paragraph by this method may seem, and sometimes be, relatively easy. You merely write a topic sentence that shows a division between two or more classes of things, and then write the paragraph to illustrate this division. In many ways, this method is like comparison and contrast (see Chapter 5). It is also like definition by contrast (see page 115 in this chapter). When you draw a distinction, you have to decide whether to keep the parts separate throughout the paper or to mix them. You have the same problem in writing both comparisons and contrasts. Also, when you attempt to distinguish one aspect of a class of things from another, you may be deeply involved in defining these aspects. The following paragraph from William Morris's "Art and the People" illustrates one way to solve these problems.

> Now the fine arts must be divided into two classes or kinds: the first what we may call the intellectual Arts, represented by painting and sculpture, address themselves wholly to the mind of man; they have no necessary connexion with any articles of material use, I mean. It is conceivable that a community might have all bodily necessaries, comforts, luxuries even, and not know what painting and sculpture meant: but besides these strictly intellectual Arts, there is a large body of art (or the pretence of it) which forms part of the matters of our daily life; our houses, our furniture, our utensils for eating and drinking, and our clothes are ornamented by this lesser kind of art, which cannot be dissociated from the things which we use every day; and this is commonly called decorative or ornamental art. I must further explain that while nations and times (though not many) have lacked the purely intellectual art, no nation or time has ever consented to do without the ornamental art; and lastly I must tell you that in all

times when the Arts were in a healthy condition there was an intimate connexion between these two kinds of art; nay moreover that in those times when art flourished most, the higher and the lower kinds of art were divided from one another by no hard and fast lines; the highest of the intellectual art had ornamental character in it and appealed to all men, and to all the faculties of a man; while the humblest of the ornamental art shared in the meaning and deep feeling of the intellectual; one melted into the other by scarcely perceptible gradations: or to put it into other words, the best artist was a workman, the humblest workman was an artist.

Note that Morris proceeds in a very orderly way: he writes his topic sentence first; then he discusses one and then the other of two aspects of art. In the middle of the paragraph he begins to alternate his comments on these kinds of art. Finally, he reflects the realities of his subject matter by explaining how both types of art are found together. In the process of making the distinction and explaining both its parts, Morris has succeeded in illustrating, also, two human qualities—craftsmanship and artistry.

EXERCISES:

A. Explain Morris's distinction by giving specific examples of your own of both kinds of art.

B. Give another list of examples that illustrate a fusion of these kinds. For each item or object in your list, explain first how it may illustrate "intellectual art," and second how it illustrates "ornamental art."

C. Explain why Morris says that both types of art were found together only "when the arts were in a healthy condition."

D. In what way does Morris imply that a good artist is also a good workman?

E. How could "the humblest workman" also be an artist, according to Morris?

F. Vocabulary: *dissociate, decorative, gradation.*

ANALOGY

An analogy is an extended comparison between two things, usually for the sake of clarifying one of them. Like a paragraph of separate comparisons, which may be divided into more than two parts, a paragraph using a single analogy is divisible into the four or five units that are the points of similarity between the things compared. Water waves and sound waves, for instance, are analogous because they are similar in more than one way. It is therefore easy to explain a sound wave to a reader who has thrown a stone into a pond and watched the concentric ripples. Likewise, you could explain what a molecule looks like to a reader who had seen a picture of our galaxy, with the planets and stars revolving around the sun. If your reader had no experience with water waves or pictures of the solar universe, you would have a more difficult job of explanation. Not all analogies are used to explain one of the units compared. Sometimes a single principle behind both elements is the object of the comparison. This is true of T. H. Huxley's analogy of life, compared with a chess game:

> Suppose it were perfectly certain that the life and fortune of every one of us would, one day or other, depend upon his winning or losing a game of chess. Don't you think that we should all consider it to be a primary duty to learn at least the names of the pieces and the way they move; to have a notion of a gambit, and a keen eye for all the means of giving and getting out of check? Do you not think that we should look with disapprobation amounting to scorn, upon the father who allowed his son, or the state which allowed its members, to grow up without knowing a pawn from a knight?
>
> Yet it is a very plain and elementary truth, that the life, the fortune, and the happiness of every one of us, and, more or less, of those who are connected with us, do depend upon our knowing something of the rules of a game infinitely more difficult and complicated than chess. It is a game which has been played for untold ages, every man and woman of us being one of the two players in a game of his or her own. The chess board is the world, the pieces

are the phenomena of the universe, the rules of the game are what we call the laws of Nature. The player on the other side is hidden from us. We know that his play is always fair, just, and patient. But also we know, to our cost, that he never overlooks a mistake, or makes the smallest allowance for our ignorance. To the man who plays well, the highest stakes are paid, with that sort of overflowing generosity with which the strong shows delight in strength. And one who plays ill is checkmated—without haste, but without remorse.

Many essayists use analogies like this one repeatedly in their writing, especially when attempting to explain to the reader a philosophy of life—something as invisible as a sound wave or a molecule, though on a different plane than either. What you should notice especially about this method of writing is that it enables you to be both clear and convincing. Also, you should observe that no analogy is perfect, simply because no two comparable things are identical.

EXERCISES:

A. Number the points of similarity, from most important to least important, in Huxley's analogy.

B. Point out the spots in the analogy that are imperfect.

C. Show how the imperfections improve the paragraph.

D. Explain why you think Huxley is really proving something, or why you think proof is not his purpose.

E. Vocabulary: *concentric, disapprobation, checkmate.*

DEFINITION (CLASSIFICATION)

A paragraph that sets out to define something may take a myriad of forms. As a compositional structure, however, a good definition by classification fills two requirements: It illustrates or identifies the thing or idea to be defined by showing a class of which it is a member, and it assists in moving the composition as a whole at least one step toward the conclusion. If you wish merely to be interesting, you can develop a paragraph simply by placing your topic in an unusual group. Thus, a topic sentence like "The short story and the novella are members of the same family" might continue with an explanation of why short stories and novellas are classed together. But if your definition must be very complete, you may have to make your paragraph more systematic.

In your themes, your purpose for defining should govern the form and structure of your paragraph. In the following passage by John Henry Newman, observe how the impression of completeness is given by the placement of a university in a great variety of different classes:

> A university is a place of concourse, whither students come from every quarter for every kind of knowledge. You cannot have the best of every kind everywhere; you must go to some great city or emporium for it. There you have all the choicest productions of nature and art all together, which you find each in its own separate place elsewhere. All the riches of the land, and of the earth, are carried up thither; there are the best markets, and there the best workmen. It is the center of trade, the supreme court of fashion, the umpire of rival talents, and the standard of things rare and precious. It is the place for seeing galleries of first-rate pictures, and for hearing wonderful voices and performers of transcendent skill. It is the place for great preachers, great orators, great nobles, great statesmen. In the nature of things, greatness and unity go together; excellence implies a center. It is the place to which a thousand schools make contributions; in which the intellect may safely range and speculate, sure to find its equal in some antagonist activity, and its judge in the tribunal of truth. It is a place where inquiry is pushed forward, and discoveries verified and perfected, and rashness rendered innocuous, and error exposed, by the collision of mind with mind, and knowledge with knowledge. It is the place where the professor becomes eloquent, and is a missionary and a preacher, displaying his science in its most complete and most winning form, pouring forth with the zeal of enthusiasm, and lighting up his own love of it in the breasts of his hearers. It is a place which wins the admiration of the young by its celebrity,

kindles the affections of the middle-aged by its beauty, and rivets the fidelity of the old by its associations. It is a seat of wisdom, a light of the world, a minister of faith, an Alma Mater of the rising generation.

Most of the paragraphs you write by this method should be informally constructed. Notice that Newman, in an informal, random way, creates the feeling that he may pick and choose any classification at all—from trade to art to "greatness"—and show how his definition of a university is appropriate to that grouping. There is no ready-made system of classes here, as there is in the example of classifying short stories and novellas. On the surface, there is no apparent ordering of details, but once you start to analyze the paragraph, you should see that beneath the appearance of natural disorder there is a clear structure and a neat arrangement. The ability to create effects like this is one of the marks of a writer of excellence.

EXERCISES:

A. Explain the principle by which Newman gives the impression of having completely defined a university.

B. Name the different subject matters that Newman uses as headings or labels for his separate classifications.

C. Choose two or three of these classifications and show how they are subdivided.

D. What words most frequently begin the sentences? Is this repetition monotonous? If not, why not?

E. Find three or four ways by which Newman unifies his paragraph.

F. Find some figures of speech and show how they are appropriate to the ideas they express and how they fit with the topic idea of the whole paragraph.

G. Find Newman's own *best* topic sentence.

H. Vocabulary: *myriad, emporium, transcendent, innocuous, celebrity.*

DEFINITION (CONTRAST)

As with the other paragraph forms, definition by contrast is usually mingled with different compositional structures. In purity, however, this method of developing an idea singles out the thing to be defined by setting it off against a background. With this thought in mind, the seventeenth-century philosopher, Spinoza, defined definition itself: "All definition is negation." By his cryptic statement, Spinoza meant that to define anything, you must first show what it is *not,* before you can show what it *is.* Thus, in the visual world, the most effective way to set off an object is to choose a contrasting background for it, to reveal its outline very sharply: for a black object, you might use a white background. Similiarly, when you wish to define a word, you should first single it out of its context, which is its natural background. To define an idea, you may have to construct a background of your own; and in this endeavor, your goal would be, ideally, to set the idea off against its opposite—just as in identifying the black object, you found it best to use a white background. In one of his definitions of truth, Henry David Thoreau uses a variant of this principle when he contrasts appearance with reality:

> Shams and delusions are esteemed for soundest truths, while reality is fabulous. If men would steadily observe realities only, and not allow themselves to be deluded, life, to compare it with such things as we know, would be like a fairy tale and the Arabian Nights' Entertainments. If we respected only what is inevitable and has a right to be, music and poetry would resound along the streets. When we are unhurried and wise, we perceive that only great and worthy things have any permanent and absolute existence, that petty fears and petty pleasures are but the shadow of the reality. This is always exhilarating and sublime. By closing the eyes and slumbering, and consenting to be deceived by shows, men establish and confirm their daily life of routine and habit everywhere, which still is built on purely illusory foundations. Children, who play life, discern its true law and relations more clearly than men, who fail to live it worthily, but who think that they are wiser by experience,

that is, by failure. I have read in a Hindoo book, that "there was a king's son, who, being expelled in infancy from his native city, was brought up by a forester, and, growing up to maturity in that state, imagined himself to belong to the barbarous race with which he lived. One of his father's ministers having discovered him revealed to him what he was, and the misconception of his character was removed, and he knew himself to be a prince. So soul," continues the Hindoo philosopher, "from the circumstances in which it is placed, mistakes its own character, until the truth is revealed to it by some holy teacher, and then it knows itself to be *Brahme*." I perceive that we inhabitants of New England live this mean life that we do because our vision does not penetrate the surface of things. We think that that *is* which *appears* to be. If a man would walk through this town and see only the reality, where, think you, would the "Mill-dam" go to? If he should give us an account of the realities he beheld we should not recognize the place in his description. Look at a meeting-house, or a court-house, or a jail, or a shop, or a dwelling-house, and say what that thing really is before a true gaze, and they would all go to pieces in your account of them. Men esteem truth remote, in the outskirts of the system, behind the farthest star, before Adam and after the last man. In eternity there is indeed something true and sublime. But all these times and places and occasions are now and here. God himself culminates in the present moment, and will never be more divine in the lapse of all the ages. And we are enabled to apprehend at all what is sublime and noble only by the perpetual instilling and drenching of the reality that surrounds us. The universe constantly and obediently answers to our conceptions; whether we travel fast or slow, the track is laid for us. Let us spend our lives in conceiving then. The poet or the artist never yet had so fair and noble a design but some of his posterity at least could accomplish it.

EXERCISES:

A. Show three ways in which Thoreau illustrates that appearance is not reality.

B. Give an example of a paragraph structure, studied above, which is found here in miniature, and which Thoreau uses to advance his definition.

C. Why does Thoreau say that the meeting-house, etc., would "dissolve before a true gaze"?

D. If appearances aren't true reality, what good are they to man—to what use does he put appearance?

E. Vocabulary: *cryptic, fabulous, still, Brahme, culminate.*

eight

Writing the essay: analysis and explication

AS A STUDENT you may have to write many papers in which you analyze the ideas in a piece of literature. If an emphasis is placed on close reading of poetry and other types of literature, you may find special use for the analytical procedures described in this chapter and in the relevant section in Part Four, "Points of Departure." In a paper of this kind, your basic concern may be to decide on the relationship between the ideas in the assigned reading material and the ideas in your proposed paper. To solve this large problem will mean that you can also solve many smaller ones. For instance, with a clear plan for how your paper will deal with the literature, you will be able to answer the following important questions: How much of the literature should you incorporate into your paper? How many of your own ideas may you use? What are the best ways to mix your own ideas with those in the literature? What point of view toward the literature should you adopt? Your answers to these questions will depend partly on the specific literature and partly on your writing assignment. But if you have a distinct plan for your own writing, it will be easier for you to connect your paper with your reading assignment. Since this connection between reading, planning, and writing is vital, you may wish to refer to the Outline-Guide at the end of Chapter 1.

ANALYSIS OF AN ESSAY BY EMERSON

The focus in the first kind of paper illustrated in this chapter is upon ideas and the way they fit together in a work of prose. To illustrate this kind of analysis, a hypothetical student paper on Emerson's well-known essay, "Self-Reliance" is included; the second kind of paper illustrated in this chapter is the explication of a poem. All kinds of literature, however, are appropriate subjects to analyze and to explicate.

To write a good analysis of ideas should require your sharpest preparatory study of the specific literature. Since you cannot analyze ideas that are vague to you, you should never strike out blind, especially on this type of paper. Therefore, have the selection and the specific passages you will write about clearly in mind. When you write, allow your clearest insights about these passages to help you decide upon your own paragraphs and selections.

Let us assume, then, that you are to write an analysis of the ideas in "Self-Reliance." After reading over the whole essay carefully, you may decide to focus upon the following paragraph:

A. Whoso would be a man must be a nonconformist. He who   1
    would gather immortal palms must not be hindered by the
    name of goodness, but must explore if it be goodness. Noth-
    ing is at last sacred but the integrity of your own mind. Absolve
    you to yourself, and you shall have the suffrage of the world.   5
B. / I remember an answer which when quite young I was
    prompted to make a valued adviser, who was wont to im-

portune me with the dear old doctrines of the church. On my
saying, What have I to do with the sacredness of traditions, if
I live wholly from within? My friend suggested,—"But these   10
impulses may be from below, not from above." I replied, "They
do not seem to me to be such; but if I am the Devil's child, I

C. will live then from the Devil." / No law can be sacred to me
but that of my nature. Good and bad are but names very
readily transferable to that or this; the only right is what is   15
after my constitution, the only wrong what is against it. A man
is to carry himself in the presence of all opposition, as if everything were titular and ephemeral but he. I am ashamed to
think how easily we capitulate to badges and names, to large
societies and dead institutions. Every decent and well-spoken   20
individual affects and sways me more than is right. I ought to
go upright and vital, and speak the rude truth in all ways. /

D. *If malice and vanity wear the coat of philanthropy, shall that*
pass? If an angry bigot assumes this bountiful cause of Abolition,
and comes to me with his last news from Barbados, why should I   25
not say to him: "Go, love thy infant; love thy wood-chopper: be
not good-natured and modest: have that grace; and never varnish
your hard, uncharitable ambition with this incredible tenderness
for black folk a thousand miles off. Thy love afar is spite at
home." Rough and graceless would be such a greeting, but truth   30

E. *is handsomer than the affectation of love.* / Your goodness must
have some edge to it,—else it is none. The doctrine of hatred
must be preached as the counteraction of the doctrine of love

F. when that pules and whines. / I shun father and mother and wife
and brother, when my genius calls me. I would write on the   35
lintels of the door-post, Whim. I hope it is somewhat better
than whim at last, but we cannot spend the day in explanation.
Expect me not to show cause why I seek or why I exclude

G. company. / Then, again, do not tell me, as a good man did
today, of my obligation to put all poor men in good situations.   40
Are they my poor? I tell thee, thou foolish philanthropist, that I
grudge the dollar, the dime, the cent I give to such men as do
not belong to me and to whom I do not belong. There is a class
of persons to whom by all spiritual affinity I am bought and
sold; for them I will go to prison, if need be; but your miscel-   45
laneous popular charities; the education at college of fools; the

building of meeting houses to the vain end to which many now
stand; alms to sots; and the thousandfold Relief Societies;—
though I confess with shame I sometimes succumb and give
the dollar, it is a wicked dollar which by and by I shall have the   50
manhood to withhold.

Stage by stage, your background study, the writing of your notes,
and the writing of the paper could proceed as follows:

1. Read the whole essay in the two ways suggested in Chapter 1;
then read the paragraph two or three times again.

2. Mark the difficult words: *absolve, suffrage, wont, importune,
titular, ephemeral, capitulate, affectation,* and perhaps *philanthropy, abolition,* and *affinity.* Write down the appropriate dictionary definitions in a notebook; for the hardest words, copy down
the sentences in which they occur—for example, "*Absolve* you to
yourself, and you shall have the *suffrage* of the world."

3. Mark the jointures between the separate ideas in the paragraph, as is done with slanted lines above. Then write down paraphrases of these ideas as follows:

A. Lines 1 to 6 admonish the reader not to accept "the name
of goodness" blindly but to decide in his own mind what is
good.

B. Lines 6 to 13 narrate an anecdote showing how Emerson
refused to accept blindly even "the dear old doctrines of the
church."

C. Lines 13 to 23 explain that since the words "good" and
"bad" can be attached to anything, one must not give in
easily "to badges and names, to large societies and dead
institutions."

D. Lines 23 to 31 narrate another anecdote to show how it is
easy to adopt a good cause (abolition) not out of true
"tenderness for black folk" but to "varnish" (a key word)
a "hard, uncharitable ambition."

E. Lines 31 to 34 justify Emerson's rough rejoinder to the

"bigot" who adopted abolition out of ambition instead of
from charity and love.

F. Lines 34 to 39 show more of what it means to rely on oneself: even though self-reliance seems whimsical to the outside world, the man of conscience does not owe the world
an explanation of his behavior.

G. Lines 39 to 51 explain that one should not be charitable to
everyone who has his hand out (to "miscellaneous popular
charities," etc.) but only "to that class of persons to whom
by all spiritual affinity I am bought and sold."

4. From these paraphrases, you should decide upon the special
idea to analyze in your paper. Your aim here is to make a study of
one or two of your marked sections, for one or two central aspects
of your proposed paper.

5. Write down detailed notes explaining all parts of the central
idea that you decided upon in step 4. For example, suppose you
chose section D, printed in italics, for this special focus. Your
notes might run as follows:

> At Line 23 Emerson launches an attack against hypocrisy. In the
> passage from Lines 24 through 26, he puts the case of an abolition-
> ist who tells him news of Barbados—a Caribbean island used for the
> infamous traffic in Negro slaves. In Lines 26 through 30 Emerson
> replies to the abolitionist, telling him not to put on a repellent false
> tenderness: "Thy love afar is spite at home." Lines 30 through 31
> explain that such a person deserves this rough "greeting" not be-
> cause he upholds a good cause but because of his falseness—his
> "affectation of love"—which is the worst kind of hypocrisy.

With this analysis as the kernel of your paper, the main outlines
of your plan should become clear and you should soon be ready to
write.

The paper may take many forms, depending upon the framework and method of writing adopted. For a longer paper, you
could show how this passage and its paragraph are related to the

essay as a whole. However, let us assume that this paper is to be short—say from 500 to 600 words. For this limited length, a good plan would be to attempt to explain the meanings of the italicized passage and to illustrate how it ties in with the other parts of the paragraph. Your study of the whole essay would not be irrelevant to your paper; it would be a check on the correctness of your interpretation. Indeed, you could write a short paper about the whole essay, but your ideas, covering more ground, would have to be more general—and you would have run the risk of being vague. The final draft of this paper might run as follows:

EMERSON'S ATTACK ON HYPOCRISY

One of several dominant themes in Emerson's essay on "Self-Reliance" is his running attack on hypocrisy. The first pronounced example of this attack is his anecdote about a hypothetical abolitionist. [Here, you could quote section D of Emerson's essay above, *but quotations do not count toward the required length of your paper. Only your own words count for this.*] The other themes bound up in the same paragraph are Emerson's doctrines against conformity, in favor of originality, and against foolish philanthropy. On first reading, the quoted passage may seem unduly bitter: the abolitionist is called a "bigot"; his tenderness is labeled "incredible," merely a "varnish" for "hard, uncharitable ambition"; his love is termed "spite" and an "affectation." Indeed, it almost seems that Emerson is against abolition itself, since "this bountiful cause" is a phrase used with obvious derision, and the "last news from Barbados" (the infamous Caribbean island used for slave traffic) is dismissed with his perfunctory retort, "Go, love thy infant . . ."

If the reader sees the passage in its context, however, he understands that Emerson is not against good causes; nor is he against love of one's fellow human being. Rather, he is in favor of standing on one's own two feet, of listening to one's own conscience. To be self-reliant means to avoid acting hypocritically, and Emerson emphasizes this concept by introducing the

paragraph with his famous watchwords: "Whoso would be a
man must be a nonconformist." Indeed, to avoid hypocrisy,
Emerson says that even the doctrines of the church take
second place to the law of his own nature. Later in the paragraph, he says, "The doctrine of hate must be preached as the   30
counteraction of the doctrine of love when that pules and
whines." Love that "pules and whines" would be hypocritical
love; the hate to be preached against such hypocrisy is fire
used against fire. Thus, Emerson's "rough and graceless" reply
to the abolitionist does not repudiate abolitionism; rather, it is   35
a tirade against a particularly repellent kind of hypocrisy—the
the cynical use of a good cause to advance one's own selfish
ambition.

  Without a clear understanding of his attitude toward hypocrisy, some readers may accuse Emerson himself of egotism   40
and of selfishness. For instance, his reply to the adviser,
". . . if I am the Devil's child, I will live then from the Devil,"
his assertion that his own nature and constitution determine
the only laws he will obey, his insistence that he will conduct
himself as if everything else were a passing show ("as if every-   45
thing else were titular and ephemeral but he")—all these statements may strike the reader as egotistical and selfish in the
extreme. But it is precisely such statements as these that make
Emerson a champion of individualism. Also, when the reader
remembers other passages in the essay, he can see how   50
egotism and independence are sharply distinguished. For instance, Emerson defines "the great man" as he who "in the
midst of the crowd keeps with perfect sweetness the independence of solitude," and he says later: "Always scorn appearances and you always may"; and still later, with emphasis: 55
"Insist on yourself; never imitate."

  In the last third of the paragraph, the attack on hypocrisy is
linked to a defense of originality and a vigorously stated position against "miscellaneous popular charities." These ideas are
ingeniously interconnected: having asserted the "rude truth"   60
to the abolitionist, Emerson shows that he owes no apologies
to society for following his own way, for occasionally shunning
even his friends and relatives. If people think such behavior
odd, he does not care, but allows them to think him merely

whimsical. The final emphatic statements against charities may 65
again seem excessively harsh; phrases like "Are they my
poor?" and the epithets "fools" and "sots" may even seem
inhumane. The key here is that Emerson is admonishing
against the weak reliance on others that such charities and
"relief societies" encourage. The reason he grudges the 70
"wicked dollar" he sometimes gives to them is that they
undermine the kind of manhood that relies on itself. Thus, the
paragraph begins and ends on the strongest possible note of
independence.

From your reading of this hypothetical student essay and the
material on which it is based, you should have discovered some
general methods and purposes behind such a work. The best
analyses of literary works are approached from a background of
reading in depth, like that illustrated in Chapter 1. The attentive
student reads and analyzes his material as he goes. The process is
a continuous one of taking notes for possible use in the paper,
marking passages, jotting marginal comments that throw searching
beacon lights over the otherwise obscure parts of the literature.
From this section, you should have noticed also that the mainstay
of much analytical writing is perception and explanation of interrelationships. The writer of a good secondary analytical essay fore-
stalls possible misunderstandings, clears up difficult or puzzling
references, illustrates how apparently unrelated parts of the literature fit into the context, and, in general, helps his reader to understand the literature by interpreting it without distorting it.

EXPLICATION OF A POEM BY FROST

The second sample study and hypothetical paper are intended to
illustrate how the close reading of a poem can result in an interesting student essay. (See *Explication* in the Glossary.) Suppose you
were to do a paper on the following poem by Robert Frost:

THE ROAD NOT TAKEN [1]

Two roads diverged in a yellow wood,
And sorry I could not travel both
And be one traveler, long I stood
And looked down one as far as I could
To where it bent in the undergrowth;

Then took the other, as just as fair,
And having perhaps the better claim,
Because it was grassy and wanted wear;
Though as for that the passing there
Had worn them really about the same,

And both that morning equally lay
In leaves no step had trodden black.
Oh, I kept the first for another day:
Yet knowing how way leads on to way,
I doubted if I should ever come back.

I shall be telling this with a sigh
Somewhere ages and ages hence:
Two roads diverged in a wood, and I—
I took the one less traveled by,
And that has made all the difference.

A 500- to 600-word paper could be introduced by your comments on what the woodland symbolism implies in the poem. From a reading of the last stanza, you would probably observe that the choice of roads symbolizes one of life's important decisions. In the body of the paper you could show why you think Frost uses a woodland scene rather than a street scene or a highway scene. Immediately, you would face the problem of sticking to the poem, since at least one-half of the words of this part of your paper might be devoted to discussions of irrelevancies (streets and highways, as well as the kind of a woodland road that Frost designates). Your

[1] From *Complete Poems of Robert Frost.* Copyright 1916, 1921 by Holt, Rinehart and Winston, Inc. Copyright renewed 1944 by Robert Frost. Reprinted by permission of Holt, Rinehart and Winston, Inc.

nine

*Writing the essay: background
and evaluative studies*

AS IS TRUE with literary analysis, there are several varieties
of background and evaluative studies, and you may be required to
do more than one such study. Also, as you will see in the final
section of this chapter, the literary or critical evaluation may involve elements from all your work in the course. A good background study may be brief or lengthy, simple or complex; it is
primarily a work of scholarship. A literary evaluation, which may
also take various forms, is essentially a work of criticism. Moreover, you may write answers to essay examinations in class, or
papers outside class, both of which draw on the techniques of
writing the background study or the evaluation. If you write an
early research paper, most likely it will be a background study; and
if your class is using one of the currently popular casebooks, or
books of research materials, you will probably write several small

background studies, topped off with a term paper, which may combine scholarship and criticism.

From your work on such papers, you should learn the meaning of literary scholarship and research. You will need both patience and skill to assemble facts gleaned from a variety of sources, and to show the bearing of these facts on the literature in question. As a scholar, you will have to be systematic and selective. Since your study may draw upon a number of topics, you will tax your powers of collation and of synthesis. Thus, you will have to note the interrelationships between different source materials and take account of how the facts bear on your proposed writing project. As a writer, your key tasks will be, first, to organize your materials into a meaningful whole and, second, to present these materials in a craftsmanlike style. Throughout both preparation and writing of your paper, you must keep in mind and in proper focus the literature or the author you are studying.

THE LITERARY BIOGRAPHY

Because one of the most pleasant kinds of literary scholarship is biography, Samuel Johnson said, "The biographical part of literature is what I love best." Everyone is curious about the lives of famous persons, and the biographical material you can find about any great author is both plentiful and fascinating. Hence, you should encounter no shortage of facts in the research, and your biographical study should be naturally interesting to your reader. Though your problems may be numerous, your job will be rewarding; and after you have made a thorough study of some aspect of an author's life, his name and his writings will always stir your enthusiasm.

Your planning for the paper and its parts should be very careful indeed. Moreover, your preparatory reading should be wide, including first a rapid skimming of your sources. Once you have decided on a topic, you should go over the sources again, reading slowly and taking relevant notes as you go, as explained in Chapters 1 and 2 of this book. One of your poorest topics would be a general survey of the author's whole life, from birth to death. In only a few pages, you could not hope to do justice to the full lives of Shelley or Keats, who died before they were thirty, much less to those of Wordsworth, Tennyson, Browning, or Bernard Shaw, who lived into old age.

Therefore, after the first reading of your sources, narrow your topic. Choose only an aspect of your total subject—a crucial few weeks, like those in which Robert Browning eloped from England to Italy with Elizabeth Barrett; a single incident, like Charles Lamb's brief commitment to a madhouse or the murder of his mother by his sister Mary; the effect of an event on a friendship, like the marriage of Coleridge to Wordsworth's sister; a personal characteristic, like the addictions to opiates of DeQuincey, Coleridge, or Edgar Allen Poe. It may be part of the assignment, also, to tie your biography to the literature you are studying in class. For instance, extensive biographical data is available about how Coleridge came to write "The Ancient Mariner" and "Kubla Khan," or about the relationship between Shakespeare and the "Dark Lady" of his sonnets.

THE HISTORICAL STUDY

If you write a historical study, make your paper relevant to your English course. Do not hand in work that could have been done for a history course, since its lack of literary relevance may fail your paper. Remember, also, that because the range of its subject matter is limited, the historical study is one of the more difficult types of background studies to write. Your success will depend on your ability to relate specific works of literature to the facts of history.

Literary history is composed in large part of literary biography; and if you write a study of the historical setting of an author or of his work, you may need to draw upon many biographical facts. In fiction, an author may use real persons as characters. For instance, Shakespeare's history plays, stocked with real kings and queens, transform much history into drama. Novels like Tolstoy's *War and Peace,* Thackeray's *Henry Esmond,* Proust's *Remembrance of Things Past,* and Wolfe's *Look Homeward, Angel* may use a fictionized version of the author himself as focal point for recounting real events or history. In nonfiction, the literary author may recount history directly from his own point of view, as in Defoe's *A Journal of the Plague Year, The Education of Henry Adams,* Benjamin Franklin's *Autobiography,* or conventionally, as in Francis Parkman's histories of the American continent. In lyric poetry, dedicatory personages may appear as characters, like Edward King in Milton's "Lycidas," John Keats in Shelley's "Adonais," and Arthur Hugh Clough in Arnold's "Thyrsis." Longer narrative poems, like *John Brown's Body* or *The Song of Roland,* may also recount real events, often idealized and made into national folklore. In a paper about such subject matter, your basic plan may well be a comparison and contrast of the actual events or persons with those treated in the literature. Though there are several other types of historical studies, you should consult your instructor before attempting them.

SOURCE AND INFLUENCE STUDIES

Source and influence studies may overlap each other and the biographical and historical types. Both kinds of background study are particularly suitable for papers about the giants in literature—Chaucer, Dante, Shakespeare, and Milton—as well as for special forms like the drama, the novel, and lyric poetry. One advantage is that your research materials may already be collected for you, so that your job is mainly to choose the facts you need and fit them together. Another point in your favor, even if you do not work with a single book of sources, is that there are plenty of separate materials about major authors and genres to choose from. Ordinarily, source and influence studies lend themselves most readily to the long term paper, which you may have to hand in at midterm or at the end of the course. But careful, shorter papers on given topics are also appropriate.

Studies of the sources of and influences on an author's works can be particularly rewarding. In your reading for these papers, your first discoveries should help you to revise the naive belief that greatness in literature depends on absolute originality of idea. For instance, Shakespeare originated only one or two of his plots; Chaucer, Dante, and Milton retold many ancient stories and fitted them to structures already used by lesser writers. Also, as indicated in the articles under *Archetype, Epic,* and *Myth* in the Glossary, some of the most important literature would not have been written without the great body of folklore upon which it is based. The primary value you may gain by your work here is a sense for style, for adroitness and appropriateness in the way your author handles the human traits of his characters, for the rightness of his taste when he adapts and changes the original materials to suit his own more particular needs.

Especially in your study of Shakespeare, you may write some excellent background papers comparing the originals with his plays. For short papers, you need only two books: Shakespeare's play itself and the original story. Consider a paper comparing the details in the relevant passages of *The Tempest* with those in Montaigne's essay, "Of Cannibals." Or if you have read *As You Like It,* try reading Thomas Lodge's novel, *Rosalynde,* and then plan a short paper on the broad differences in structure or characterization. For the history plays, or for tragedies like *Julius Caesar,* check out Holinshed's *Chronicles* or *Plutarch's Lives* from the library, find the specific passages that show literary influence, and make comparisons to illustrate changes in diction made by Shakespeare.

In this work you should keep the over-all plan for your papers simple. Moreover, *you should concentrate on the study and the writing of the paper*—not simply on running around the library for a multitude of sources. Contrary to a popular student theory, most teachers are not impressed by a long bibliography for its own sake. Rather, they appreciate careful reading of the literature assigned in class, and proof of the depth of this reading in class themes, outside papers, and examinations. Therefore, in an essay comparing Shakespeare with one of his sources, do not make an issue of simple busy work. It is best simply to go to work with your books and not make a great to-do of how difficult they were to find. Every good edition of Shakespeare includes the titles of his sources; and for a brief essay, one or two of these titles may be all you will need. In your paper, if you give simple and exact credit in footnotes or in the text, you will most likely satisfy the requirements here; it may pay you, however, to consult the articles on *Footnote* and *Bibliography* in the "Checklist of Grammar and Mechanics."

THE CRITICAL EVALUATION

The critical evaluation of how well an author accomplished his purposes may constitute one of your best essays about the literary subject matter of your English course. Though, as noted on page 61, and also in the article on *Purpose* in the Glossary, such an investigation may be subject to the intentional fallacy, you may still write a searching and worthwhile essay. For instance, suppose that for one of your theme assignments you are asked to discuss and evaluate purposes and goals in *The Ox-Bow Incident,* by Walter Van Tilburg Clark. If you keep your paper curious and speculative, not dogmatic or narrow, you may do the kind of work

that will improve and deepen your own and your reader's understanding of the book.

The Ox-Bow Incident is a novel about justice. Several ranchers
of the frontier West discover that their stock has been rustled.
When one of them finds the body of a ranch hand who has apparently been murdered, the central character, who is also the
narrator, becomes involved in a cattlemen's lynching party. The
middle chapters of the novel describe the journey of the posse in
pursuit of the supposed thieves and killers. After reading this
novel, let us assume that you decide to write a paper asserting that
Clark's story is more than an ordinary Western novel. A careful
plan for your essay would reveal several facts about this kind of
paper.

First, such an essay would be based upon a significant kind of
major premise: that the author's goal in writing the literature is
higher, or more difficult (or at the very least, simply different)
than it may seem upon first reading of his work. In this case,
Clark's apparent goal is simply to write a traditional Western,
replete with a chase, gunplay, and a lynching.

Second, if the purpose of your essay is to explain the essential
nature of the literature, the evidence you cite should be in every
way *representative of and directly relevant to the literature itself*.
In the present example, the basic statement—that Clark's novel is
of a totally different kind from what it appears to be—would require you to cite details that are both typical of the book and
relevant to your paper, in order to illustrate the essential difference
in kind that you are attempting to prove.

Third, in this kind of paper the facts used in support of the
major premise should be specific and should go deeply into the
texture of the literature. In the paper about Clark's novel you
would need to cite definite examples of incident, character, and
even setting that illustrate your contention that Clark's book makes
an important assertion about justice, and is not merely another

cowboy story. Your choice of these "facts" would be a crucial matter for the validity of your paper.

Fourth, and very important, since this paper is evaluative, not simply analytical, the comments should include a statement of how well the author has fulfilled the deeper purposes of the book. These purely evaluative remarks may occur piecemeal throughout the paper, especially if the discussion is long or complex; or they may be placed at the end, if the essay is brief. In either case, the evaluation should follow naturally and inevitably as a consequence of the assertions and evidence in the paper, and there should be no cryptic, tacked-on conclusion. (See Chapter 4, on the conclusion, for further discussion.)

ten

Exercises for class and for self-help

IN THIS CHAPTER some practical exercises are suggested to help you strengthen your reading and writing abilities. If the marks on your papers indicate that your reading background is not thorough enough, or that your writing is of low quality, doing these exercises on your own—without handing them in to be graded—can show you where your specific weaknesses lie. Your instructor may call for some of these papers from the class; if you do some of them purely for your own practice, you will understand better how to fulfill other assignments. In the directions for each of the five kinds of papers described in this chapter, you are shown how to write very directly about your reading. Except for the critical review, all the writing you do in these five forms should be based on the book—the book of readings, the novel, the epic poem, the play, be it what it will—that you are reading and discussing in class.

The main idea behind this chapter is to get you to form the habit of reading first, *really* reading, before you write. Too many student papers, supposedly about literary topics, are written without a clear and adequate background in reading. This shortcoming often shows up in vague, wordy, and wandering compositions lacking in the depth and the supporting evidence that come from realizing specific details, the content of your reading. One way to make this content part of your own individual experience is to learn to summarize it, or to report on it, or to explain it in words of your own.

Certainly, in these exercises, you should have no pretensions to capturing literary quality. Literature as an art never has been "canned" in this way, and it never will be. The papers that you write for this chapter should be repeatedly compared with and referred to the original literature upon which they are based. In this comparison you will note how difficult it is for you, in your own writing, to express the flavor and spirit of the original. Nevertheless, comparison of your own work with that of literary authors will help you to see your own virtues and shortcomings of composition. With these two insights you should be on solid ground as you progress in acquiring the skills both of creative reading and of critical writing.

THE PRÉCIS

The précis is a restatement of a piece of literature in condensed form. It retains the structure, proportions, and point of view of the original. Condensing good literature can give you an excellent sense for literary structure, which you cannot gain so thoroughly and so fast in any other way. The first thing you must notice, in reducing the length of any piece of literature—if you would avoid violating the relative proportions of its parts—is its form and structure. A second advantage in this kind of writing is that to do it well, you must become aware of the best literary styles and the most concise ways of phrasing. Since such condensation requires you to use your own words, not those of the original author, you feel the sharp necessity both of writing economically and of increasing your vocabulary of words, phrases, and compositional structures.

The best procedure to follow in writing a précis is to set yourself a word limit and to determine to stay within this limit. For most essays, short stories, single chapters in novels, and single acts of plays, your word count should be about one-tenth of the length of the original. Since the point is to miniaturize the literature, you should not make your précis more than 500 words long, regardless of the length of the original. If setting a minimum becomes a problem, since it is possible to distill down to almost nothing, 250 words should ordinarily constitute the minimum length for longer pieces, 100 words for very short pieces. For every condensation you make, count every word in your paper to be sure you stay within these limits.

Before doing the writing, you must necessarily scrutinize the passage to be condensed, so that your précis does not misrepresent it. Since the object is to provide yourself and your reader with an accurate bird's-eye view of the original material, you should not include any ideas that you do not find in the original itself. Your précis should reflect both the structure and the content of the original, so that your reader can see its main outline parts—its major emphases, its internal relationships, the movement and direction of its theme. To summarize accurately, of course, you need to know what these aspects of the original are. Thus, several readings of the material should usually precede your first writing efforts. When you do attack your writing problem, unless your instructor directs you to do otherwise, you should have the book open before you, so that you do not unconsciously duplicate phrasings or key words.

You may choose any compositional structure to condense, but your early attempts may succeed best with rather short factual essays as originals. For your first précis, select an essay that is divided into readily discoverable sections, with each of its parts devoted to a clearly different aspect of the main subject matter. Write separate paragraphs, numbered or headed like the original, for each of these sections. In this writing, do your best to avoid leaving out the important facts or violating the order of items in the original. Attempt, also, to reflect the original in number of words devoted to subtopics, so that if about 300 words of the original are used to explain a subtopic, and your précis is written to a scale of 10 per cent, you would use about 30 words for the same subtopic.

EXERCISES: *For all exercises on the précis, use no quotations, even of short phrases. Make an accurate word count and enter this count and the scale that it observes (e.g., "500 words: 10 per cent of the original 5,000 words") at the end of your paper.*

A. Condense a short essay of three or four pages (1,000 to 2,000 words) into a single paragraph of 85 to 100 words. Replicate in miniature the structure of the essay, using your own phrasing.

B. Reduce a longer essay of 10 to 12 pages (3,500 to 5,000 words) in a précis of 250 to 500 words. In your own words, reproduce the main ideas of the separate parts of the original. Keep the order and emphasis of these ideas as you find them in the original.

C. With your classmates, make a composite précis of the sections in a long essay or of the chapters in a book. With the class divided into groups of two, three, or four, staying strictly within specified word-count limits, each student should condense in his own words the part of the original assigned to his group. The instructor may then choose the best précis from each group. He may decide to mimeograph these papers, assembled in the correct order, for one or two sessions of criticism by the class.

D. Write a synopsis of a one-act play, or of one act in a longer play. Reduce this to about 300 words. Do not use dialogue or stage directions; simplify by indicating only the important turnings of the plot, and by using only three or four central characters.

E. Condense a short story, a chapter in a novel, or a part of an epic poem in 400 to 500 words. If there are two or more threads to the plot, reveal this structure in your précis. Do not distort or falsify the original, and do not comment upon it, but try to illustrate its unity of effect.

THE EPITOME

An epitome attempts to compress the main idea of a piece of literature into only one or two sentences. Like the précis the epitome may have any literary form—the novel, the drama, the essay, epic or lyric poetry—as its subject matter. In writing epitomes, no matter how long the original, you should take care to stay within the suggested length limits. These limits would allow you to write a maximum of three or four sentences, but two sentences are about average.

Writing epitomes is valuable in helping you to remember your reading; it is a good method—in preparing for examinations, for instance—to fix the central ideas of the literature in your memory. With this method you can distill out all irrelevancies and decorative ideas, pinpointing your single most essential concept as concisely as possible.

There are as many different classes of the epitome as there are aspects of literature to epitomize. Thus, besides setting down the main emphasis of a work or passage, you can slant your epitome to serve your more specific purposes. Even short pieces can be epitomized in different ways; but the longer the work, the more numerous these ways are likely to be.

Quite possibly, the author of the original that you epitomize will have written his own covering statement, or statement of the purpose of his work, which would serve as an epitome. However, when you are framing your own idea of the over-all content of the literature, and when you write your epitome, it is best not to study such statements in detail. Doing this would be like looking in the back of a mathematics book for the answer to a problem. The best method is to wait until you have considered the whole assignment deeply and have written and rewritten your epitome several times. Then look at the author's first and last paragraphs, where you may most likely find his statement of intention or the conclusions he has arrived at. (Of course, these statements may be found elsewhere.) In this way, the author may provide you with good clues as to whether your reading has been adequate and your concept of its central idea has been accurate.

EXERCISES: *For each exercise on the epitome, give an exact word count at the end of your statement.*

A. Write separate epitomes of not more than thirty-five words each for every section in a subdivided essay. Number these epitomes to correspond with the section numbers. Then assemble them and revise your phrasing so that each statement helps to show how the essay moves toward a complete statement of its topic idea. Finally, write an epitome of fifty to sixty words that clearly states the topic idea of the whole essay. Do not repeat your own phrases or those of the author.

B. After careful study of a reading assignment, write an epitome of it in a sentence or two. Then find the author's own best statement of his purpose and compare your epitome with this statement. In most cases, they should be quite similar in idea.

C. In an epic poem, or in a novel like Fielding's *Tom Jones,* observe the "Arguments" that precede the sections, books, or chapters. Choose several of these and compare them closely with the literature they refer to. Then explain, in writing or in class discussion, what purposes are served by the author's epitomes of his own work. Note any differences in point of view or in attitude between the epitomes and the literature itself.

D. In your own words, write a single-sentence epitome of a paragraph in a reading assignment and compare your sentence with the author's topic sentence. Assess your own sentence for compression by noting how well it covers the central idea of the paragraph.

THE LITERARY REPORT

In writing a literary report, you have freedom to express the central idea of the literature without the necessity to reflect the exact sequence of its development or the precise order of its details. Nevertheless, you should remember that no usage that wastes words, or that is pointlessly vague or roundabout, is good style. In the report, you should not evaluate the literature. Rather, you are asked to choose its salient aspects, its point or theme, and set these down in your own words. The literary report is written to inform, and in it you avoid the tendency to expend many words explaining your own ideas. In the précis, you reflect the details as you find them; but in the more informal report, you choose only the important details for emphasis. Notice especially the difference in generalization, in order, and in phrasings in the following examples from Conrad's *Lord Jim:*

PRÉCIS	REPORT
Jim stood before Doramin; the ring he had given to Dain Waris dropped to the floor as the old chief struggled to rise with his pistols. Then Doramin shot Jim through the chest.	Jim has caused Dain Waris's death, but he will not run now from the old chief's wrath. Doramin shoots him where he stands; his symbolic ring has fallen to the floor.

The literary report is thus concerned with the central content of your reading, with adequacy of exposition, rather than with replication or even compression of details. Being more informal, it may be, or seem to be, easier to write than a précis, though your reading background should be equally thorough. Writing a précis is an exercise in polishing your sentences down to fit a pre-established mold, the over-all structure of the original. Writing a literary report is an exercise in making up your own over-all structure, in which you describe the content of your reading. The literary report is therefore useful in cases where the structure of the original is too complex to be reflected in a précis—as in intricately plotted novels and plays, in which the action twists and turns tortuously. Similarly, the report is valuable in describing literature in which structure is only a minor consideration, or where (except for special studies) it would be pointless to try to reflect this structure—as in some familiar essays and familiar letters.

EXERCISES: *Make your work for these exercises primarily explanatory writing. Do not evaluate.*

A. Write a report of a reading assignment in which you (*a*) define the topic in about 100 words; (*b*) explain the author's attitude toward his topic in another 100 words; and (*c*) describe the structure and the style in a final 100 words. Unify! Total word count: about 300 words.

B. Write a report of a reading assignment in which you explain how the subject matter is divided. Reveal the relationship between the subject matter and the way in which it is broken into parts by the author.

C. Write two slanted interpretations of a reading assignment, one in favor of and one against the author's position. Then write a third paper which incorporates both slanted versions into a single, unbiased report. In this report try to balance the biases from the two earlier papers, using neutral words when possible.

THE CRITICAL REVIEW

The reader of your critical review may not have read the material that you are writing about. In the exercises for this section, therefore, you will do some reporting, but you are asked also to include some brief interpretative comments. Up to now, you have had to consider only the literature itself, and any statements of your own have been excluded. In writing a simple critical review, your primary job is still to describe the contents of your reading; but once you have done this, you are free to add your own comments. The reporting that you do need not come first, but you should make it your main emphasis. In more elaborate critical reviews, giving proper credit in footnotes, you may even supplement or contrast your interpretations with those of other writers on the subject.

In the following passages from a literary report and a critical review of Part III, Chapter 2, of Swift's *Gulliver's Travels,* note the objectivity of the description in the report. Contrast this with the critical review, which both describes the book and tells the reader what Swift means.

REPORT	REVIEW
On the flying island, Gulliver discovers that the mathematical Laputans must be flapped on the mouth and ears so they will not forget to speak and listen . . .	Swift's contempt for impractical thinking is shown by the mathematical Laputans, who are so absent-minded that they must be flapped on the mouth and ears to be reminded to speak and listen . . .

In writing a review, you must have your reader in mind just as much as the material you are reviewing. The report, the précis, and the epitome, on the contrary, require you to think mainly of the original that you are describing or condensing.

EXERCISES:

A. Read book reviews of the same book, if possible in issues of *The New Yorker, Time* magazine, and *The New York Times* Book Review section. Note the relative number of words devoted to explanation of the subject of the book, to description and evaluation of the book, and to the reviewer's comments on related topics. Write a theme in which you compare and contrast these reviews.

B. Write a review of a book you have read. (*1*) Describe its content, and (*2*) evaluate the author's treatment. Then compare your own review with as many magazine reviews of the book as you can find. Note how different purposes and points of view result in different structures of the reviews.

C. Read the review sections devoted to plays and to movies in *Time* and other magazines. In a theme, compare and contrast some specific reviews in these sections with articles in the book-review sections. In your theme, note how different subject matters cause the reviewers to adopt different emphases and points of view, which in turn result in different structures and styles of the reviews.

D. In a unified critical review, compare and contrast a novel with a movie that was drawn from the novel. Do not make your review tedious and boring by lengthy retelling of the story, but outline the plot deftly and interestingly.

THE PARAPHRASE OF A POEM

Although a paraphrase of a poem is no substitute for the poem itself, it makes sense to record your poetic discoveries in a paraphrase, just as it makes sense for an explorer to draw out on a map new territories he has traveled. And just as the explorer does not pretend that his map is more than a reminder of the specific details of his adventures, neither should a writer pretend that his paraphrase is more than a reminder of his poetic experience. True, both the map and the paraphrase are devoid of the beauty of the landscape, of the richness of the experience itself; yet, quite often, both map and paraphrase are found to be indispensable.

Consider the following delicate little four-line poem by Emily Dickinson:

> Lay this laurel on the one
> Too intrinsic for renown
> Laurel! veil your deathless tree,—
> Him you chasten, that is he!

Without paraphrase or explanation, this poem could hopelessly puzzle many a reader; understanding its idea unlocks its beauty, even though the beauty consists not so much in the idea as in the way it is expressed in the poem. The paraphrase is therefore merely the key, not the house. Emily Dickinson's poem may be paraphrased as follows:

> Give this praise to one whose value is too personal for public ac-
> claim. Such public applause should be quieted for one who is
> humbled by it.

When you compare the paraphrase with the poem itself, the one-
dimensional paraphrase can make clear many of the poem's multi-
dimensional meanings that may have escaped you before.

You may see, for instance, that the poet is complimenting someone for whom the limelight ("renown") is only an embarrassment,
someone whom it would "chasten." Also, you could see that the
poet addresses the laurel itself, a symbol of praise, in line 3. The
leaves of a laurel come from a tree, which is used here to symbolize
the public renown. This renown, though "deathless," is too crass
for one whose value is personal ("intrinsic"); the laurel is asked
in line 3, therefore, to "veil" its tree of renown. Because of the
paraphrase you could also notice the beautiful paradox in the last
line: the poet, anxious that there be no mistake about who should
receive this special laurel, tells it on whom it should be placed—
not one who would be made proud by it, but one who would be
humbled, "chastened," by it. That is, the poet uses this exceptional
trait in the person she is complimenting as a mark to distinguish
him from others, who might otherwise also deserve the laurel.

EXERCISES:

A. Choose a short poem or a brief passage from a long poem in which
the meanings puzzle you. Spot the difficult points by attending to
specific words and phrases that at first seem odd, obscure, or out of
place. Read the whole poem over and over, until you solve the puzzle
by seeing why these words and phrases are used instead of others. Then
write a prose paraphrase that makes the difficult passages clear.

B. To see how inadequate a paraphrase is to express all the meanings
of a poem, write two or three paraphrases of a sonnet or other short
lyric. Make each paraphrase restate a different set of meanings that
you find in the poem, and note that however many prose statements
you write, you cannot reproduce all the meanings and effects in the
poem.

C. A modern critic has written that "For its life a poem cannot be said otherwise." To see what is meant here, do your best to write down an accurate prose paraphrase of one of your favorite poems. Then write a theme in which you explain why you could not capture all the ideas and emotions of the poem in your paraphrase. Specify words and phrases in the poem for which you feel that there are no adequate substitutes.

D. In a theme, distinguish the content of a poem that can be paraphrased. Then try to explain the feelings in the poem by taking sample words and illustrating all the possible meanings the words may have. Do not introduce irrelevant meanings, but stick to the shadings and nuances in the poem itself. In this way, you will be pointing toward the content of the poem that cannot be paraphrased.

eleven

The essay examination:
preparation and writing

AN EXAMINATION on reading materials may take a variety of forms. It may emphasize facts, interrelationships, ideas, even opinions and attitudes. But whatever its nature, the essay examination has one constant purpose: to reinforce your knowledge of the literature. Students are always curious about the nature of a test, and rightly so. To be safe, however, it is best, not to depend upon some limited guess of what the examination questions will be. When you expect a test, your preparation should cover all aspects of the material, not just a segment of it. When you finally do see the questions, you will thus have guarded against the hollow feeling that you studied the wrong things.

SYSTEMATIC PREPARATION

One important key—there are several—to writing a good examination is systematic preparation. System in your study means regularity of application, intensity of effort, and perspective of details. The memory and the intellect should function together when you study. To attempt to cram your mind full of literature to get through an examination is an especially bad mistake, because by its nature literature requires a long process of mulling over. The mind that approaches a work of literary art in the right way achieves a kind of spongelike saturation. Such close familiarity with your reading material cannot be gained in one or two frantic sessions, no matter how long and sleepless these sessions may be. To rush from reading the last page of a novel, a play, an epic poem, into the writing of an examination is therefore likely to cause you some disappointment.

Let us say that you are to take an examination on Shakespeare's *As You Like It*. This play is often presented before an audience in a little over two hours, and it can certainly be read in a single evening. Such a rapid overview would be excellent preliminary preparation. Suppose, however, that you have budgeted your time to spend four evenings on this play, instead of just one. In this case, even if you are not very systematic, you will probably write more thoughtfully about the play than the student who studies it in one sitting. With a system your chances improve even more. Therefore, the question is: How can you spend each one of these four sessions with maximum effect?

One method can be ruled out immediately: breaking the play into four consecutive parts and spending one evening on each of these parts. As explained in Chapter 1, a rapid overview is usually needed; therefore, in the first session you would read all five acts of the play. For the other three sessions, your interests should help to guide you.

During the second session, you could run down the list of characters in the play, choose three or four of them, and spend a half hour in close reading of the speeches of each one. The chief characters would be best for this purpose—Orlando, Oliver, Rosalind, and Celia. Your second study session should make some important advances: you would begin to see the play as a pastoral fantasy, depending for its interest not upon realistic settings but upon delightful plays of wit and fancy. You would also observe that the character of Rosalind is the central focus of the play and that her personality sheds light, by its contrast, upon the others. Another important insight would be the manner in which the affairs of these four young persons form the major plot of the play.

Your third study session would continue from previous interests. In this case, you would probably focus upon the relationship between the two plots in the play. With a possible contrast between the plots in mind (that you could write about later, in detail, if need be) you would study the minor characters—the two Dukes, and especially Jaques, Touchstone, and the country folk. By now, the deeper lines of the play, its particular kind of truth, should be absorbing your whole attention. For instance, you would not merely "know" that Jaques makes the speech about the "seven ages of man"; you would also feel that you understood the kind of person Jaques is, in comparison, for instance, with Rosalind, with Duke Senior, and with Touchstone.

Your final study session should be at least one-half review. Also, you may spend a good deal of this time in writing. It may pay you to set down some of your impressions in a practice composition. As long as you do not narrow your thinking about the play, such a practice theme can be a very good warm-up for the examination. The caution here is simply to avoid setting your mind to write about one aspect of the literature, when you may be asked in the examination to write about something totally different. In the practice theme you can limber up your mind for fluency in writing. You can review your lecture notes and plan for having them mentally accessible during the examination. The practice theme can also help you digest your reading and writing notes, and help you achieve clarity and vision into the depths of the play.

AN UNWRITTEN TEST OF YOUR STUDY SESSIONS

Besides a practice theme, you can also apply an unwritten test to assess whether your study sessions have been worthwhile. This concerns the intensity of your application. When you are finished with all your books and notes, ask yourself whether you were able to increase your interest in the play as you advanced from one session to the next. After spending about eight hours reading, re-reading, and studying details, do you wish you had even more time to investigate Shakespeare's characterization, plot, setting, or style? If so, if you have achieved not a satiation but an appetite for more detailed knowledge, you have also gained maturity in approaching other works of literature. On the other hand, if you have not become absorbed by your own, self-initiated investigations of the literature, each of the eight hours would have become an increasingly painful business of clock watching.

We have presented an ideal situation—four evenings of increasingly engrossed study of Shakespeare's *As You Like It*. Let us now ice the cake by assuming that you get a good night's sleep and begin the day of the test in your best frame of mind.

THE LAST–MINUTE REVIEW

To these advantages, you may add another—a final five- or ten-minute review at your desk in the classroom before class begins. For some students, these minutes are only an invitation to become excited and worried. But let us say that you find yourself capable of steeling your mind against these emotions and can use the time to advantage. It is possible, now, to make either some serious mistakes or some important advances. Your goal is a bird's-eye view of everything you have studied in your four study sessions. Thus, in your last-minute review, there would be little profit in trying to skim, say, the fifth act of the play. Reading details in the book that you know already would also be a waste of time. Possibly the only part of the book you should look at is the list of characters—the *dramatis personae*. (In other books, a table of contents or a list of characters in your notes would serve this purpose.) Observing each character's name separately and distinctly should bring to your mind whole sections of the play, and give you a mental set or stance for thinking in the examination. Your notes should be approached in the same way—as reminders of larger sections of the literature, not as a set of guesses about obscure questions that might be asked. If you find yourself hastily flipping through your books and notebooks to regain a confidence that you find rapidly slipping away, you had best disregard the last-minute review altogether. In that case, simply calm down and regain your readiness for systematic thinking.

WRITING THE EXAMINATION

When the examination begins, your fullest attention will of course be focused upon the questions. The phrasing and organization of your answers, the amount of time you devote to each section of your paper, even the physical appearance of your pages, should all be determined by the nature of the questions. Though it seems obvious that every student will scrutinize the questions and the directions carefully, excitement or haste often causes errors, especially at this point. Therefore, be sure you read through the whole examination, paying special attention to directions, before you answer any part.

Not all essay examinations are alike. Your first step, in reading a set of questions, should be to discover the purpose of the test as a whole, as related to the literature and to the course. You may be asked for facts; if so, philosophical digressions will weaken your answers. You may have to defend or attack a position; if so, you will need to display the best evidence for your side of the case. The question may ask you to state your opinions about the reading assignment. If so, you will need to show how your opinions are solidly grounded, and you may have to specify the relevant parts of the literature in some summarizing touches. The more specific the questions, the clearer your purpose for writing should be, and your answers to sharply outlined examination questions should not be generalized, vague, or evasive. The question, which grew out of the subject matter, should always control your purpose, which in turn should determine the type of answer you write.

SAMPLE QUESTION AND ANSWER

Let us consider a possible examination question about *As You Like It* and a hypothetical response to it:

> *Question:* Show how *As You Like It* follows the classical pattern of comedy, how it progresses from a set of specific problems to a set of solutions.

This question invites you to structure your answer around specific points that you think of yourself. If you could spend an hour on it, you might be able to refer to all five acts of the play; let us assume, however, that you have only twenty minutes. In this case, you must compress your reply and limit the number of problems you deal with. You may make a crucial error if you begin writing before you decide on the problems, and the parts of the play, you will deal with. Here, your plan could allow for reference mainly to the beginning and the end of the play. In this limited time you could plan for at most, three or four full paragraphs. Observing that specifics are asked for, you would waste no words on general truths about Shakespearean comedy. Your first paragraph might set the topics for your later comments as follows:

> In Act I, Shakespeare presents a special problem for each character in the play, but by Act V all these problems are solved. One group of problems is caused by the banishment of Duke Senior into Arden; a second group centers around Orlando's undeserved, degraded

position and the obstacles to his proposed love affair with Rosalind.
It is Rosalind who is the focus of the play, who ties these two
groups of problems together, and who finally solves them all.

This is probably a better beginning than one which attempts to
list all the problems and their separate solutions. The writer allows
for statement of specific problems in his second and third paragraphs. The pitfall of vagueness has been avoided by the writer's
immediate distinction of the two classes of problems. This distinction, and the statement that every character has a special problem,
could not have been made without a fairly close knowledge of the
play. In the second paragraph, the writer should focus on specifics:

> The two Dukes—one banished, the other tyrannical—present focal
> points and separate atmospheres for specific problems. Duke
> Senior's problem will be solved when in Act V he is recognized by
> all as the true ruler, Duke Frederick's when in the magic of Arden,
> his character is transformed. Orlando's problem is like Duke
> Senior's, and Oliver's is like Duke Frederick's; moreover, their solu-
> tions are parallel: Orlando marries the noble Rosalind and so is
> recognized as of noble blood, and Oliver's character is reformed,
> partly by his love of Celia but mainly by the beauty of Arden. The
> two sets of brothers, old and young, thus contribute to the sym-
> metry of the play.

The writer has only five or six minutes left, but he has completed
about two-thirds of his plan to answer the question in detail. Keeping his eye on the specific problems and their solutions, he has
also given structure to his paragraphs. In this brief time, however,
he has not launched any complicated explanations. A clear, simple
paragraph plan helps him progress in fulfillment of an over-all
pattern for the answer. The final paragraph of the answer takes up
the problems that are most central to the play:

> Rosalind's problems, for which these background matters allow a
> sharpness of outline, are typical of comedy as a form. In the spirit
> of the play, she plays at love with Orlando, banters acidly with

Jaques, and chides the country folk, using her delightful, light-hearted wit that helps the play to transform hard reality into lyrical fantasy. At the end of the play, the simple act of removing her disguise is in keeping with this atmosphere: automatically it gives her Orlando, transfers the love of Phebe from her to Silvius, and allows the multiple wedding to begin.

In this example, we have concentrated on the compression and brevity that would be required under time pressure. With these carefully constructed paragraphs as a third or a fourth of an examination, the writer could hope to do justice to his hours of study. One of his pervasive goals would be to recapture and to reflect some of the absorption that he had achieved in his study sessions. Examples of other kinds of examination questions would reinforce the lessons of this brief sample question and answer.

Possibly the most important of these lessons is that to write an effective essay examination, you must use your writing skills to the utmost. Because you must exercise all kinds of these skills, practice in writing papers other than examinations may help you a great deal. Moreover, an answer to an examination question may be nearly identical in structure and in content to the writing of a critical paper. Therefore, the instructions and suggestions for writing offered in all the other parts of this book may have important applications in writing the essay examination.

part two

A checklist
of grammar
and
mechanics

TO THE INSTRUCTOR

THE SYMBOLS for the items in the following Checklist, for the most part, are simply the letters of the alphabet; occasionally two or three letters (*Sp, Cap, CF, PV*) are used, and there are a few common symbols (¶, ‖, #, ⌒). The author has found that most errors in student writing could as well be classified under simple alphabetical headings as under complicated systems of numbers or abbreviations, which take time to remember and cause errors of reference. Also, one can write *D* or *M* or *F* in the margin more quickly than "Diction is not accurate" or "Meaning is not clear" or even "Frag." Moreover, if the student knows where to look for advice on correcting his error, there is usually little need for lengthy marginal comment. Therefore, for instance, the symbol *Pn* is used to indicate all errors of punctuation, and the common punctuation marks are treated alphabetically under this one heading. The instructor may validly check the spot where the punctuation error occurs, mark *Pn* in the margin, and read on. The student should learn punctuation well enough not to need "A comma is omitted here" or "Semicolon is misused" written out in the margin. (Please note that mistakes in the apostrophe are treated as spelling errors, but that the apostrophe receives its own symbol.) The grammatical matters in this checklist, including punctuation marks, are treated in a fairly thorough manner, and cross references are provided as guides to the student. Also, brief instructions on footnotes and bibliographies are given under *FN* and *Bib*. The instructor may wish to add his own special correction symbols to the list.

TO THE STUDENT

The headings in this checklist correspond to the correction symbols listed on the following pages. When your instructor marks your paper with one of these symbols, look it up, read the entry carefully, and revise the mistake.

160

correction key

Symbol	Meaning	Page
A	Apostrophe is misused or omitted.	163
Ab	Abbreviation is incorrect.	165
B	Read the book. Also, do not merely rewrite the book.	166
Bib	Bibliography.	166
C	Construction and coherence. Sentences are formless or choppy.	167
Cap	Use a capital letter.	168
CF	Comma fault. Use a period or semicolon.	168
D	Diction. Use the right word.	169
E	Emphasis. Do not bury your central ideas.	170
F	Fragment. Repeated fragments (and CF's) can be serious errors.	170
FN	Footnote.	171
G	Good!	173
I	Idiom. Write in English.	174
K	Awkward.	175
L	Logic. Your statement does not make good sense.	176
lc	Use lower case, not capitals.	176
M	Meaning is not clear.	177
N	Negative statements are weak or illogical.	178
O	Order of words or of ideas is awkward or incorrect.	178
P	Passive voice is weak here; use the active voice.	179
Pn	Punctuation is incorrect.	180

Symbol	Meaning	Page
PR	Pronoun reference is inexact.	187
PV	Point of view shifts awkwardly.	189
R	Repetition is awkward.	189
S	Subordination is inaccurate or lacking.	190
Sp	Spelling.	190
S&V	Subject and verb do not agree.	190
Tns	Tenses of verbs are awkward or illogical.	190
Tr	Transitions are inadequate or awkward.	191
U	Underlining is needed (or not needed).	192
V	Vague. Give examples.	192
W	Wordy. Omit needless words.	193
¶	Paragraph structure.	193
‖	Parallelism is incorrect.	193
#	Use a space. Also, use two words, not one.	194
⌒	Close up. Also, use one word, not two.	194

references for correction key

A *Apostrophe is misused or omitted*

The apostrophe is often incorrectly used in papers about literature. Probably it is best to think of the apostrophe not as a punctuation mark but as a unit in spelling. Just as you spell *he, him, his, they, them,* and *theirs* differently because of differences in case and number, so you should spell *fox, foxes, fox's,* and *foxes'* differently for the same reasons.

Possessives and other genitives
One of the most common errors in student themes is the omission of the apostrophe in singular possessives. For any single thing that takes the genitive case, add apostrophe and *s,* regardless of whether or not the final consonant is *s:*

R. C. Sherriff's *Journey's End*
Shakespeare's *Love's Labour's Lost*
Chaucer's *Nun's Priest's Tale*

> Hobbes's philosophical works
> Dorothy Dix's column

For many nouns ending in *s,* however, the phrase may often be more graceful if rewritten: *The Corn Is Green,* by Emlyn Williams; *The Well Wrought Urn,* by Cleanth Brooks; the pseudonym of Samuel Clemens.

The rule for plural possessives is to add only an apostrophe after the final *s,* or *s* sound, when it occurs:

> The collaborators' revision
> The Brontës' novels
> The Walpoles' literary works

(Note the singular spelling of the above names: *Brontë, Walpole.*) For plurals not ending in *s,* add apostrophe and *s:*

> A children's book
> The deer's tracks

For inanimate objects, it is usually best to rephrase the expression to avoid awkwardness. Thus, instead of "the novel's conclusion," "France's king," "*Little Women's* style," it is better to say "the conclusion of the novel," "the king of France," "the style of *Little Women.*" In older poetry, however, such usage as the following is often accepted:

> The Soul's dark cottage, battered
>   and decayed,
> Lets in new light through chinks
>   that time hath made.
>   *Edmund Waller*

It is for reasons of style and euphony that Henry James titled his books *The Wings of the Dove* and *The Turn of the Screw,* rather than *The Dove's Wings* and *The Screw's Turn,* and that Otto Jespersen titled his book *Growth and Structure of the English Language* rather than *The English Language's Growth and Structure.*

For dual or multiple joint authorship, add the correct possessive punctuation to the last name only:

Charles and Mary Lamb's *Tales from Shakespeare*
Gilbert and Sullivan's *H.M.S. Pinafore*
Wordsworth and Coleridge's *Lyrical Ballads*

If the authorship referred to is independent, however, separate apostrophes must be used for each name:

Wordsworth's and Coleridge's poems

Plurals and contractions
The rules for apostrophes in these forms are intended as aids for the reader, not merely as sticklers or problems.

For nonpossessive plurals use the apostrophe and *s* only in the following three cases:

1. Letters of the alphabet:
   Babbitt is spelled with two *b*'s and two *t*'s.
2. Words used as words:
   Using *The*'s in titles is often a matter of style.
3. Nonlinguistic signs:
   In proofreading, use ¶'s to mark paragraphs.

For contractions, use the apostrophe where a letter would be if the words were spelled out: *don't, doesn't, can't, isn't, haven't, he's, they're, it's.* Note especially that *it's* means only *it is.* The possessive of *it* is simply *its:*

It's a pleasure to read the poem; its meaning, however, is difficult to grasp.

Ab *Abbreviation is incorrect*

This error occurs most often when papers are written in haste; a companion error is the improper use of the ampersand (&). It is generally true that students abbreviate too often and that they tend to overuse the ampersand.

B   *Read the book, or, do not merely rewrite the book*

These rather cryptic admonitions may be in order when all or part of your essay misinterprets, gives misinformation, or merely summarizes your reading assignment. The remedy for these ills is twofold: First, study your text so that your ideas are accurate; second, heed your writing assignment. See Chapter 3, especially the diagrams.

Bib   *Bibliography*

For most of your brief papers about literature, you may not require a bibliography. If you write a research paper, however, you may need to show the sources of your information both in footnotes and in a bibliography. If the paper is long, you may study these matters in class, with special attention to methods of research and work in the library. For shorter research papers, you may need to use a bibliography only of the sources you actually use in the footnotes. Such a bibliography should show, in alphabetical order, the same references in the footnotes.

The following sample bibliography lists one accepted form for the sources referred to under *FN* (Footnote) in this list. Note the differences between the items in the bibliography and those in the footnotes. In the bibliography, indention is reversed; the last name of the author is put first; more publication data are included. Also, material for which no author is given is in its alphabetical place, listed by the first word of the title. The bibliography is on a separate page.

Bibliography

Aristotle, *The Poetics*, in *Aristotle on Poetry and Style*, tr. G. M. A. Grube, Indianapolis, The Bobbs-Merrill Company, Inc., 1958.
"Aristotle's Tragic Catharsis," *Time* Magazine, April 24, 1934.

Forster, E. M., "The Ivory Tower," *Atlantic Essays,* ed. Samuel N. Bogorad and Cary B. Graham, Boston, D. C. Heath and Company, 1958.

Grube, G. M. A., tr. and ed., "Translator's Introduction," *Longinus: On Great Writing (On the Sublime),* Indianapolis, The Bobbs-Merrill Company, Inc., 1957.

Oliver, Egbert, "The Existentialist," *College English,* January, 1961, 22:4.

Randall, John Herman, Jr., *Aristotle,* New York, Columbia University Press, 1960.

Ross, W. D., *Aristotle: A Complete Exposition of His Works and Thought,* New York, The World Publishing Company, 1959.

Solmsen, Friedrich, "Introduction," *The Rhetoric and the Poetics of Aristotle,* tr. Ingram Bywater and W. Rhys Roberts, New York, Random House, Inc., 1954.

C Construction and coherence. Sentences are formless or choppy

Formless and choppy sentences are two of the most common faults in student writing. (For an example of the formless sentence, see lines 4 to 8 of the hypothetical student theme beginning on page 48. Choppy sentences are found in lines 15 to 19 of the paper beginning on page 48.) *Formless sentences* can result in over-all incoherence, problems of meaning, and an amorphous style. Your sentences should reflect the rhythms of cultivated informal speech, not the careless lack of depth and form that are likely in slangy, immature gossip, or the frequent triteness and awkwardness of idle chatter. The student who writes about profound subjects in a style of trifling chitchat, paying little or no attention to diction and sentence structure, may not always understand why his compositions do not succeed. At times, he may think deeply, but the reader cannot respect his thoughts if they are couched in slipshod sentences that lack form or that continue endlessly. The reader may rightly suspect that there is no coherent plan behind the remarks at all. In such a case, the writer allows his sentences to carry his ideas haphazardly and at random, and the reader must either go along on a pointless journey or stop reading altogether.

An essay full of *choppy sentences,* each of which contains only eight or ten words, may cause similar problems. In this case, the writer may believe that the only real test of good writing is to make no obvious errors of punctuation and to write no fragments or comma faults. Thus, the main reason for his baby sentences may be that the writer has a healthy fear of making grammatical errors, but an undeveloped capacity for the job of mature, literate composition. If he reads his own work objectively, such a student may see how childish is the style that results. Like the writer of endless, formless sentences, he should make a special study of sentence structure while he fulfills his reading assignments. In this study, he should emphasize methods of subordination and transition. (See Chapters 4, 7, and 10.) For specific passages marked with a *C* in your papers, you should rewrite the offending sentences with both clearer structure and more effective diction.

Cap   *Use a capital letter*

CF   *Comma fault. Use a period or semicolon*

The comma fault is an example of the futile attempt to hook complete sentences together with nonterminal punctuation. (With no punctuation at all, the mistake is called "run-on," or "contact clauses.") Terminal punctuation should be used unless, as is quite possible, the sentences should be rewritten into a single unit, with one part subordinated to the other, or more directly without subordination at all. If simply inserting a period or a semicolon causes wordiness or choppiness, it is worth the effort to rewrite the passage. Thus, the comma fault in the following example should be corrected to avoid wordiness:

> Bret Harte's stories were typical of the frontier, their rough, bragging humor was part of the American tradition.

When because of hurry or carelessness you have committed a comma fault, make up for it in your correction by a greatly improved version of the original. Experiment with various structures until you get the one that best fits your needs. Thus, the fault in the example above would be eliminated in any of the following versions, and the emphasis you need would determine which revision you would finally use:

> Bret Harte's stories, typical of the American frontier, were full of rough, bragging humor.
>
> The rough, bragging humor in Bret Harte's stories was typical of the American frontier.
>
> The kind of rough, bragging humor used on the American frontier also characterized Bret Harte's stories.

D *Diction. Use the right word*

Flaws of diction in student papers are among the most difficult to correct. Certainly no student should ever feel perfectly satisfied with his choice of words for anything of consequence that he writes. Revision after revision may be needed, with substitution, addition, and subtraction of words and phrases at every stage. To choose the exact word for a key spot is rarely a matter of good luck; much more often—especially for the beginner—it is grinding, hard work. On this point, it may be good advice to distrust the things you write with great ease, to read them later with an eye for the accuracy of your word choice, as well as for the flow of your style. For these purposes, you should always have access to a good dictionary and, if possible, a thesaurus.

Matters of diction embrace the whole vocabulary and the universe it designates. Therefore, as a writer, you should always concern yourself with the separate meaning of each individual word and phrase you employ. Make each word pull a bit more than just its own weight; be sure that it is accurate, that it points to just the right thing, quality, action, idea, or connection. Finally, be sure that individual words go naturally with each other and are appropriate in tone and mood to the over-all context. Your diction should neither shock the reader nor put him to sleep. Double-checking your word choice can be your most valuable writing habit.

E   *Emphasis. Do not bury your central ideas*

If you find an *E* in the margin of your paper, the mistake may be that you ignore or slight the most important aspect of your topic in favor of some secondary aspect. The error may be one of sentence or paragraph structure, or it may be a flaw in your over-all plan. In all three instances, remember that the ends of the units of your composition are the most emphatic places. Next are beginnings, and last are middle sections. To make an idea more emphatic, try placing it at the end of a sentence or paragraph. Other methods of emphasis are underlining—which, in print, corresponds to italics— the use of extremely short paragraphs, and, as in this sentence, placing an idea between dashes. *Quotation marks are not acceptable signs of emphasis.* To correct weaknesses of emphasis in sentences and paragraphs, see *S* in this list, and study paragraph structure in Chapter 7. For mistakes in over-all structure of your paper, study again Chapters 3 and 4.

F   *Fragment. Repeated fragments (and CF's) can be serious errors*

The sentence fragment can be a valuable tool of style, but if used unconsciously, it can betray a lack of literacy. In general, the habitual use of fragments for stylistic effect is to be discouraged. The primary reason is that the fragment often causes problems of vagueness and undesirable ambiguity. Also, intentional fragments may cause a halting, awkward rhythm, or an affected coziness of style. Moreover, your reader may confuse an intentional fragment with an unintentional one, especially if the device serves no evident purpose. In this case, the most reasonable conclusion is that the writer does not fully understand what a complete sentence is. Such elementary knowledge should have been mastered long before the student enters the college classroom.

FN *Footnote*

In many of your brief interpretations and analyses of specific works of literature you may have little occasion to use footnotes. In a term paper or a research paper, however, the use of correct footnotes is important. If your instructor wishes you to have practice in footnoting, he may ask for a minimum number of sources in a research paper—say ten or fifteen, with two or three footnotes per page. In this case, he may specify a style to follow, with close attention to order of items, punctuation, and underlining. For this purpose, you may find detailed instruction in the *Modern Language Association Style Sheet* and other sources. For short essays, it is a mistake to collect a great many sources just to have footnotes at the bottoms of pages.

In general, a guiding principle may help: In a formal work of scholarship, for which you collect many opinions or facts on your subject, you may have to use many footnotes. The more formal and derivative your paper, the more acknowledgments you will need to make in footnotes. Informal essays, on the other hand, may carry less of the apparatus of scholarship, because their basic purpose is not to amass ideas or facts from outside sources. In the informal paper, therefore, it is acceptable to indicate the sources in the text itself, usually in the introduction.

Footnotes are of various kinds, but their purpose is always (1) to show the sources of facts, quotations, or paraphrases; or (2) to record added information that would be out of place in the text of the paper itself. The second type of footnote admits an irrelevancy into the paper and should therefore be avoided whenever that is possible.

In footnotes for sources, the superscript (the raised number) for each note is repeated from the text of the paper, where it follows the exact quotation, paraphrase, or fact that is to be identified. A line may be used above the footnote, to separate note from text; also, in a manuscript, the note is flush with the left margin of the text. In print, it is indented like a paragraph.

Each note gives author, title(s) and publication data, volume number (if published in more than one volume), and page number. Following are examples of accepted forms of footnotes, given in their order of appearance in a hypothetical paper. The material in brackets explains the details of some fairly complex problems solved in the notes. Since these forms vary, you may need to consult your instructor about his own requirements.

[1] John Herman Randall, Jr., *Aristotle* (New York, 1960), p. 294. [Chapter title is not required; book title is underlined (to indicate italics); only one terminal period is used.]

[2] *Ibid.*, p. 141. [Randall's *Aristotle* is referred to again; no other note intervenes between this and the preceding note. *Ibid.* is an abbreviation for *Ibidem* and means "in the same place."]

[3] Aristotle, *The Poetics*, in G. M. A. Grube's translation, *Aristotle on Poetry and Style* (Indianapolis, 1958), p. 41. [The student wishes to direct his reader to a particular translation of Aristotle; it is Aristotle in Grube's translation, not Grube himself, who is quoted or paraphrased.]

⁴ W. D. Ross, *Aristotle: A Complete Exposition of His Works and Thought* (New York, 1959), pp. 81–82. [Complete title is used; more than one page is referred to here.]

⁵ Randall, p. 296. [Randall's *Aristotle* is referred to again, with other notes intervening between this and the first note.]

⁶ Friedrich Solmsen, "Introduction," Roberts and Bywater translation, *The Rhetoric and the Poetics of Aristotle* (New York, 1954), p. xviii. [Solmsen, not Aristotle, is the source referred to.]

⁷ G. M. A. Grube, tr. and ed., "Translator's Introduction," *Longinus: On Great Writing (On the Sublime)* (Indianapolis, 1957), p. xiii. [Grube is the source, not Longinus. Also, note that *On the Sublime,* in parentheses, is written as part of the title of the book, since it is printed this way on the title page. *On the Sublime* is the conventional title of Longinus's work.]

⁸ E. M. Forster, "The Ivory Tower," in Samuel N. Bogorad and Cary B. Graham, eds., *Atlantic Essays* (Boston, 1958), p. 83. [This is a typical footnote for a selection in an anthology or a collection of essays.]

⁹ Egbert S. Oliver, "The Existentialist," *College English,* 1961, 22:252. [For a signed item in a periodical, use quotation marks for the article and underlining (italics) for the periodical title. Then give the date. Volume number precedes the colon, and page number follows it.]

¹⁰ "Aristotle's Tragic Catharsis," *Time* Magazine, April 24, 1934, p. 36. [In this case, no author is cited in the source itself. Also, since *Time* begins each issue with page 1, the date is shown instead of the volume number.]

G *Good!*

One reason many instructors are very sparing with this comment on student themes is that it may tend to throw the writer off balance. Therefore, even when you succeed, a caution should be offered to you: the only reason your instructor puts red marks on your papers is to help you improve your writing. Remember that each of his marks takes his time and should receive your closest objective attention. When you find a *G* in the margin of your essay, your instructor is pointing out an example of your best style. If you strive to come up to this quality in your other work, you may receive more *G*'s—and perhaps some A's for grades. But if you do not observe what is good about the passage, the mark has served no purpose, and you may not receive another. Thus, you should read the successful passage carefully and compare it with parts of your writing that are marked down. If the instructor could be sure that all students would judge their own work in this way, he might be more disposed to put *G*'s on all the papers.

I   *Idiom. Write in English*

The English language is both logical and illogical. For instance, the words *no* and *not,* the prefixes *un, in,* and *im,* all usually express negation. Similarly with comparatives and superlatives: an *-er* or *-est* suffix ordinarily implies greater or greatest quantity or quality. It has not always been so, however, and it is not always so now. Consider the word *flammable,* for instance. If the prefix *in* always meant *not* (as is true with *independence, inexperienced, insanity, insensitive,* and a host of others), you should be able to light a match to an inflammable mixture—but do not try! The point is twofold: Even prefixes may have more than one meaning, and the usage of sometimes illogical persons invades the language and becomes accepted as idiomatic.

Prepositions are often what should be changed when you find an *I* on your paper. It is no more logical to back *up* than to back *down* or even to back *away;* each expression has its own meaning and to confuse one with another is to violate an idiom. Some words —for no logical reason—seem married to certain prepositions. It would be as logical to say "belief on" as "belief in" or "conscious with" as "conscious of" or even "to think around" as "to think over," but in each case the former expression has "lost out" to the latter. These examples, and many others, show that, to make his style natural as well as simply logical, a writer must tune his ear to the idiomatic way of saying things.

K *Awkward*

Even if your writing is relatively free from simple flaws of grammar, you may find a great many *K*'s on your papers. For each *K*, try to see how your reader would regard the offending passage. Observe that a phrase or word may be unpleasing or out of rhythm, or that a simple transposition of words would smooth out your style. For instance, you may have put a transition in a rather ineffective place, and hence require a pair of commas where one should serve:

> It, for example, would have been difficult for J. F. Cooper to write a social novel.

Here, "for example" should probably be placed first. The most direct way of expressing your meaning should usually determine the placement and diction of your phrases. You may occasionally need to interrupt your sentence with transitional expressions, and you may often employ subordination that qualifies but does not interrupt. But you should be careful not to slow your reader down excessively or to make him backtrack. To read sentences that are chopped in pieces with irrelevant interruptions may be as irritating as to drive over a road with detours every mile or so.

L   *Logic. Your statement does not make good sense*

Your instructor will usually indicate whether this comment applies to over-all form or to an individual passage. In both cases, you should check to see whether the framework of your paper is causing you to contradict yourself. Step back and observe the nucleus of each broad section of your essay, and notice how the assertions go together. For instance, suppose that in your introduction you set out to prove that Shakespeare's King Lear is the real cause of his own troubles, and that he treats his daughters Goneril and Regan unfairly. If, in the middle of the paper, you begin to emphasize how his daughters' ingratitude and greed overwhelm the old king, the strength of your second idea may overpower your original thesis. Consequently, when you look at your essay in logical perspective, you may see that the body of your paper does not support your introductory thesis at all, but its opposite. To write with solid logic in support of an argument requires good control over your emphasis, and over the sequence and details of your main concepts.

In shorter passages, you may find that one paragraph or sentence tends to contradict another. Consider, for instance, two parts of the same hypothetical paper on *King Lear*. If you say in one part of your paper: "Gloucester, Lear's parallel, is as quick-tempered and foolhardy as the king," you should beware of saying later on: "But Gloucester's more careful and prudent temperament saves him from the madness that overtakes Lear." Usually, the illogical passages in student themes result from failure to qualify correctly. This cause prevails especially in comparisons where the first part is a blanket statement: ". . . as foolhardy and quick-tempered as . . ."; and the second part must be hedged: ". . . more careful and prudent . . ."

lc   *Use lower case, not capitals*

M   *Meaning is not clear*

Problems of meaning in student writing often center on the accuracy of individual words, which, if chosen carelessly, can make a whole sentence or paragraph unclear. Hence, if a word carries key meaning, it must be precise. But even little function words or punctuation marks in otherwise unimportant places can throw your reader off the track. Like the signals on a railroad, where one wrong green light can cause a disaster, a single wrong expression can wreck your whole composition.

Sometimes the error is a less serious one of simple logic:

> D. H. Lawrence's "The Rocking Horse Winner" is a boy who tries too hard to please his parents.

At other times, meaning is obscured by inaccuracy of diction (see *D* in this list), compounded by faulty pronoun reference (see *PR* in this list) or illogical order of elements (see *O* in this list):

> Money dominates his uncle's part in this story in regard to Paul. He tries to win this by betting on the races after riding his rocking horse. He strains his intuition to the bursting point. He hopes this will bring happiness back to the family.

In such a passage, the reader is thrown into a maelstrom, where meanings are left haphazard and entangled. The remedy, of course, is to be more direct. Usually, you would find that your problems would be greater if you tried to patch up such a muddle than if you merely started out anew. Sometimes, however, you can use a few of your original phrases:

> When his uncle shows him how to bet on the races, Paul tries to control his luck by riding his rocking horse. In this childish and superstitious activity, he strains his intuitive powers to the bursting point; his goal is to win the money with which he hopes to regain his family's lost happiness.

As you may realize, from your own reading, problems of meaning that should have been straightened out by the writer can be very irritating. This is true especially when the reader sees that the confusion is needless and that a little thought would have cleared it up.

N   *Negative statements are weak or illogical*

It is often a good idea to avoid a negative statement when an affirmative one is possible. One reason for this suggestion is that a needless negative may cause another negative:

> Congreve's *The Way of the World* is based on a not uncomplicated plot.

Two negatives like these may take the reader through a slightly painful mental twist. The problem can obviously be solved by saying simply:

> Congreve's *The Way of the World* is based on a complicated plot.

In this example, the stylistic fault is caused by an awkward attempt at emphasis. This emphasis, however, is gained more effectively by the brevity and simplicity of direct statement.

O   *Order of ideas is awkward or illogical*

The order in which you express your ideas is a prime element in the flow of your style. When ideas are simple, it is usually not a good practice to make difficulties by placing them in unnatural order. Often, however, it is valuable to slow down the pace of your writing by inserting a qualification or a subordinate idea (see *S* in this list). For this reason and others, it is good to vary your compositional structures and the order of the elements in your sentences. The writer who merely links all his thoughts together with *and's,* as if they were all of equal importance, needs practice in variety of structure, and in subordination.

When you find an *O* in the margin of your paper, test the passage first for logic, simplicity, and directness. Try reading it aloud, to see whether your statement is expressed naturally. Finally, check your emphasis (see *E* in this list) to be sure that you have placed the important part of your idea in the most emphatic position.

P *Passive voice is weak here; use the active voice*

Passives where they are not needed may cause style to be flat and lacking in vitality, and can even contribute to vagueness and ambiguity. Moreover, the passive voice may require at least two more words than the active—the auxiliary verb and the preposition *by,* in italics below:

> Johnson's *Dictionary,* which *was* given to her *by* Miss Pinkerton, *was* thrown out of the carriage window *by* the spiteful Becky Sharp.

Probably (depending on the emphasis desired) the passage should be revised to read:

> The spiteful Becky Sharp threw Johnson's *Dictionary,* a gift from Miss Pinkerton, out of the carriage window.

Sometimes the passive voice is a makeshift solution to a problem of information or meaning. Because the subject can be omitted, the writer may conceal the doer of the action:

> Johnson's *Dictionary* was thrown out of the carriage window.

If you are not sure of your facts, check them, and do not use the passive for evasion. Used judiciously, however, the passive voice is a valuable writer's tool.

Pn   *Punctuation is incorrect*

We shall discuss punctuation marks alphabetically, except for underlining (italics) treated separately under *U* in this list. For the
comma fault, also, see the separate treatment under *CF* in this list.

Brackets

Brackets are used to interrupt a quoted passage with editorial comment or explanation, as in the following sentences from *The
Journals of Arnold Bennett:*

> Friday, April 25th [1914]—Yesterday we went over to see the Velsa
> [his barge-built yacht] in Brightlingsea creek.

> Sunday, December 31st [1916]—I finished the first part of my
> London novel [*The Roll Call*] this afternoon. 35,000 words.

Comma

The best way to study punctuation, especially the comma, is to
attend to its use in good, current prose style. The comma is such a
frequently used mark that it would be impossible to give examples
of all acceptable uses. However, the most common of these uses
are illustrated below.

1. For nonrestrictive modifiers, interrupters, and appositives.
The word *restrictive,* as applied to sentence elements, means necessary to meaning; *nonrestrictive,* on the contrary, means *not*
necessary to meaning. If an element of a sentence should be set
apart by comma or a pair of commas, it is nonrestrictive and can
be lifted out of the sentence without damage to the essential meaning. This use of the comma holds for words, phrases, or clauses, as
long as the elements are nonrestrictive. Consider the modifying and
transitional elements in the following sentences:

> *War and Peace,* however, is less powerful as a novel than *Anna
> Karenina.*

> The sprawling length of *War and Peace,* which in one edition is printed in 1,370 pages, does some harm to artistic unity. *Anna Karenina,* on the other hand, is a product of Tolstoy's best writing craftsmanship.

"However" and "on the other hand," in the first and third sentences above, are nonrestrictive transitions; the "which" clause, in the second sentence, is a nonrestrictive adjective modifier. In the present sentence, and in the preceding sentence, all phrases beginning with *in* are also nonrestrictive. Notice, too, that in the first sentence above, the phrase "as a novel" is restrictive, and that the meaning of the word "powerful" would be changed if the writer had set this phrase apart with commas. Likewise, the phrase "in one edition" in the second sentence above is restrictive. (As is true in the preceding sentence and in this one, many sentences are introduced by nonrestrictive adverbial or transitional elements that should be set apart from the main clause with a comma.)

2. *Between clauses in compound sentences, and with other coordinate elements.* If a compound sentence is short, the comma may be omitted before the conjunction:

> Twain's invention was a failure and he knew it.

Usually, however, it is best to use the comma; for instance, even short compound sentences connected with *but* or *for* should use it:

> Parkman's eyes were going bad, but he kept on writing.

In sentences that contain nonrestrictive appositives, it is desirable to help the reader by placing commas around them:

> To read Dostoyevsky's or Conrad's novels without knowing about the lives of the authors, without realizing their problems with language and money and women and gambling, is to miss part of the astonishing effect.

Parts of sentences connected by *and* do not usually require a comma:

> Milton was in trouble for writing pamphlets against the government and for his views on divorce.

With rather long or complicated coordinate elements, however, a separating comma may be a help to the reader. In such a case, it should be used before the conjunction even if the elements are not independent clauses:

> At about this time, he was employed in composing his inflammatory but extremely convincing statements on freedom of the press, and in writing his pieces for the dissident groups who labeled themselves by their initials.—*Smectymnuus*

3. Items in a series. This is one use of the comma that almost everyone understands and observes. But even here, past usage has not been consistent in using the comma before the last item in the series. The present preferred form, followed by most editors and teachers, is to use it:

> The titles in Joyce Cary's *First Trilogy* are *Herself Surprised, The Horse's Mouth,* and *To Be a Pilgrim.*

If extremely short independent clauses are in series, commas may be used, but the student always runs the risk of incurring a red *CF* marked on his paper for the comma between the first two elements (see *CF* in this list). This may happen because grammatically the two elements are complete sentences:

> Cary was on his death-bed, he could barely wield a pencil, but he was virtually able to finish *The Captive and the Free.*

Colon

The colon is like an arrow, pointing to what follows. In most textbooks, including this one, it is used after a phrase or sentence introducing an example. Also, it is used in formal letters after the salutation, and in time references:

> Gentlemen: 6:30 p.m.
> Dear Professor Hayward: 10:15 a.m.

Also, remember not to confuse the colon with the semicolon, and do not use the colon in the middle of an ordinary sentence after a linking verb. To introduce lists, quoted materials, and illustrations, the colon is usually acceptable. It may also be used, however, between closely linked sentences when the first one clearly points to and anticipates the second:

> Lamb's troubles had only begun: the next day, his father died.

Dash

The dash is to be used sparingly, primarily because, like parentheses, it tends to detour the meaning. Its best use is probably for emphasis. If you look at a page without reading it, probably the first punctuation marks you will notice will be the dashes. To set an item between these marks, therefore, tends to impress it upon the reader's attention. In reading the page, you should find that the dash may interrupt a thought abruptly almost at any point, just as an informal speaker may interrupt himself in midsentence with a new idea. Too many dashes are a symptom of an excessively colloquial style.

Ellipsis

Use three spaced periods to indicate a word or passage left out of a quotation. The ellipsis is also used somewhat like a dash, for abrupt interruption of an idea. But in one particular, it differs from the dash, since the three dots indicate that the writer could continue but chooses not to do so. In this use, the ellipsis is gradually replacing the abbreviation *etc.* When a sentence is concluded by a period, and an ellipsis follows, four dots are used.

Exclamation point

Unless there is a pronounced need for it, you should try to avoid this mark. Its too frequent use is a symptom of false enthusiasm.

Hyphen

Consult your dictionary for the rules on correct division of words at ends of lines. For particular problems, take the time to look up the word in question. Usually, simple spaces between syllables, centered dots, or accent marks indicate points at which a word may be divided.

Parentheses

The best use of parentheses is for explanatory matter, to help clarify a word or phrase. But even this use is to be avoided when possible, since too many parentheses, like dashes and ellipses, tend to interrupt rather awkwardly. Another acceptable use is to enclose numbers or letters that label the items in a list or series. For this second use, especially when the items begin paragraphs, it is permissible to use the right-side half-parenthesis: 1), 2), 3) . . . ; but it is equally permissible and just as common to use full parenthesis: (1), (2), (3) . . . .

Period

Do not omit periods at the ends of your sentences. Use them also after abbreviations, for decimals, and for money: Nov., $20.63, $5.26. In quotations, at the end of sentences, the period goes inside the quotation marks:

Stephen Crane wrote "The Open Boat."

Question mark

Place the question mark outside the quotation marks if the essential question is found there:

Why should John Donne write a poem titled "The Flea"?

Conversely, if the question is in the quoted material, keep the question mark inside the quotation marks:

> In a way, it is idle speculation to ask, "Why should John Donne write a poem titled 'The Flea'?"

In general, it is best to avoid rhetorical questions (statements made in the form of questions used for emphasis or other rhetorical effect). The caution applies particularly to questions for which the writer does not immediately supply answers, and to a series of unconnected questions, as in the following example, a hypothetical introduction weakened by the bewildering effect of repeated interrogations:

> is served by using such petty devices? Is Donne's poetry really worth the trouble of serious analysis?
> Why should Donne write a poem about a shadow or a flea? Would it not be better to write about love and hate directly? What purpose

Quotation marks [see also *U* (Underlining) in this list]

1. Titles: Do not use quotation marks around your own titles. Quotation marks are used for titles of units smaller than book size, or for subunits of books, magazines, or pamphlets: titles of articles chapter headings, section headings, lyric poems, essays—all are used with quotation marks and are not normally italicized.

2. Sources: Do not use quotation marks for paraphrased material. However, you must give credit in footnotes, or in the text of your paper, for ideas taken from other sources. If you paraphrase, check to be sure you are not unconsciously quoting; if you do quote, be precise, use quotation marks, and indicate the exact source by author, title, page number, publisher, and date. [See also *FN* (Footnote) in this list.]

3. Length and method of quotations: Do not try to fill up a paper by quoting at unnecessary length. The words you quote do not count as part of the required length of the paper. If you quote poetry, or prose of more than five typed lines, do not use quotation marks, but indent and single-space, to set the quotation off from your own writing; in longhand, simply indent. In print, smaller type is used, as in this book. (See also Chapter 6.)

For quotations of less than a sentence, and for quotations out of context, use the three periods of the ellipsis to indicate that material has been omitted:

> In his Stockholm Address, Faulkner said modestly, ". . . this award is only mine in trust . . ."

For quotations within double quotation marks, use single quotation marks; for quotations within single quotation marks, use double quotation marks, and so on, alternating types. Always begin with double quotation marks.

For conversations, indent for each new speaker if the material is given for its own sake. (Your model here is any nonexperimental novel or short story.) For illustrative conversations, keep quoted matter in regular paragraphs.

4. With other marks: Place commas and periods inside all final quotation marks. For other terminal punctuation, use the principle explained in this list under *Question mark.*

Semicolon

Except for the comma and the apostrophe, no punctuation mark is more commonly misused by students than the semicolon. Nevertheless, the mark is relatively simple to use; and once you master its two main functions, it should give you no trouble.

1. Use semicolons to separate complicated items in a series, items that are themselves punctuated with commas:

> We know the following dates of publication: 1593, *Venus and Adonis;* 1594, *The Rape of Lucrece;* 1623, the First Folio.

> The female characters in *As You Like It* are Rosalind, daughter of Duke Senior; Celia, daughter of Duke Frederick; Phebe, a shepherdess; and Audrey, a country girl.

Obviously, this use of the semicolon is simply a device to keep the items clearly separated. If only commas were used, the reader might tend to confuse one item with another.

2. Use the semicolon to balance independent clauses. In this use, the semicolon is like the fulcrum of a teeter-totter:

> *As You Like It* is one of Shakespeare's lighter comedies; *The Merchant of Venice*, on the other hand, is more somber. ^

The ideas balance; they are parallel grammatically; they are also expressed in complete sentences. The semicolon here could be replaced with a period or with a comma and a conjunction, but the writer wishes to show that the two parallel ideas are part of a single concept. To do this, he uses a mark of balance—the semicolon. Most students use far too many semicolons. Use them sparingly, adroitly, and you will improve your style.

PR   *Pronoun reference is inexact*

Because pronouns are such inconspicuous words, you may tend to pay slight attention to them in both reading and writing. Nevertheless, these little words often carry large burdens of meaning and perform Herculean structural tasks. Therefore, in your attempts to improve your style, you should study the multiple possibilities of pronouns very thoroughly. If you let them become a problem, the pronouns in a passage can snarl your ideas into a hopeless jumble. If you use them with respect, however, they can tie your phrases and sentences together neatly and with great economy. As with other specific skills, to use pronouns well requires practice and care. The errors marked *PR* on your papers will usually be obvious once they are pointed out to you. Consequently, your real problem is to revise them gracefully and with improvement of clarity.

Pronouns are substitutes for other, larger words; they are used frequently to avoid the awkwardness and tiresomeness of repetition. For instance, suppose that for a passage from the above paragraph, all possible care was taken to avoid pronouns. If the writer merely repeated the antecedents, the passage would read as follows:

> If the writer lets pronouns become a problem, the pronouns in a passage can snarl the writer's ideas into a hopeless jumble. If the writer uses pronouns with respect, however, pronouns can . . .

And so on. This would be a bit like talking to a small child. The awkward repetition of "pronoun" and "the writer" gives the effect of not trusting the reader to follow the thought. Of course, if you place your pronouns too far from their antecedents, or if they may logically have more than one antecedent, you can confuse your reader seriously. In writing, therefore, you should give your reader credit for normal ability to connect your pronouns with their correct antecedents, but you should not demand backtracking or clairvoyance from him.

Some pitfalls to avoid in pronoun reference are:

1. Vagueness.   This flaw is most frequent when the pronoun points not to a specific word or phrase, but to an idea. If you do not give your pronouns clear antecedents, the passage can be unclear or awkward and vague:

> The letters of Charles Lamb are among the highlights of epistolary literature. He enjoyed doing this only at times . . .

It is usually best to avoid the vague reference of *it, they, you,* and *that,* when these words point to an unclear, nondescript group, person, or thing.

2. Misuse of which and that.   Reserve your relative *which's* for use after the comma; also, use *that,* not *which,* for close linkage to specific antecedents, as in the following:

His accountant's job, which he hated, served only to make the money that kept the family together.

3. Ambiguity. If there are too many possible antecedents, the reference is ambiguous:

Writing letters to personal correspondents took up many of Lamb's creative hours. They were surely worth it.

PV *Point of view shifts awkwardly*

Point of view, pronoun reference, and problems of tense are all interrelated. In a composition that moves forward, slight shifts in point of view that do not violate good logic may be acceptable. Within a single sentence, however, it is best to maintain consistency of person and number of pronouns and of verb tenses. The following are examples of pronoun shift and tense shift that involve a shift in point of view:

Pronoun shift: One should begin *War and Peace* early in the summer if *they* expect to finish it by fall.
Tense shift: Natasha *falls* victim to her own romantic imagination and *tried* to elope with Anatole.

R *Repetition is awkward*

Repetition of unemphatic words may be necessary and relatively inoffensive. Also, it is a mistake to put an awkward phrase or clause into a graceful sentence merely to eliminate a minor repetition. However, when the repeated word or phrase is unusual or in an emphatic position, or when it begins to toll like an annoying bell, it is best to attempt a revision. To avoid awkward repetition, try reading your composition out loud.

S   *Subordination is inaccurate or lacking*

One mark of an accurate, mature style is ample subordination of the minor elements in sentences. Also, if your writing lacks vigor, depth, and interest, one reason may be the monotony or formlessness of your sentences (see *C* in this list). To be accurate, you must subordinate the less important aspects of an idea rather than place them all on an equal footing. Contrast the passage on the left below, which gives the ideas equal status, with the example on the right, which employs the needed subordination:

Sinclair Lewis's *Babbitt* shows up modern American conformity for what it is. Dullness and stupid habit are what make up this conformity. Babbitt himself is a typical middle-class executive. He does not know how to be an individual.	In Sinclair Lewis's *Babbitt* modern American conformity, with its dullness and stupid habit, is shown up for what it is. Babbitt himself, a typical middle-class executive, does not know how to be an individual.

Sp   *Spelling. Check your dictionary*

S&V   *Subject and verb do not agree*

Tns   *Tenses of verbs are awkward or illogical*

In writing about literature it is common and conventional to use the present tense. The logic of this usage becomes apparent especially in discussion of fiction. For example, consider the following parallel passages:

Othello realizes his mistake the instant after he has made it; this rapid discovery of his error causes the tragic irony to be more poignant.	Othello realized his mistake the instant after he made it; this rapid discovery of his error caused the tragic irony to be more poignant.

In the example on the left, the writer avoids the impression that the events in *Othello* happened, like history, in the past. Also, when he wishes to comment on the tragic irony, this writer can use the present tense without a shift. In the example on the right, the writer's use of the past tense before the semicolon causes him to use another illogical past tense after it.

Tr *Transitions are inadequate or awkward*

As explained in the second part of Chapter 4, the best transitions are linkages in thought. A number of devices and expressions, however, are used to connect ideas. Some of these are indicated in the following brief paragraph from "Dante Gabriel Rossetti," by Walter Pater:

> What is important, then, is not that the critic should possess a 1
> correct abstract definition of beauty for the intellect, but a
> certain kind of temperament, the power of being deeply moved
> by the presence of beautiful objects. He will remember always
> that beauty exists in many forms. To him all periods, types, 5
> schools of taste, are in themselves equal. In all ages there have
> been some excellent workmen, and some excellent work done.
> The question he asks is always:——In whom did the stir, the
> genius, the sentiment of the period find itself? Where was the
> receptacle of its refinement, its elevation, its taste? "The ages 10
> are all equal," says William Blake, "but genius is always above
> its age."

In line 1, *then* links this paragraph with the preceding paragraph, and *not* anticipates *but* in line 2. In line 3, *temperament* and *power,* two appositives, also help to tie the paragraph together. The *he* of line 4 points back to *critic* of line 1 and forward to *him* and *he* in lines 5 and 8. Repetition also is a powerful transitional device in this paragraph. The words *all* and *always* repeated in lines 5, 6, 8, and 11, are examples of repetition of unemphatic words used for transitional purposes. The repetition of *excellent* and *genius* and of the question form add further cohesion.

U *Underlining is needed (or not needed)*

In typing or longhand, underlining corresponds to italics, which are used for emphasis and to indicate titles (see *E* in this list). The rule for titles is to italicize any title of a work that is first printed in book-unit form, and to use quotation marks for titles of articles, poems, short stories, essays, and chapter headings, first printed as subunits of books. Thus, the titles of plays, for instance, are italicized because they are normally first printed as separate units.

V *Vague. Give examples*

One of the most common flaws in student writing, vagueness can be corrected by getting down to cases. Excessive generalization is the most frequent cause of vagueness. Always try to be sure you are doing justice to your own detailed knowledge, not just expressing your broadest conclusions. Do not merely link easy statements one after another, but work progressively toward subconclusions and, finally, toward a thoughtful over-all conclusion. It is true that some of your first and last statements may necessarily be more general (though not more vague) than your middle ones. (See Chapter 4.) Moreover, to avoid general ideas altogether would be as fallacious as to rely on them completely. Therefore, a good plan to avoid vagueness is to construct the framework of your paper out of your more general conclusions, which are like the large timbers and beams in a house. The bulk of your writing will be the specific details, the small items which, like brickwork, give meaning and validity to your general structure. Also, for specific errors of style that cause vagueness, study reference of pronouns, under *PR* and meaning, under *M,* in this list.

W   *Wordy. Omit needless words*

One of the most valuable skills in writing is the ability to cut deadwood efficiently. In most early student papers, the number of words per idea is far too high. Such wordiness occurs not because the writer tries consciously to pad, but because he is used to talking, not writing. In colloquial speech, words are cheap, but in writing, it is best to treat them as expensive. To use too many words usually results in formlessness or obscurity. (See *C* and *V* in this list.) When you learn to cut the needless verbiage out of your papers your ideas will be both clearer and more pleasant to follow. Most of your papers written out of class should be read aloud before you make a final draft. In this reading, be sure that your composition observes economy, but be sure also that you have not cut so drastically that it sounds like a telegram.

¶   *Paragraph structure*

See Chapter 7.

‖   *Parallelism is incorrect*

One of the ways to give your style distinction, form, and vigor, is to use parallel constructions in the right places. Any two or three items in a series (for example, *distinction, form,* and *vigor* in the preceding sentence) must be parallel grammatically. The error most often committed is to have one of the items a different part of speech from the others.

> Writing poetry for the Elizabethan gentleman had to come with ease, grace, and be full of meaning.

Here *ease* and *grace* are nouns, while *be* is a verb and *full* is an adjective. It is true that *meaning* is a noun, but this word is out of the normal position for the third item in a series. The sentence is therefore awkward and rather unclear.

In the same way, when the sentence structure indicates parallelism for more complex elements, the same construction must be used in each parallel unit. In the following example, the connective *. . . as much . . . as . . .* is a false indicator of parallelism.

> Tolstoy objected as much to the historians' accounts of political affairs as he felt that their descriptions of specific battles necessarily had to be incorrect.

For separate sentences that are parallel, a recognizable recurrence of sentence structure is an important clue to the reader. The following example promises parallel construction and then fails to fulfill the promise; the second sentence is therefore awkward and the pronoun reference *he* is ambiguous.

> How can a historian know the feelings in the breast of a private soldier before a charge? How can he fail to be worried about the battle, and often very much afraid?

As a start toward understanding parallelism, it would be good practice for you to correct the flaws in the above examples.

In the other exercises you do to improve your style, and to give your sentences clearer structure, you should include plenty of experimenting with parallelism. Once you have mastered the device, however, you should be careful to avoid the monotony and the affected tone that would result from too many parallel elements. In this, as in other matters of style, the best counsel is simple: try to hit a happy medium.

\#   *Use a space. Also, use two words, not one*

⌣   *Close up. Also, use one word, not two*

part three

A glossary
of
literary
terms

EXPLANATION OF THE GLOSSARY

THE LITERARY terms in this Glossary are defined with the needs of the student writer in mind.[1] Often, definitions of terms can stimulate ideas for papers about specific literary works. This is true of nearly all terms treated here at length: names that distinguish one *genre* of literature from another (e.g., *Comedy, Drama, Epic, Essay, Lyric, Novel, Poetry, Tragedy, Short story*); terms that designate literary qualities (e.g., *Classicism, Humor, Irony, Naturalism, Romanticism, Satire*); labels for aspects of, approaches to, and attitudes toward literature (e.g., *Ambiguity, Analogy, Antithesis, Audience, Belief, Catharsis, Identification*, and examples of *Figurative language*, like *Metaphor* and *Symbol*). The Glossary may be used, also, as an aid to literary analysis. For instance, the mechanics of versification are indicated under terms like *Prosody, Stanza*, and *Meter*, so that the student may learn to scan lines of poetry. Because the definitions of many literary terms extend into areas of literary criticism, the Glossary may often be used in conjunction with the Outline-guide for Literary Study, pages 19 to 27, and with the relevant sections of Part Four, "Points of Departure." After studying a specific work of literature, the student would do well to browse around in all three before he makes his final decision on a topic for writing.

---

[1] Literary terms defined in the Glossary discussions are italicized. Look for the definition in alphabetical order in the Glossary, and watch for cross references.

index to the glossary

glossary terms and discussion

ACCENT

See *Prosody*.

ALEXANDRINE

A line in a pattern or stanza of *iambic pentameter* verse with an extra foot (see *Prosody*); the *alexandrine* is thus not pentameter but hexameter. It is sometimes used to close a stanza or to lengthen one line of a *couplet*. Spenser, in the *Faerie Queen*, used the alexandrine in the final (ninth) line of his Spenserian stanza:

> And in the wine a solemn oath they bind
> T' observe the sacred laws of arms that are assigned.

See also *Stanza*.

ALLEGORY

The use of a connected system of *symbols*, whereby a fiction has meaning of two kinds. Bunyan's *Pilgrim's Progress* and Dante's

Divine Comedy are allegorical stories narrated by the central characters, who are also symbols of all mankind. Thus, Pilgrim climbs
a particular mountain and Dante makes a particular journey, and
the reader is interested in the stories as narratives of particular
events. But he should also find embodied in the allegory a moral
meaning applicable to all human beings. In this second meaning,
the characters and even the settings form a coherent symbolic
structure that admonishes or invites the reader to heed the author's
moral warning or message.
See also *Narration, Symbol,* and *Metaphor.*

ALLITERATION

Repetition of sound in verse or prose, usually of initial consonants,
as in Lyly's

> Cupid and my Campaspe played
> At cards for kisses—Cupid paid; . . .

Here the *K* and *P* sounds begin alliterative syllables.

ALLUSION

Hidden or indirect reference; in literature, usually for the purpose
of connotative enrichment (see pages 12 to 15). Modern poetry is
particularly allusive; among the poets adept at the device are
Ezra Pound and T. S. Eliot. Eliot's poem, "The Love Song of
J. Alfred Prufrock," is packed with classical and Shakespearean
allusions.

AMBIGUITY

Multiple meaning. An ambiguity may be intentional or not; but if
it is not intentional, it is not at all likely to achieve a valid literary
or artistic effect. The intentional ambiguity helps the author to
carry his meanings on more than one level at a time, and thus

assists his work in achieving the complexity and depth that are often necessary in a work of art. Today, in the age of science and technology, ambiguities are often frowned upon. In former ages, like those of Dante and Shakespeare, it was good form to make one's words carry as many consistent meanings as their context allowed. Thus, literature flourished in an atmosphere more conducive to ambiguity than it does today, when the scientific habit of mind is not always oriented toward literary complexity and depth.

Ambiguity is thus an important critical term, to be understood as thoroughly as possible by the student who writes about literature. He should study it consciously in his daily conversation, as well as in his reading and writing. He should notice not merely the obvious *double entendres,* the separable meanings and the accidental puns, but more important the varying degrees of meaning that he finds in even the most common words in different contexts. In literature, uncontrolled ambiguity can destroy an author's work, but the controlled use of multiple meaning can be the central literary value. For several reasons, words and their meanings may reveal to a skillful author even greater possibilities of artistic power than do paints and their colors to a painter, or notes and their harmonies and discords to a musician. For one thing, verbal effects are universally accepted modes of expression, and everyone trains himself to use them as well as he can every day. A literary author thus, in a sense, is writing to an audience of authors and can therefore indicate deeper lines of meaning. In addition, the readiness with which words can carry different meanings in different situations gives them immediate effect when and where it is needed. It is as though the painter or the musician had vast actual and potential audiences of trained painters and musicians, without the need for art galleries or concert halls. Thus, the actual and potential ambiguity of a word is characterized not only by its ability to mean different things at the same time but by its ability to shift its meaning, its range, and its depth according to time and place (that is, according to its context). A word is thus a living thing, dependent on its surroundings for its character and its livelihood. When its surroundings change, it changes.

ANALOGY

An extended comparison usually for the sake of clarifying one of the things compared, for instance, a comparison of the organization of the solar system with that of a molecule. The *analogy,* which is not ordinarily figurative, is sometimes to be distinguished from the epic simile and from other figures of speech which are used to show similarities. Analogy is a teaching instrument to be used consciously and logically. It is usually couched in literal language, and the author may even attempt to exclude imaginative and emotional overtones. The logical aspect of the analogy is found in possibilities of inference: if one finds some qualities of the things compared to be similar or identical, it is possible that other similarities or identities also exist.

The analogy as a literary device may be similar in form and dissimilar in context to the *simile.* One could call many similes analogical if the purpose for comparison were not to entertain but simply to teach. Also, one can discover the teaching purposes of authors by noting how poets, novelists, and dramatists often imply analogies, without stating them explicitly. Thus, T. S. Eliot implies an analogy between the church and a hippopotamus, and in this way indicts the church for being sluggish and stuck in a mire of convention. Also, an author may use simple symbols to imply intended analogies and thus reveal a teaching or reforming purpose. In *Gulliver's Travels,* for instance, Swift belittles human pride and war by implying a comparison between human society and his society of pygmies up in arms over which end of an egg to crack and whether or not high heels should be worn. In this way, analogy is often found, upon analysis, to be buried in an author's work. When the reader unearths such an analogy, he probably discovers also that the comparison was put there in order for him to make the discovery. One literary effect of such a discovery is to allow the reader to consider on his own other points of similarity that the author may not always exploit fully. But whenever there is a discoverable analogy, there is likely also to be some kind of *didacticism,* even if this is merely the author's urgency that the reader see or understand something that had been obscure before the comparison was made.

ANAPEST

See *Prosody.*

ANTAGONIST

A character or force opposed to the hero, or the *protagonist,* sometimes called, simply, "the villain."

ANTITHESIS

The opposing of one effect to another, often in parallel form. Like many literary devices, antithesis may be simple or complex. Pope's line, "Man proposes, God disposes," if considered as two opposite ideas, is simple antithesis. But obviously opposition of ideas is not always clear, since in one way the ideas may be quite compatible and in another incompatible. Point-blank assertion and denial is probably the clearest form of antithesis, and yet even when someone says no to your yes, you both have a common proposition in mind. The prefix *anti* must not, therefore, be taken in isolation from the root word *thesis,* and the two halves of the antithesis are always fused together in a common universe of discourse.

This fusion may be broken, destroying the antithesis, by simply adopting a new topic. But changing the subject to avoid answering

an assertion may be itself a kind of subsurface denial of the assertion, so that although in such a case the antithesis seems to have
been destroyed, it lives on underground. Thus, even as a small
literary device, antithesis can be extremely complex and deep.

As a large, structural concept, antithesis may command a
writer's whole output, since his being in favor of something probably implies that he will defend it—that is, that he is against something else. To discover the pros and cons in a writer may therefore
assist in discovery of an over-all "Pro-and-Con" that unifies his
whole work. The larger the concept the easier it may be to identify,
so that some writers like Dante, Milton, Hawthorne, and even
Whitman, may be readily placed in a movement, especially if this
movement is so encompassing as Christianity, or liberalism, or
humanism. Some writers, however, elude a much closer identification with broad causes. Shakespeare, for instance, may or may not
have been a Christian, a democrat, a mystic; William Faulkner's
true position on the South may be no position at all. It is a good
critical exercise first to try to discover both parts of a commanding
antithesis in a writer's work, to discover both what he is for and
what he is against.

Such a study should be undertaken, like every kind of critical
work, with an open mind. For the kind of understanding of the
works that one aims to achieve, Shakespeare's religion may be a
minor consideration, and Dante's a major one. The student must
keep his balance and his perspective intact, and he must question
his own assumptions. To assume a major, commanding antithesis
when there is none, or when the opposition of ideas is only a
small aspect of the writer's attitudes, would probably throw the
student off the track.

APHORISM

A concise statement of a real or apparent truth, like a proverb.
A proverb, however, is more often than not a popular saying taken

from folklore; an aphorism may or may not be popular, and often it is coined by a literary author or even by a philosopher. Thus, in spite of attempts to distinguish between them, there may be an area of overlap, where an aphorism is a proverb, and vice versa. This overlapping is common to most synonyms, and it is what links together the string of words that may, on given occasions, be used in place of the term *aphorism: proverb, saying, maxim, adage, motto.*

In literature, the spirit of an author's aphorisms may be his attempt to create proverbs. If one were to sum up a work of literature as concisely as possible, the resulting statement would be called an *epitome* (see Chapter 10). But insofar as this distillation contained in miniature all the wisdom and value of the book, the summary could be called an *aphorism.* And insofar as the author was recommending this wisdom for popular use, he would be attempting to transform his aphorism (the epitomized book, or poem, or whatever) into a proverb (a way of regarding the world by the world).

ARCHETYPE

A more or less universal way of behaving that in literature receives more or less specific treatment. Archetypes can be primitive ways of meeting problems that have survived through centuries of modification. To discover an archetype in literature is to show it divested of its idiosyncratic, local *texture* in its most pristine simplicity. *Oedipus Rex,* illustrating universal, deep-seated anxieties about patricide, incest, blindness, and concentrating upon the fate of a king and his people, represents a grouping of archetypes from which Sophocles has formed a classic tragedy. The more fundamental motives of human nature are incorporated into the archetypal pattern, and the author who displays these motives effectively in the work of art has a greater chance to achieve lasting, widespread appeal.

The literary artist, however, must write for his own age, and this requirement robs him of the universality he could achieve if he were able to ignore his contemporary scene and write only about timeless forms of behaving. Under the necessity of reflecting the changes and complexities of the life he observes, the writer must overlay the ageless archetypal aspects of his work with decorative material taken from his own period of time—or from some other period also characterized by change and complexity. Literature that is simply archetypal and not involved with the passing scene would attempt to ignore that mankind by definition is complex and changing. Although, as Milton and Dante have shown, human beings are interested in literary treatment of the archetypal Human Being, and although it is possible even to dramatize him in literature, yet he cannot be the only subject matter of the literature. He must be regarded by temporal, changing, mortal beings in a complex world. And the audience of such literature finds itself, willy-nilly, interested as much in these mortals as in the Archetypal Being.

In literature, then, both the age in which an author writes, as well as the age he writes about, must qualify the embodiments of archetypal human motives in his work. Despite these disclaimers, the study of archetypal patterns in literature is extremely rewarding. When such a study is made, as it should be, together with studies of the age of literary production and subject matter, the literature can be fully explicated.

(See also Maud Bodkin, *Archetypal Patterns in Poetry,* New York, 1934.)

ARGUMENT

This term is sometimes used as a synonym for *argumentation.* Also, the term is used to designate a summary of a section of an *epic* poem or of a *novel.*

ARGUMENTATION

The method or style of rhetoric usually emphasizing formal logic; also, one of the four classical types of composition, the others being *description, exposition,* and *narration.* In one way or another, every genre of literature may be used for persuasion, and so may employ a style that is argumentative in some degree. Thus, the terms *argumentation, persuasion,* and *rhetoric* may often overlap in meaning. Moreover, the correspondences between argumentation and *didacticism* are evident: in order to teach or preach, one must be able to persuade the *audience* to be of the same mind, to have the same opinions, ideas, attitudes as those of the author. One reason for the interinvolvement of the members of this cluster of terms is that any literary work may include some element of argumentation that is not evident on the surface. For instance, in a *lyric* poem, the persuasion is not always directed toward an obvious goal, but may be simply the expression of an attitude which the reader is invited to share.

See also *Question begging.*

ASSONANCE

Repetition of vowel sound in prose or verse. Assonance is to be distinguished from rhyme by the difference in final consonant sound:

> I speak for each no-tonguéd tree
> That, spring by spring, doth nobler be . . .

In these lines from Sidney Lanier's "The Symphony," assonance is the repetition of the *ee* sound in *speak, each,* and *tree,* since each of these words differs in its final sound. Rhyme, of course, is found in the end words, *tree* and *be.*

In prose, assonance can be one method of obtaining a melliflu-ous flowing style, but its too obtrusive employment soon becomes a mannerism. Together with other acoustic and rhetorical devices, like *consonance* and balanced periods, assonance contributed to the artificiality of a style called "euphuism" (after Lyly's *Euphues*), cultivated by several sixteenth-century authors.

See also *Alliteration, Consonance,* and *Rhyme.*

AUDIENCE

A term used to designate the reader, the spectator, or more generally the agents who react to a work of literature. Audience studies may bear more or less immediately upon the literature itself. At one extreme, the student may almost ignore the specific literary work itself and concentrate on how it has been received through the years since it was produced. This study of social history as related to a literary work could specify aspects of the work that receive different emphases during different ages. Audiences found *Hamlet,* for instance, to be a more romantic play during the early nineteenth century than during the eighteenth century, when the more thoughtful aspects of the play were exploited.

At the other extreme, the student may study the literature as a set of stimuli for audience reaction. This more psychological approach would focus attention less on specific audiences than on the literary elements designed to stir their thoughts and emotions. As the historical approach describes specific sets of audiences apropos of the literature, the psychological approach describes literature as stimulus apropos of audience reactions. I. A. Richards, a pioneer in literary psychology, early coined the term *appetency* (in *Principles of Literary Criticism,* 1949) to refer to literary reactions, which he tried to chart and study in detail. Richards's later work, however, repudiated overemphasis on the clinical aspects of audience study and disclaimed the early hypotheses that literary reactions were of a kind differing from ordinary reactions. One tendency of the clinical study of audiences was to slight the study of literature in favor of hypothetical responses.

Audience studies, both of the historical and of the psychological kinds, however, can be valuable. If conducted in proper balance and in a perspective that includes proper emphasis on the literature, historical studies can help to reveal appeals in the work that may be hidden or inactive today but that were overt and functioning in a former age. Thus, one age may blind itself to meanings that are quite visible in another age, as the Age of Reason may often have blinded itself to intuitive values. Psychological studies, moreover, may enable the student to discover deeper, often hidden meanings by focusing, for instance, upon phenomena like *identification* of audience with the central characters in a work. Thus, psychological studies of *Oedipus Rex* have revealed and helped to explain depths of the human character that had remained buried, or that had not been explicitly analyzed.

BALLAD

A story in verse, usually episodic and often with a refrain. Many ballads are of folk origin and are therefore anonymous. In any case, the genuine ballad is a story intended to be set to music and sung to the accompaniment of a lyre, a guitar, or other stringed instrument. The subject matter is often grim; death, bereavement, and lost love and loyalty are frequent occasions of the ballad. Because of its lyrical nature, the ballad is usually composed in one or two forms of *stanza*. (Sargent and Kittredge's *English and Scottish Popular Ballads* is the definitive source for many ballads.)

BATHOS

The dropping into emotion or pettiness after intellectual or serious discourse. Bathos is sometimes a valid literary device and sometimes a flaw; it is not often considered deeply by critics, who have ordinarily labeled it as a simple error of taste. For instance, Milton's *Paradise Lost* has been criticized adversely because it does not maintain, throughout, a tone of high seriousness proper to the epic as a form. The extreme length of this poem has mitigated these criticisms, since no poem of more than 3,000 lines could be written on a single plane of high philosophical thought. And, indeed, bathos may damage the literary quality—where the spirit of the poem is violated by uncalled for emotionalism or sensationalism (as Book VI, "The War in Heaven," is said to be outlandish and improbable).

Nevertheless, more critical studies of bathetic effects that contribute to literary value could profitably be made. There is no reason why the term *bathos* must be reserved to designate a loss of literary effect, but a new term for its obverse—a gain of literary effect—might be found. For one thing, bathos is a natural rhetorical device; Cicero might have included it as the emotional aspect of one of his terms. In Shakespeare's *Julius Caesar,* Antony, in his "Friends, Romans, Countrymen" speech, illustrates its effectiveness by using bathos to sway the populace from one political position to its opposite. The tendency of this speech is to juxtapose high philosophical reasoning with the low, personal self-interest of the crowd. The fact that Antony's own motives are well hidden, and that he controls his use of emotional appeal, only reinforce the power of his bathos where it does occur—as in his turning aside to weep, at the sight of Caesar's wounds.

BELIEF

Wordsworth coined the phrase, "the willing suspension of disbelief," to indicate what he thought should happen when a reader is thoroughly absorbed in a work of literature. Fiction—novels and short stories—best illustrates what he meant: when the reader gives himself thoroughly to a fictional piece, he allows himself to disregard the fact that the story is not "true," that it has never really happened. This phenomenon is readily noticeable in children, who while being told a story, may live in a fantasy world; that is, they willingly suspend their normal disbelief in the untrue aspect of the fiction. Another analogy is found in daydreaming— allowing a part of one's critical faculties to sleep while idly contemplating an imaginative situation, event, or series of events. The daydreamer, in effect, is constructing his own fiction and is his own best reader. The fact, however, that one's critical faculty—the ability to assess, to evaluate, to judge—is relatively inactive can allow the fiction to be incoherent, to lack the qualities of good art. The problem of belief, then, involves the degree to which, in a given literary work, the reader should be uncritical.

This is one of the most complex problems in literary criticism, and a brief definition can only indicate the areas in which it is involved. What John Crowe Ransom (*The World's Body,* 1938) has called the ontological problem is perhaps most central to the problem of belief. Ontology is the study of what constitutes truth itself. As related to literary criticism, ontology asks questions like: Where is the truth of a literary fiction? What should one believe about literature? Is there a kind of literary truth, as distinct from other kinds of truth? Does this truth exist on the page, in the reader's mind, in the author's intention, or in some combination of these loci? An ontological study of a literary work would also explain the methods of writing used by the author in encouraging the reader to "suspend his disbelief" in the fiction.

The problem also involves the question of literary value and usefulness. Since, by suspending his disbelief, the reader willingly allows his judgment to be guided by the story, under this influence he may allow himself to accept ideas that he would otherwise reject —or fail to notice at all. Thus, to the author who knows how to command it, an area of his reader's mind is available that may be appealed to only by the special techniques of literary fiction. The author may choose merely to entertain his reader by taking him, temporarily, out of the humdrum into a world of happiness or adventure. But if the author has a special view of life—a philosophy, a set of ideals, or even a complaint about mankind—he may embody this view in a fictional story. When the story has captured the reader's imagination, the author may use this receptive frame of mind to set forth his attitudes or his philosophy to its best advantage.

See also *Didacticism.*

BLANK VERSE

Unrhymed, iambic pentameter verse. Much epic poetry is in blank verse; Milton's *Paradise Lost* and *Paradise Regained* are two famous examples. Many Elizabethan plays, and some modern dramas, also, use the form. Thus, Shakespeare's dramatic poetry contains long passages in blank verse, and plays like T. S. Eliot's *The Cocktail Party* use it frequently. Probably of all metrical forms of poetry, blank verse is the most common in English. The term is sometimes used erroneously to mean *free verse.*

BUCOLIC

Rustic literature, usually of the *pastoral* tradition; sometimes loosely applied to any *verse* or *poetry* that treats of country life.

BURLESQUE

An imitation intended to ridicule by exaggeration. The burlesque mocks its subject by caricature. A burlesque is usually a humorous example of a style or a characterization, neither of which need be very specific. In contrast, the parody lampoons a more specific subject. An example of a burlesque of literary criticism is Ring Lardner's "How to Write Short Stories" (pages 354 to 358).

See also *Hyperbole, Parody, Satire,* and *Travesty.*

CADENCE

The rhythm usually of *prose* or *free verse. Cadence* is a convenient term to designate the measured repetition of emphasis and accent that is found in nonmetrical discourse. In contrast, the term *meter* is applied to more regular verse.

See also *Alliteration, Assonance, Consonance, Prosody,* and *Meter.*

CAESURA

A pause between feet in the middle of a line of verse. In scansion, the caesura is marked by two vertical lines. It may or may not be indicated by a punctuation mark. In the following, from William Browne's "Britannia's Pastorals," the caesuras result from slight shifts in the advancement of the meaning:

Gentle nymphs,//be not refusing,

Love's neglect//is time's abusing.

See also *Prosody.*

CATHARSIS

Aristotle's term to indicate a cleansing or purging of undesirable emotions or characteristics in an audience subjected to *tragedy.* The theory of catharsis is likely to endure, although it has had its adversaries throughout critical history. The basic idea is that tragedy presents in a harmless form, on the stage, attitudes that, if acted out in real life, would be injurious to society. The audience comes to the drama with individual problems that have stirred unhealthy confusions and emotions. These emotions demand release in some form, and Aristotle considered tragic drama to be the most efficient vehicle for this release. If the drama has been constructed according to Aristotelian principles—foremost of which are the nobility and the tragic flaw of the hero and the fated defeat of the hero by his problem—the audience will participate emotionally in the dramatic action and will go away psychologically cleansed and elevated, able to function more effectively in their services to each other and to the state.

Catharsis thus requires, as its central ingredient, a focus of attention in the drama that would allow the fullest audience participation to occur. Therefore, Aristotle specified that the ideal tragedy should concern itself basically with the fortune of the tragic hero, who receives the major increment of attention and sympathy from the audience. The dramatist so constructs his play that in sympathizing with the tragic hero, the members of the audience identify themselves with him, while the drama is being presented (see *Identification*). They share the hero's problems and his temporary victories; and they feel, vicariously, his ultimate defeat, which ordinarily is illustrated by his death or suicide. At the death of the tragic hero, the audience observes that the tragic flaw has likewise received a death blow, and although they live on, their weaknesses symbolically but nonetheless effectively have died together with the hero.

The tragic hero, then, contains symbolically within himself the weaknesses in the audience that the dramatist dooms to an irrevocable death. Since from the first this heroic death has been inevitable, an element of fate is also essential to tragic catharsis, and religious concepts are often used to reinforce the tragedy. The gods often play important parts; and the audience, trained in their religion as well as in the conventions of the drama itself, are encouraged to resign themselves to the death of their hero. If they have identified themselves with him (more or less thoroughly, according to the skill of the dramatist), they have been spared anxiety that the tragic flaw may survive; and they have satisfied their religious impulses by having bowed, symbolically, to the decrees of the gods.

CHARACTERIZATION

The treatment of human nature in literature. Most literary theory
that is critically acceptable rests on the thesis that the human element cannot and should not be eliminated from any phase of
literary production and study. Literature is always by human
beings and most often *about* them, and even though an author may
write extensively about other subject matter, his utterance is always
directed to human beings. Since the *audience* of literature is always
considered by the author, in discussing even the most scientific
topics he often humanizes his discourse in some way. Sometimes by
virtue of his very attempt to eliminate human error from his discussion he uses a special vocabulary—mathematics, symbolic logic,
chemical or physical formulas—which vocabulary is the more
limited and fallible the more it assumes that the people who use it
are machines.

In fictional and dramatic literature, the general term *characterization* subsumes the functions of such terms as *protagonist* and
antagonist, hero and *villain;* and minor characters and even characteristics may be discussed under this heading. Characterization
may permeate novels, plays, and lyric and dramatic poems, since
the focal point of conflict is usually the actor, the agent himself.

One may find much matter for thoughtful discussion by comparing traits of different characters or of the same character at
different times. A good idea, however, is always to link the character to be discussed with the main action in the *plot*, with its
scene, its *style,* its *purpose*—or with a combination of these four
elements as the background against which a writer can most effectively silhouette the character he is contemplating.

The plot as a whole, and specifically the reactions of characters
to situations and episodes, can help form ideas for papers. Also the
student may find much to say by comparing two characters in relation to the same act or scene, which can also give perspective and

depth of understanding about literary characters. Consider, for instance, the scenic overtones to human character, and how the same person may act so differently in two different settings that he seems to be two different individuals. Or observe how different characters in a literary work have different styles, different ways of meeting the same problem. Or notice that the goals and intentions of a character change in relation to those of a different character. Thus, it should be apparent that when a literary work is divided into separate elements, with one of them serving as focal point, the student may discover valuable ideas and insights about any specific work of literature.

CHIASMUS

An interlinking in idea or in *point of view* between the parts of a parallel structure; also, a reversal of parallel elements. The following lines from Thomas Campion are examples of the chiasmus:

Love me or not, love her I must or die;
Leave me or not, follow her needs must I.

See also *Figurative language.*

CLASSICISM

The term *classicism* has been used by T. E. Hulme and other modern critics, who contrast it with *romanticism.* (See Hulme's *Speculations,* 1924.) Hulme uses the terms to designate two states of mind, radically different from one another, which alternate through the ages and which thus characterize literary history. The basic emotional trait of classicism is pessimism, since the classicist believes that man is evil by nature, that he requires much religious and secular education to make him good. Classical literature (as distinguished from romantic literature) is therefore likely to be didactic, and the function and position occupied by the church and by the gods in this literature may be very definite and prominent. Another characteristic of the literature of classicism is its dependence upon strict form. Just as classical architecture is spare and austere, employing economy of line and simplicity of structure, so classical literature may rely upon sharply defined verse forms and clearly outlined plots stated simply and cogently.

In practice the traits of classicism and of romanticism are rarely found in purity; and ordinarily, the critic's problem is simply to discover, by its emphasis, and by its period of composition, which tradition a given literary work belongs to. Also, the terms are useful in characterizing long periods of time, like the eighteenth century (classical) or the early nineteenth century (romantic). If used with perception and critical understanding, the terms may be extremely useful in analysis of individual literary styles. The procedure in this analysis could distinguish the classical and romantic elements in an author's work in order to estimate how effective is their blending, to discover how well the states of mind are expressed, and to specify which state of mind, classicism or romanticism, prevails. Poets like Dante, who lived and wrote during a transitional period and whose work clearly illustrates both states of mind, would be especially interesting and challenging to analyze in this way. For instance, the implications of Dante's attitude toward Beatrice, his guide through the *Paradiso,* are romantic, but the structure of his poem and his attitudes toward the function of Christianity are classical.

COMEDY

Aristotle's term which together with *tragedy* distinguishes the drama from other literature. Essentially, the pattern of a comedy is simply the obverse of the pattern of a tragedy. Whereas the tragedy begins in happy circumstances and ends in disaster, comedy begins in difficulty and ends happily. One should note that this definition does not specify that the comedy must be humorous or even lighthearted, although most comedies have these traits. Dante's *Divine Comedy,* which begins in hell and ends in heaven, is serious in tone and intent, and is still correctly named according to the Aristotelian definition.

The minor characteristics of comedy vary much more widely than do those of tragedy. For example, a tragedy is felt to be imperfect if it contains no central character (the tragic hero) and if it does not abide by some kind of unity—preferably the unities of time, place, and action. A comedy may dispense with these characteristics or modify them according to the needs of the plot. Thus, in Shakespeare's *As You Like It,* the central character is a woman (Rosalind) whose character, however, makes two concessions to the tragic requirement: (1) she is a member of the nobility (a duke's daughter); and (2) she disguises herself as a man (Ganymede). The same play lacks the more formal unities of place and time but is strongly unified in the last act by Rosalind's magic touch. When she doffs her disguise, all the sympathetic characters get their hearts' desires, or what the audience perceives would be even better for them. Examples like this one illustrate that comedy and tragedy have several important traits in common. Not the least of these traits are conflict and appeal to an audience, which one may say are essential to any dramatic literature.

CONCEIT

A figure of speech that orders the expression or *form* of a piece of literature. Behind the conceit is an ingenious or witty analogy, which on the surface may seem fanciful or even farfetched. The conceit calls the reader's attention to an unusual, many-sided idea; it is thus at once metaphorical and purposely ambiguous. The *metaphysical poetry* of sixteenth- and seventeenth-century poets like Donne, Herbert, and Crashaw often employs the conceit. The following typical example is only one of ten stanzas describing a lady's eyes in Richard Crashaw's "The Weeper":

> Hail Sister Springs!
> Parents of silver-forded rills!
> > Ever bubbling things!
> Thawing crystal! Snowy hills!
> Still spending, never spent; I mean
> Thy fair eyes, sweet Magdalene.

See also *Ambiguity* and *Wit*.

CONNOTATION

See Chapter 1.

CONSONANCE

Repetition of consonant sound, usually at the ends of words. The consonance of a literary style, however, may be simply its euphony, its ability to please the ear by a happy combination of sound and meaning. The term may thus be used either narrowly, as in *prosody,* or broadly.

COUPLET

A pair of rhymed lines of *verse.* Couplets are of several kinds. Heroic couplets are in iambic pentameter—that is, two lines of ten syllables per line, alternating unstressed and stressed syllables. The heroic couplet may be "closed," having its meaning complete within itself, as in the following lines from the "Epilogue" of Dryden's *Tyrannick Love,* a typical heroic drama:

> I come, kind gentlemen, strange news to tell ye;
> I am the ghost of poor departed Nelly.
> Sweet ladies, be not freightened; I'll be civil;
> I'm what I was, a little harmless devil.

This type of couplet may often employ the *caesura*. Couplets may also be "open," with the meaning running on from one couplet to the next, as in the following well-known lines from Keats's *Endymion: A Poetic Romance:*

A thing of beauty is a joy for ever:
Its loveliness increases; it will never
Pass into nothingness; but still will keep
A bower quiet for us, and a sleep
Full of sweet dreams, and health and quiet breathing. . . .

The final line, above, with eleven syllables, is sometimes erroneously called an *alexandrine*. Nonheroic couplets may contain any length of line. Though both lines of the couplet are usually of the same length, they may occasionally differ, as in the following from a *lyric* of Sir Philip Sidney:

Ring out your bells! Let mourning shows be spread,
For love is dead.

See also *Stanza*.

DACTYL
See *Prosody*.

DECADENCE
A term used by Yvor Winters (in *In Defense of Reason,* 1937), to be compared with *primitivism*. Winters uses the term *decadence* to indicate a pervasive flaw, a failure to reflect the particular truths that a given literary *form* is capable of reflecting. The primitive poet, by contrast, sees these truths, but he expresses them only in disconnected, partial flashes of insight. Since the decadent poet may not see the details of his subject matter, his work is likely to be characterized by excellence of over-all form or *structure,* and by a corresponding weakness in *texture*. Late Victorian poets like

Swinburne and Oscar Wilde could be called decadent because they often illustrate errors of taste or understanding that cause them to fail to record details with mature and balanced insights and emotions. The excellence of structure in a decadent work of literature may almost make up for these errors. Moreover, an author who represents a classical or a neoclassical age, when formal literary structures received great emphasis, is more likely to exemplify the errors of decadence than is, for instance, a romantic poet. Thus, Pope and Dryden may be more decadent, according to this definition, than Wordsworth and Shelley, who, by comparison, would be called primitive.

In second-rate literature, decadence and primitivism may both be present, and an author may fail in respect both to his expression of details and to his portrayal of a literary form. For example, a tragedy that fails to illustrate any real truths about life, and that also ignores the classical tragic structure, would embody the flaws both of decadence and of primitivism. Taken together, these terms designate contrary aspects of the act of perception and cognition. Decadence is a failure to see clearly the individual members of a class, although the class as a whole may be distinguished; primitivism is a failure to understand the class as a whole, although its individual members may be distinguished.

DENOTATION
See Chapter 1.

DESCRIPTION
One of the four classic types of composition; the others are *argumentation, exposition,* and *narration.* Description may be concerned with both the human and the nonhuman. Preeminently, the descriptive writer tries to capture or evoke an atmosphere, usually of a physical *scene,* but also, sometimes of a human per-

sonality. Strong examples of scenic description are in the novels of
Scott and Hardy and the poems of Keats and Wordsworth. But a
literary artist may also delineate human nature in descriptive
writing that takes psychological as well as physical *characterization*
as its basic concern. Proust's *Remembrance of Things Past* is an
example of this kind of descriptive writing, as are the novels of
Henry James.

DIDACTICISM

The teaching or preaching of facts or morality by way of literature.
With a few exceptions, literary critics today ordinarily regard
didacticism in literature as a flaw, but the issue of whether poetry
(that is, literature) should be useful in an educational way has
been debated since the earliest philosophers. Plato considered the
didactic element in poetry to be more powerful and more dangerous to society than a drug; therefore, he advocated strict literary
censorship. Aristotle's *catharsis,* on the other hand, is one of the
most specific and widely accepted explanations of how poetic
didacticism may contribute to the psychological health of a society.
In Sir Philip Sidney's "Apology for Poetry," the fact that poetry
entertains while it teaches is a major thesis, and Sidney ranks
literary teaching as superior too all other methods.

Present-day opposition to the advocates of didacticism constitutes one of the main rallying principles of the "new criticism."
This movement, led by John Crowe Ransom and Allen Tate, is
one aspect of a larger critical complaint against the age we live in.
These "new critics" accuse the twentieth century of overemphasiz-
ing utility at the expense of esthetic values. As evidence they point
to the high development of modern scientific and technological
utilitarianism, which results in more gadgets and instruments of
destruction than we need or know how to control. In the same
indictment, the critics cite the low level of modern cultural and

literary attainment, which presumably results from twentieth-century preoccupation with usefulness. Our tendency to make this usefulness, or didactic purposefulness, the criterion of literary worth, the new critics assert, has lowered the essence of poetry from esthetic to utilitarian values. The critical reaction against didacticism, violent and pervasive in the thirties and forties, but less so in the fifties and in the present decade, is one source of paradoxical statements that the best poetry is "perfectly useless," that to the extent that it is useful, poetry is unpoetic. I. A. Richards, the earlier T. S. Eliot, and a group called "The Chicago Critics," headed by R. S. Crane and Richard McKeon (see *Critics and Criticism,* ed. R. S. Crane, 1952), have opposed this position, often using Aristotle as their champion. But a considered and un-biased assessment of the last forty years of literary criticism would still tip the balance against didacticism as being a true poetic element.

DRAMA

One of the largest genres of literature, divided into *comedy* and *tragedy,* each of which has subdivisions of its own. Extended discussions of the drama are found under these terms and in the section entitled "Drama" in Part Four.

A good account of the origins, history, and nature of the drama in English is *British Drama,* by Allardyce Nicoll, published in 1925.

DRAMATIC MONOLOGUE

A poem narrated in the first person by one of the chief characters. In most cases, the speaker is addressing another character, whose presence may be inferred by what is said. The speaker reveals the traits of other persons as well as his own, and elements in dramatic conflict are made evident. The conflict may exist in the present,

past, or future, or in a combination of these times, as in Browning's "My Last Duchess" (see Chapter 1). The monologue may be, but is not always, a *lyric*. Browning's *The Ring and the Book*, a poem of epic proportions, is a series of dramatic monologues, each of which consists of the same story retold by each of the characters. Other practitioners of this form are Tennyson, E. A. Robinson, T. S. Eliot, Allen Tate, and Carl Sandburg.
See also *Characterization*.

ELEGY

A thoughtful poem on a serious topic—usually, the death of a friend. The elegy may be an example of *occasional verse;* a poet may write a poem commemorating the passing of his friend and use this subject as the focal point of a wide, nonspecific poetic meditation. Thus, Milton's "Lycidas," Tennyson's "In Memoriam," and Shelley's "Adonais" are typical of many elegies in their concern with matters of the church, politics, and social justice.

Genuine grief may be expressed at the poet's personal loss, but this emotion is made consistent with other feelings in the poem, like indignation at conditions of life endured by the deceased subject, and even subdued wrath at the general causes for the death. Thus, the elegy, although a formal poem of mourning, is very likely also to be a protest against one or more of the evils of society.
See also *Ode* and *Lyric*.

EPIC

Traditionally, the oldest form of poetry, the other two types being the *drama* and the *lyric*. Although the definition and the origin of the epic are still debated by critics, one may find general agreement that the Germanic *Nibelungenlied* and the English *Beowulf* are examples of the folk epic. In contrast, such varied poems as Dante's

Divine Comedy, Spenser's *Faerie Queen,* and Milton's *Paradise Lost* may be called art epics. On the borderline between these two types may be poems like Homer's *Iliad* and *Odyssey* and Virgil's *Aeneid.* The distinction between kinds is mainly one of degree of artistic arrangement by the author of materials arising primarily out of history and folklore. Thus, the critic who finds more evidence of single authorship in the *Iliad* is more likely to call it an art epic than a critic who believes it to have been composed by a variety of authors. The assumption that the art epic is the inferior form, since it attempts to imitate the folk epic, ignores the fact that all literature is imitative in some way.

Folk heroes and the wars of antiquity are fit subjects for the epic; and even in highly sophisticated variants like the poems of Dante, Spenser, and Milton, there is ordinarily strong emphasis on war and heroic battle. Cervantes and Byron, in *Don Quixote* and *Don Juan,* exploited epic glorifications by making their heroes into parodies of epic heroes.

The epic as a serious form has several important similarities to *tragedy.* In the first place, the central figure is of the nobility, and in the course of the poem he proves his high birth by such acts as Achilles' mediation between his mother (the goddess Thetis) and the kings and princes of mortal birth on the battlefield. Secondly, the hero, who in one way or another is doomed, has a tragic flaw in his character: Achilles, though half god, is petulant and jealous, and he knows he will die a mortal death; even Christ, in the art epics named above, allows himself to carry the burden of human sin, which is his tragic flaw. Tragically, Christ is therefore doomed to die on the cross.

The differences between the epic and tragedy are just as important, though perhaps not always so concrete, as the similarities. In an epic, the subject matter may include more territory—in terms both of geography and of time—so that the topic of Homer's *Odyssey* may include the whole known Mediterranean area and many years of Odysseus' life. More important, perhaps, since Shakespeare wrote tragedies like *Antony and Cleopatra* that cover as much ground and as much time, good epic subject matter can be derived from more barbarous, warlike cultures, and the sense of vastness and of length should contribute to the glorification of the more primitive qualities of the hero. Moreover, the sense of structural unity is not always as pronounced in an epic as it is in a tragedy. The obvious differences are that the tragedy, a subclass of drama, is meant to be acted, and the epic was originally meant to be sung.

EPITOME

See Chapter 10.

ESSAY

A discussion expressing the author's views or attitudes on any conceivable topic; often today, written in an informal style and having the tone and form of a conversation from the author to the reader. Much early philosophical literature of the Orient, India, Greece, and Italy resembles the essay form, and the Epistles in the Christian Bible also reflect an essaylike tendency. Books written to patrons of the arts like Lucretius' *On the Nature of the Universe* and Machiavelli's *The Prince,* may also be ancestors, direct or indirect, of the essay form. The essay as a *genre,* however, received its name and matured its modern character in eighteenth- and nineteenth-century France and England. Two strong formative influences of comparatively recent times were the development of mass periodical literature and the more sophisticated postal services of the nineteenth and twentieth centuries.

In England, as early as the sixteenth century, the familiar letter became a literary form, and as illiterate and awkward as some of these early specimens were (for example, the *Paston Letters*), their intimate personal tone and rambling structure are the first distinguishing influences on the modern essay. The great seventeenth-century essayists, Montaigne and Bacon, treated subjects from the most superficial to the most deeply philosophical; and by the end of the eighteenth century, when periodical literature began to flourish, the essay had broadened to include so many topics and styles that the word *essay* almost lost its restrictive meaning. To show this development: Locke's "Essay Concerning Human Understanding" is an abstruse prose work on epistemology; Dryden's "Essay on Dramatic Poesy" is a dramatic dialogue; and Pope's "Essay on Man" and "Essay on Criticism" are poems in heroic couplets.

Throughout the nineteenth century, the essay is probably the most frequently employed literary genre in spite of the fact that both poetry and the novel also received great impetus from the burgeoning periodical. Charles Lamb, whose personal letters are today regarded as highly as are his essays, may represent the individualistic turn taken by the early nineteenth-century essay. His "Essays of Elia" are written in archaic style and say things "by the way," with long, complicated sentence structure. In the Victorian period, when social and political issues began to engross a vastly increased audience, the essays of Newman, T. H. Huxley, Ruskin, and Mill, are less idiosyncratic, less casual in style, since the form more and more begins to reflect the urgency of practical affairs. The twentieth-century essay may sometimes partake of early nineteenth-century casualness and charm, with its style a mirror of the author's mood. More often, however, our grim concern about such matters as disarmament, bomb testing, and racial tension infuse the contemporary essay with a typical Victorian seriousness, which may, according to the proficiency of a given essayist in this style, deprive the form today of some of its former literary excellence.

EXPLICATION

The detailed analysis of a passage of prose or verse to unravel or explain its meaning. Explication is used in contemporary literary criticism more than any other technique. Its advocates—for example, William Empson and John Crowe Ransom (in *Seven Types of Ambiguity,* 1949, and *The World's Body,* 1938) point out many of the advantages of explication over other possible approaches to literature. The chief advantage, they claim, is that the explicator must analyze the text of the literature itself. The historian and the sociologist, for instance, may study literature mainly as a reflection of an age or a society, and pay only secondary attention to artistic values, which are the explicator's first concern.

Any literary work is suitable subject matter for explication. Modern critics like T. S. Eliot and Yvor Winters, however, have chosen to focus attention upon the *metaphysical poetry* of the sixteenth and seventeenth centuries, because its complexity presents interesting challenges to textual analysis. The poetic *conceit* is often an example of such complexity. Other writers of various genres to whom the explicators have paid special attention are Shakespeare, Hawthorne, Blake, Joyce, Eliot, and Faulkner.

EXPOSITION

One of the four types of composition; the others are *argumentation, description,* and *narration.* Explanation is the burden of expository writing, and facts, either fictional or true, are its usual subject matter. The essay as a genre is more often expository than descriptive, narrative, or argumentative. It is true, nevertheless, that no example of literary composition is likely to be purely of one type. In most cases, all four types are blended, and the clearest example of one type is likely, on analysis to reveal merely an emphasis.

FIGURATIVE LANGUAGE

Nonliteral statement. The definition of figurative language is elusive, but it is good practice for the beginning student to identify the different figures of speech in a literary work. Obvious examples are easy to spot though sometimes difficult to classify; and borderline figures of speech, which are literal in one instance and figurative in another, are interesting and challenging problems. A rule of thumb is to label as figurative any phrasing that does not mean, literally, merely what it says, but may imply more than it says, like the following *metaphor* from *Macbeth:*

> Life's but a walking shadow, a poor player
> That struts and frets his hour upon the stage
> And then is heard no more.

Another frequent identifying mark is that the figure of speech is an unusual expression in order or in phrasing, not the ordinary way of saying something, like the following alliterative passage from *Paradise Lost:*

> Him the Almighty Power
> Hurled headlong flaming from the ethereal sky.

Both these criteria, however, may seem to be absent, and the example could still be figurative in one sense or another (for example, the leg of the table, the foot of the hill). The point here is that language itself is figurative, and because words can give only hints of the things they refer to, it is impossible for anyone to be truly literal in what he says. There is thus no final authority on whether a given expression is figurative or literal. Moreover, there is no absolute measure of the "ordinary" way of saying anything.

Nevertheless, one does not need to go on the premise that language is either fully literal or fully figurative in order to profit from extensive study of figures of speech. The more common classical types of these figures—*antithesis, hyperbole, irony, metaphor, metonymy, personification, simile, synecdoche*—should be identifiable by the beginning student of literature, and the advanced student should also understand the folk and literary origins of some examples of these types, which he can find and label without critical help.

FLASHBACK

The interruption of the sequence of a *narration* in order to present an antecedent action or *scene;* also, this action or scene itself. Since every writer of fiction must make frequent use of the flashback, many different variations upon the basic pattern have been invented. Essentially, the flashback is very simple: the author merely stops telling one part of his story and begins another part at a point earlier in time than the last episode of his first story. Devices for making this shift in time vary in type from the awkward and hackneyed "Meanwhile, back at the ranch . . ." to the depiction of the activity remembered by a character and presented from his *point of view* in the *stream of consciousness* technique.

For the dramatist, the flashback is much more difficult than for the novelist or short-story writer, but with the help of the *soliloquy,* stage machinery, and scene shifts, playwrights from Sophocles to Arthur Miller have experimented with graceful ways of presenting past action. In the novel, Tolstoy may use the device most simply; and perhaps Faulkner, Proust, or Joyce most intricately. In the short story, Hawthorne, Poe, and Stevenson present interesting examples. The device is used even in the *epic,* which like the novel must carry more than one strain of action in a *plot.* Milton's *Paradise Lost,* for instance, begins *"in medias res"* and must flash back to the creation of the world in a later part.

FOOT

See *Prosody.*

FORM

In literature, a combination of *structure* and *texture,* a framework and a detailed style. John Crowe Ransom (*The World's Body,* 1938) has said that the best literary form is a molecular fusion, like salt, *NaCl,* in which the textural or stylistic element is joined chemically with the structural element. Ransom has contrasted this close combination with lemonade—a solution in which, though the sugar and lemon are dissolved in the water, the components are not fused in larger molecules. The point of the analogy is that in good literature texture and structure constitute a single substance. The more mechanical or forced the union of parts, the less effective the literature will be.

One could also say that its form is whatever the *audience* reacts to in the literature. Using this definition, a good formal study could be conducted by showing how an author creates and satisfies *suspense.* In a paper resulting from such a formal study, the writer should indicate such mechanical devices of structure as the degree to which the author keeps his reader in puzzlement, gradually solving the puzzle or allowing it to be solved, as in many Shakespearean tragedies and in the popular modern mystery story. Since literary form is also textural, a formal study of a literary work should also illustrate the ways by which the style reinforces these structural devices.

For works of nonfiction, the student could first analyze the literature into its structural parts. It may already be divided into numbered sections, but this study would analyze the commanding idea around which each section is organized. The material could next be subdivided further, until one or two samples of the smallest structural atoms are discernible. The progress in the first part of the study would be from section to paragraph to sentence to phrase; the second part would be a textural or stylistic analysis, showing how attitudes of the author and details of subject matter are fitted into the structure.

FREE VERSE

Poetry that uses *cadence* instead of *meter* and that finds its basic unit in the *stanza* or verse paragraph, instead of the line. Thus, free verse may have any length of line, with any number of syllables, and except for devices of rhythm, occasional rhyme, and typographical appearance, it may be indistinguishable from *prose*. Free verse has been widely used since the earliest times and is not a twentieth-century invention.

See also *Meter, Prosody,* and *Blank verse.*

GENRE

The type into which a piece of literature may be classified. Since literary types may overlap, and since there is no final authority on what constitutes a given type, genre study may be simple or complex, practical or theoretical. A simple and practical study is explained on pages 89 to 91, where Aristotle's definition of a tragedy is the criterion against which a specific play is measured. A more difficult and original study of the same kind could be composed of a student's definition of a genre—say, of tragicomedy or an item from Polonius' list—which would be used to delineate and to analyze a literary work. The student's definition would be more limited than that of Aristotle, but the study itself could still have the seriousness of any other literary analysis.

As normally used, the term *genre* should not be confused with *form.* A formal study may proceed in relative disregard of considerations of genre. As long as generally accepted classifications are observed, the student may simply assume, in his study of the form of a work, that this work belongs to a certain genre. His analysis could proceed along the lines of the plan discussed in the definition of form above.

Studies based on literary classification would properly fall under the heading of genre study. One aspect of this kind of work may be an analysis of literary conventions, in which the student would attempt to describe and define what literary types were emphasized during a given age. In this analysis the student would take note of the frequency and the degree of development of special kinds of literature, perhaps comparing and contrasting one age with another. For instance, the Renaissance and the early nineteenth century both saw a great flowering of lyric poetry in England, but in the latter age, the drama was drastically reduced in scope and quality. These facts, if discovered from an overview of literature itself, rather than merely from commentaries, could help the student gain valuable perspectives.

HUMOR

The laughable in literature, often based on simple contrast. As distinguished from *wit, humor* is gentle, good-natured, light-hearted, and primarily emotional; wit is sharp and intellectual, often an example of persuasive *rhetoric.* Humor is nearly always blended with wit because it requires intellectual insight to perceive subtle contrasts and because emotional and intellectual elements in literature are rarely found in isolation. The traditional contrast between body and mind is thus discoverable in the two terms: *wit,* which refers to the mind, leaves to the term *humor* some vestiges of its seventeenth-century designation of the four liquids in the human body.

Humorous contrasts in literature may provide an alert student with much to write about. For instance, it may be valuable to ascertain the relative degrees of wit and humor in a given work and to distinguish between pointed contrasts and contrasts not directed toward or against a cause or opponent. A different study could investigate the degree of exaggeration that contributes to separate humorous effects in the literature. The student could measure the exaggerations on a scale from the greatest to the least difference in the terms contrasted and then classify and evaluate the effects.

A third type of study could observe how and when the human traits of the author or his characters result in a humorous tone. These traits could be identified, and a character sketch (see pages 95 to 97) could form an integral part of the study. A similar type of study could be made using situations rather than persons as subject matter.

HYPERBOLE

Exaggeration, in *figurative language* with the purpose of intensifying the meaning, or for humor. The following lines from Andrew Marvell's "To His Coy Mistress" are composed almost entirely of hyperboles:

> My vegetable love should grow
> Vaster than empires, and more slow;
> An hundred years should go to praise
> Thine eyes and on thy forehead gaze:
> Two hundred to adore each breast:
> But thirty thousand to the rest;
> An age at least to every part,
> And the last age should show your heart;

The figure of speech is often quite appropriate also for prose—especially for humorous fiction. For instance, American frontier humor, in the tall tale, used many rather wild hyperboles. Among the characters in this literature were the braggart rivermen, who competed in loud braggadocio, full of hyperbole. An amusing example is the following, from Mark Twain's *Huckleberry Finn:*

> Then he jumped up in the air three times, and cracked his heels together again and shouted out:
> "Whoo-oop! I'm the original iron-jawed, brass-mounted, copper-bellied corpse-maker from the wilds of Arkansaw! Look at me! I'm the man they call Sudden Death and General Desolation! Sired by a hurricane, dam'd by an earthquake, half-brother to the cholera, nearly related to the small-pox on the mother's side! Look at me! . . ."

It should be made clear that hyperbole as a figure of speech is not just literal exaggeration; rather, it is nonliteral and is consequently most often a form of *metaphor.*
See also *Style.*

IAMB
See *Prosody.*

IDENTIFICATION
Broadly, any specific definition. In literature, the drawing upon sympathy and antipathy so that the audience shares emotions and feelings with the central character(s) in a fiction. To identify a thing, one singles it out (see *Analogy*), or defines it. Similarly in literature, when the audience identifies itself with a character, a kind of definition takes place: the character is singled out to receive special attention. With particular care, the audience notes what makes this dramatic personage an individual, resents the obstructions to his success, and exults when he overcomes these obstacles. It is this concern with the fortunes of the central character that allows the audience a distinct *point of view* from which to experience the work as a whole. The details in the work are noticed by definitions on a smaller scale; these little definitions are for the purpose of clarifying the single master identification.

Identification is one of the central ingredients of the *catharsis* that occurs in *tragedy* and of the interest that is necessary to *suspense.* The audience cannot be absorbed by something totally outside their spans of sympathy and interest. Therefore, a work in which identification occurs must embody at least some of the values of its audience. As *rhetoric,* the work may use these values as part of its persuasion toward new values. Similarly, as a teacher must gain at least some of the sympathies of his class, *didacticism* in literature cannot occur without some degree of identification.

Wordsworth's phrase "suspension of disbelief" indicates part of what happens in identification, and the study of literary *belief* would aid and complement that of identification.

IMAGE

An idea, usually of a sense impression, created most often by *figurative language*. An image may rely upon any of the senses for its effect, and as the blind poet Milton has illustrated, visual mental pictures may be only one classification of the image. The following passage includes images—one or more per line—from Book IV of *Paradise Lost,* drawing upon each of the five senses:

SENSES:

smell	"Groves whose rich trees wept odorous gums and balm,
sight	Others whose fruit burnished with golden rind
taste	Hung amiable, Hesperian fables true,
	If true, here only, and of delicious taste:
touch	Betwixt them lawns, or level downs, and flocks
	Grazing the tender herb . . .
hearing	The birds their choir apply; airs, vernal airs,
	Breathing the smell of field and grove, attune the trembling leaves. . . ."

The last three lines mix a single, commanding auditory image (birds singing) with an olfactory one ("smell of field and grove") and a predominantly tactile image ("trembling leaves"). This mingling of sense impressions, called synesthesia, is an embellishment on simple imagery. Some critics—for example, Caroline Spurgeon (in *Shakespeare's Imagery,* 1935) imply that figurative language is the fountainhead of all images. Literal phrasings, however, as in line 5 above also seem adapted to the creation of ideas of sense impressions.

As Miss Spurgeon's valuable study has shown, one may learn much about an author's mental equipment, his tastes and interests, by noting the areas of life from which he draws his images. Also, a deeper appreciation of the literature may result from the discovery of imagery that is repeated in different contexts: William Empson has shown how the image of ill-fitting clothes recurs throughout *Macbeth,* as Macbeth finds that his new kingship fits him poorly and uncomfortably. Another type of study could classify images according to the different senses appealed to, and thus show the degree to which the work is visual, auditory, tactile, etc. Or one could continue a study of figurative language with one of imagery, to discover the frequency and the types of figures that may embody the different images.

IRONY

Assertion by contrast, often, in drama and other fiction, dependent upon a character's ignorance of the full import of a situation that should concern him. For instance, Oedipus, in search of his father's murderer, is, ironically, the guilty party himself. Rosalind, in love with Orlando, disguises herself as a young shepherd, and tricks him into learning the arts of love from her. Falstaff, during a highway robbery, runs away and leaves his loot when his own masked companions frighten him. Later he entertains them with wild tales of his heroic stand against terrible odds. Irony may thus be tragic or comic, and it may function as a plot framework of a complete work or of a minor scene.

Irony may also be simply an isolated figure of speech or a single element in an exchange of repartee. As a figure of speech, it is convenient to call ironic a statement that means the opposite of what it says. In repartee, one may need to distinguish irony—assertion by contrast—from sarcasm, which is a simple, direct attempt to wound. One of the main forms of literary irony is *satire,* which combines the attempt to reform, with pointed and humorous *wit.*

Studies of the ironic in literature may be varied and challenging.

For instance, one may discuss a character's ignorance of what should concern him. Such a study could illustrate how *suspense* is dependent upon bits of knowledge being gradually unfolded to the character in question. Or the student could analyze the human source of the irony by investigating the character traits—the tragic flaw or other idiosyncrasy—that sustains the ironic situation. For instance, the character of Othello could be analyzed to discover why he places his trust in Iago, who destroys him. The section on "Writing the Literary Character Sketch," in Chapter 6, should help to solve some of the problems in such a study. Another type of analysis could explain the implications of situations that may not appear to be ironic at first. This study would be a valuable aid in the discovery of deeper lines of meaning in the literature.

LITOTES

Understatement. The logical obverse of *hyperbole,* litotes may seem, and be, close to the poetic equivalent of hyperbole. But as hyperbole exaggerates in larger terms, litotes exaggerates in smaller ones. In the following stanzas from a poem by Sir John Suckling, litotes dominates the first stanza and hyperbole the second:

> Out upon it! I have loved
> > Three whole days together!
> And am like to love three more,
> > If it prove fair weather.
>
> Time shall moult away his wings,
> > Ere he shall discover
> In the whole wide world again
> > Such a constant lover.

The effect here is one of *lyric irony*.

LYRIC

The type of poetry not designated by the terms *epic* or *drama.* Since poetic types overlap, no type being found in purity, the terms are most exact when used to indicate qualities of mind, rather than as labels of strict *form* or *genre*. The term *lyric* emphasizes the vocal and musical aspects of poetry, rather than its expansiveness, proper to the epic, or its conflict, germane to the drama. Some lyrics are best understood as being pure songs, so that the emotions and feelings are focal points, rather than ideas or lessons. When analyzing a lyric, therefore, one may go wrong by demanding *didactic* material from it. Although, as in the poems of Blake and Donne, such material may be inseparable from emotional expression, the single requirement of the lyric as such is that it be a verbal expression of emotion and feeling. The lyric, thus, may be somewhat like an *essay* set in poetry—a statement of or a reproduction of an attitude or state of mind. Kenneth Burke has called poetry "the dancing of an attitude," indicating that lyric expressions are like dramas in which the conflicting actions are arrested at some single, interesting point.

A great variety of studies of the lyric is possible. Original ideas for analyses are particularly appropriate, and if the student sticks closely to the poem, his special approach may have real merit. The warnings in this book, especially on pages 41 to 44, should make clear why digressions from the literature itself are undesirable. Ideas about structural interrelationships within specific lyrics may be most lucrative of good papers. As in the sample study of Robert Frost's "The Road Not Taken," in Chapter 8, a special kind of *image* may also provide a good principle of organization for analysis of a lyric. Usually, the goal of such studies is to understand and explain meanings that are deeper than those found merely on the surface. Finally, since it is so various in form, including such subclasses as the *sonnet,* the *ode,* the *elegy,* and the *ballad,* the lyric is excellent subject matter for studies of *prosody.*

MASQUE

Originally, a parade of masked citizens through a community; then a lavish spectacle, part of a celebration, with little or no dramatic conflict. Before Milton, the masque was often merely a religious or secular tableau, using expensive costuming and scenery. Beginning with Milton's *Comus* in 1634, however, the masque included more narrative and dramatic content. Milton's play presents a series of moral episodes, with symbolic *protagonists* and *antagonists*. The masque has retained its formal, episodic nature, and is much less an example of drama than of sheer *spectacle*. See also *Symbol*.

METAPHOR

A term (1) for *figurative language* in general and (2) for the broadest classification of figures of speech. In the first use the term *metaphor* implies that it is impossible to say literally what one means, since language is selective, not reflective. The writer must choose his words out of a larger reservoir of possible words, all of which are only sounds in the air or marks on the page, and which can only partially represent the things they signify (see also *Symbol*). Metaphorically, words can symbolize objects, actions, ideas, because users of the language have previously agreed to attribute given meanings to given expressions. The binding force which holds the language together is primarily this general agreement about meaning.

As a broad kind of figure of speech, a metaphor consists of two elements which are always in some tension with each other—the meaning and the expression or the *symbol* itself. In the sets of symbols of chemistry and formal logic—the ideal is a 1-to-1 relationship of sign to thing signified. Literary language may sometimes strive to be thus exact, but it may also encompass more meaning per expression than is possible in scientific terminology. The extra meaning can be carried by literary expressions which utilize the *connotation,* or suggestion, of words, as well as their *denotation,* their narrow, scientific ability to identify.

The metaphor, in placing more emphasis on suggestion than on identification, is the example par excellence of literary, as distinct from scientific, language. Often, the metaphor denotes something seemingly unrelated to what it connotes, and thus the meaning is carried by an apparently irrelevant expression. For instance, Marlowe's line,

> Is this the face that launched a thousand ships?

is a personification that *denotes* Helen of Troy and the Greek army, but it *connotes* the whole myth of how Helen's abduction began the Trojan War. A good metaphor may command a paragraph or a poem, as when Shakespeare uses a tree that is shedding its leaves to designate the autumn of life (see page 48). This sonnet contains metaphors within metaphors, and Shakespeare is referring to the branches of the tree by the word "choirs" in the famous line:

> Bare ruin'd choirs where late the sweet birds sang

Studies of metaphor in literature may center upon specific figures of speech, upon a general, commanding metaphor that orders overall *form,* or upon a combination of the specific and the general. Isolated figures of speech should be studied in some systematic way, though the system used may be very simple. One good approach may be to show how the metaphors are linked together to help give the literature its *structure.* Another may be to illustrate how the work is affected in its tone and style by repeated use of a specific kind of metaphor or of a general metaphor that informs the whole work.

METAPHYSICAL POETRY

Poetry using the extremes of *figurative language* to analyze and express intellectually and emotionally the deeper content of life. Love and religion are typical subjects of the metaphysical poem, and a frequently used device is the *conceit.*

The earliest metaphysical poets were sixteenth- and seventeenth-century lyricists like John Donne, Andrew Marvell, Richard Crashaw, Richard Lovelace, and Abraham Cowley, whose verse shocked their readers with its colloquial tone and its earthy subject matter. In recent years, T. S. Eliot, John Crowe Ransom, and Allen Tate have returned to the metaphysical poem; moreover, much modern criticism is devoted to both the earlier and later masters of this type of verse. Eliot's poetry in particular reflects his deep concern with the subjects and methods of the metaphysicals.

The following stanza from Richard Crashaw's "Epithalamium" embodies many of the characteristics of metaphysical poetry—its concern with mingled love and death, its preoccupation with physical aspects of what is not physical, and its employment of irregular *meter* and *stanza:*

> Yet Love in death did wait upon her,
>   Granting leave she should expire
> In her fumes and have the honour
>   T'exhale in flames of his own fire.
>   Her funeral pile
>   The marriage bed,
>   In a sighed smile
>   She vanished.
> So rich a dress of death ne'er famed
> The cradles where her kindred flamed;
> So sweet her mother phoenixes of th' East
>   Ne'er spiced their nest.

METER

The rhythmic structure of verse, the unit of which is the foot (see *Prosody*). A given metrical system may be quantitative, as in Anglo-Saxon poems like the *Beowulf,* or qualitative, as in most other English verse. In quantitative meter, the rhythmical units are based on long and short syllables; qualitative meter uses a fixed

number of accented and unaccented syllables to comprise the feet in a line.
See also *Poetry* and *Verse.*

METONYMY

The use of one word for another that it suggests: The *crown* for the *king.* Metonymy is much like *synecdoche,* but a metonymy does not necessarily designate a part of what is referred to.
See also *Metaphor.*

MYTH

In literature, a folk story or a body of literary subject matter. As a folk story, the myth may give imaginative reasons for some objective phenomenon: the story of Helen of Troy is a myth, used in the *Iliad* and a great deal of other literature, to account for the Trojan War. There is no requirement that the myth be either true or untrue as history, and elements of fantasy readily become part of the warp and woof of mythical accounts, which may grow more improbable as they are retold. Each new retelling may make additions to or subtractions from the earlier forms, so that the student may sometimes discover several versions of a widely used myth. In the *lyric,* the folk ballad is the most striking illustration of this imaginative freedom and variety. A good example of scholarly work in this field is *English and Scottish Popular Ballads,* edited by Sargent and Kittredge, 1904, a fairly definitive edition that illustrates a large number of mythical, folk stories in their different poetic variants. Ordinarily, the basic myths are anonymous, and in the true folk ballad, the anonymity of the myth is retained in the literature itself.

Examples from every *genre* of imaginative literature may be found to embody or to be constructed around specific or general mythical materials. Several of Shakespeare's plays—notably, *King*

Lear, The Merchant of Venice, and *A Winter's Tale*—are built around stories told and retold so often that they are virtually myths whose original authors are unknown. The term *myth* may designate not merely old stories, but in a broad sense the whole corpus of human materials from which literature receives its meaning and its subject matter. Thus used, myth has much in common with *archetype,* since both terms may imply universal, or general, patterns of behavior. Myth, however denotes literary subject matter specifically, and this use of the term is apparent in the comment that twentieth-century literature may be inferior to that of other ages because it does not grow out of a coherent myth. For further discussion on this point, see *Ambiguity.*

NARRATION

The form of composition that focuses specifically upon action. *Description, argumentation,* and *exposition* are the other three divisions of composition classified according to mode or type. *Narration,* the principal agency of the novel and the short story, is the representation by an author of events or episodes. Like the other three compositional types, it is rarely found in absolute purity, since in order to tell a story the author must ordinarily give some indication of a setting and characters and must therefore employ also description and exposition. Narration may be either straightforward or plotted. In the first case, the story is simply chronological, marching forward from one event to the next. In plotted narratives, by far the most common in literature, the author may stimulate *suspense* by interrupting the story with events from the past with *flashbacks,* or with events projected in the future.

NATURALISM

A theory of literature formulated by Émile Zola, in "The Experimental Novel," by which the author attempts to use fictional materials to illustrate scientific theories about the effects of environment on human nature (see Part Four). Naturalism was especially strong in the first two decades of this century. American writers like Theodore Dreiser, Stephen Crane, Jack London, Frank Norris, and James T. Farrell put naturalism into practice, using the economic and political—even the biological and geological—ideas of theorists like Marx, Lyell, Malthus, Darwin, and Herbert Spencer. Ordinarily, the naturalist in literature is a determinist, one who posits a closed system of cause and effect in human affairs, who denies free will, who places the ultimate causes of behavior beyond the control of the individual.

Life in naturalistic fiction is thus a matter of survival of the fittest, and the characters are often at the mercy of superior powers —of economic hardship, as in Dreiser's *Sister Carrie;* of political and economic tyranny, as in Norris's *The Octopus;* or even simply of hunger and want, as in Stephen Crane's *Maggie, a Girl of the Streets;* or of animal fear, as in Crane's *Red Badge of Courage.* Such novels may be written in simple reportorial style, illustrating combinations of environmental factors operating usually to destroy the weaker, and to further brutalize the stronger characters. Frank Norris's *McTeague,* in which the bestial tendencies of the title character are strengthened by victory, and Dreiser's *American Tragedy,* in which Clyde Griffith's efforts to free himself result in his downfall, may illustrate this more general naturalistic pattern.

Naturalism is thus deterministic, pessimistic, often concerned with defeat, indignity, misery that is undeserved or simply fated. Some elements of naturalistic fiction may thus be common to *tragedy,* and interesting analyses may be made to determine whether or not a given work measures up to the requirements of the more classical genre. Another type of study could attempt to uncover the system of causes of behavior in a given writer's work. Part or all of such a study could describe the relative importance of separate causes—for instance, of Dreiser's "chemism" and of social and individual responsibility for the defeat in *An American Tragedy*. Finally, a good study could be made of the relations between a writer's style, his theory of composition, and his subject matter, to measure how deeply and how well the author illustrates his particular naturalistic thesis.

NATURE

A term used sometimes to denote broadly the laws of the universe, including the laws of human nature, or more narrowly the natural, scenic world outside man. In both cases, there is a wide overlap in meaning with the term *scene*. Nature as "scenic environment" is one of the most frequently used topics in literature, and writers from the unknown author of *Beowulf* through Shakespeare to such moderns as Frost and Eliot have expressed a great variety of feelings and emotions toward it. In the middle ages, for instance, Chaucer and Dante reveal such diverse attitudes as simple joy in the springtime to terror at being lost in a dark wood.

Any period of literature may exemplify such variety of attitude, but there may also be a strain of consistency within this variety. The eighteenth century felt and expressed the orderliness in nature: the fine art of cultivating precisely outlined gardens was reflected in poetry, where the distinct limits of the heroic couplet were used, in Pope, Cowper, Gray and others, to illustrate sharp dividing lines between the elements in nature itself. For English romantics in the nineteenth century like Shelley, Wordsworth, Keats, and Coleridge, nature was often a grand mystery, an inspiration not to be violated by systematic or pseudoscientific analyses.

Nature as a set of laws is also a frequently used concept in literature. Henry David Thoreau, in the passage on page 115 illustrates this idea and shows also a general tendency, common to writers like Emerson and Rousseau, to describe natural law as it operates both in man's environment and in man himself. The implication in these writers is often that if man lives in harmony with nature, its laws are benign—not destructive as in *naturalism,* but constructive of the higher, finer aspects of the human being. This attitude may result in a typical plea of *romanticism,* for the individual to live his own life away from the conformities that may influence him to live as the crowd directs.

NOVEL

A term used to designate any long prose fiction, whether plotted or unplotted. If one delineates a set of requirements that a book must fulfill in order to be called a novel, however long the list or however loosely he defines the term, exceptions to the definition may be found. For instance, unity of treatment or of topic, artistic portrayal of character, singleness of purpose, fictional reflection of actuality—all are reasonable criteria, but all may be ignored in one sense or another and the work in question may still validly be called a novel.

It is probably best, therefore, to treat the term as a convenient description, which can denominate a great diversity of materials, rather than as a strictly outlined prescription, by which a book must qualify to receive this label. Specific works that seem borderline cases—like Benet's *John Brown's Body,* which is in verse; Malory's long tales of King Arthur, which were called *fabliaux;* or Boccaccio's *Decameron,* which today might be called a collection of short stories—may be at least compared with novels, and the student may do little damage to the term by using it for these examples also. His experience in reading about literature will teach him the most frequently used label.

Subspecies of the novel, however, may sometimes present the student with interesting problems and opportunities for study. Since it exists in a large variety of types, the novel may be classified in several ways. Thus, rarely would a study of the novel in general be of value, but analysis or comparison and contrast of specific novels may yield good results. For example, in one type of analysis, the student may set out the criteria for the kind of novel he is analyzing: picaresque novel, gothic novel, novel of manners, epistolary novel. He could then attempt to illustrate by what details and in what ways the work fits, or does not fit, the form he has described.

OCCASIONAL VERSE

Poetry written for a special occasion, as for a coronation, victory in war, or the death of an eminent person or friend of the poet. The *elegy,* the *masque,* and sometimes the *ode,* may be examples of occasional verse. The subject may be either solemn or happy, but the treatment is usually formal and serious. All poets laureate write occasional verse, in celebration of important national events.
See also *Lyric.*

OCTAVE

See *Sonnet.*

ODE

In English poetry, odes are of three kinds: Horatian, Pindaric, and irregular. The ode originated with the Greek chorus, which sang the poems at festivals; the chorus moved to one side for the *strophe,* to the other for the *antistrophe,* and stood still for the *epode.* These movements were intended to reflect the ebb and flow of the emotions. Except for the Horatian ode, the form in English still retains some vestiges of these three movements. Though the *Horatian* ode uses only one type of *stanza,* this may be varied internally, as in Collins's "Ode to Evening," written in four-line, unrhymed stanzas. In the *Pindaric* ode, strophe and antistrophe have identical stanza forms, with a variant for the epode. Gray's "The Progress of Poesy" is a Pindaric ode in which the six strophes and six antistrophes are stanzas of twelve lines in a complex rhyme scheme. The three seventeen-line epodes are structurally even more complicated. The *irregular* ode was invented (presumably by accident) by Cowley, who is supposed to have thought he was writing the Pindaric form. Cowley thus infused a refreshing freedom into the ode, so that lengths and numbers of line in any given stanza could vary, and so that the rhyme scheme could also depart from its first-used form. In all three types of ode, the poet invents his own stanzas; in the Horatian and Pindaric odes, however, once he adopts a structure, the poet must retain it. In tone, the ode reflects a heightened emotion and is especially suited for typically *lyric* feelings and attitudes.

OMNISCIENT OBSERVER

Usually, the narrator of a fiction, who sees all and knows all about his story. In reading a story that is narrated by one of the characters, it is a good idea to contrast his *point of view* with that of the other characters. To do this, the reader should note the limits of the narrator's supposed knowledge of the story and his function as an active participant in the action. Also, the narrator's position in regard to the reader (see *Audience*) is indicative of this point of view. The main function of the omniscient observer may be simply to tell the story; as storyteller, he may, for example, withhold a crucial part of the narrative because this method is more suspenseful than to give it away at the start.

The omniscient observer is more often an onlooker than a very active character. Since he looks back on the events, he can see all the relevant time and space simultaneously. A fine distinction is thus usually necessary between the author who writes as author—who steps out of the story and speaks of himself as, for instance,

Henry Fielding does in *Tom Jones*—and a background character whose only real function is to recount the events in the plot.

Thus, varying degrees of participation by the omniscient observer in the events of the story are possible. One device is to string the events together by occasional meetings in life between the narrator and the chief characters, as in Conrad's *Lord Jim* and the other stories using Marlowe as narrator, and in stories like Somerset Maugham's *The Razor's Edge*. Henry James, notably in books like *Portrait of a Lady* and *The American,* also uses this device and experiments deeply with this point of view. James shows how a high level both of complexity and of artistic unity can be achieved when the omniscient observer himself receives varying degrees of the reader's full attention and sympathy as a character. To study the development of James's literary artistry may be in large part to discover how his omniscient observer implies greater intricacies of pattern and *form.*

ONOMATOPOEIA

The use of words whose sounds suggest the things referred to. The following anonymous poem of the thirteenth century illustrates how far a poet can go into the spirit of his subject when he obeys the dictum of Alexander Pope: "The sound must seem an echo to the sense." In the anonymous poem below, it is not merely the sound of "cuccu" that makes for onomatopoeia, but also the special *assonance, consonance,* and general euphony, in which the sounds are those of the springtime. (The poet is not distorting his words but writes in his own dialect of Middle English.)

> Sing cuccu, nu! Sing cuccu!
> Sing cuccu! Sing cuccu, nu!
> Sumer is icumen in,
> Lhude sing cuccu;
> Groweth sed and bloweth med,

And springeth the wde nu.
    Sing cuccu!
Awe bleteth after lomb,
   Lhouth after calve cu;
Bulluc sterteth, bucke verteth;
    Murie sing cuccu!
      Cuccu, cuccu, well singes thu, cuccu:
Ne swike thu naver nu.

Nu, *now;* lhude, *loud;* sed, med, *seed, mead;* wde, *wood;* awe, *ewe;* lhouth, *loweth;* cu, *cow;* verteth, *hides in the green wood;* murie, *merry;* swike, *cease.*

See also *Image, Meter,* and *Prosody.*

OTTAVA RIMA

See *Stanza.*

PARADOX

A statement that seemingly contradicts common sense or reality but that may be true in a deeper sense. In *The Well Wrought Urn* (1947), Cleanth Brooks sets forth a strong argument that paradox is at the root of all poetry. One may say, at least, that most poets who are adept at pithy, epigrammatic statement often excel in the paradox—for example, Alexander Pope, John Dryden, William Blake, Emily Dickinson, and G. K. Chesterton. In the following poem, "Parting," by Emily Dickinson, the superficial meanings run counter to the deeper meanings as the poetess piles paradox on paradox. When reading the poem, one may well recall the Biblical paradox that one must lose his life in order to save it.

My life closed twice before its close;
    It yet remains to see
If Immortality unveil
    A third event to me,

> So huge, so hopeless to conceive,
>   As these that twice befell.
> Parting is all we know of heaven,
>   And all we need of hell.

See also *Aphorism.*

PARAPHRASE
See Chapter 10.

PARODY
An imitation, usually satirical, in which a rather specific target is made to seem ridiculous. Just as the cartoonist may exaggerate a physical oddity, so the writer of a parody exaggerates a particular set of characteristics—usually of another author. There are wide areas of overlap between the terms *burlesque, parody,* and *travesty,* but the main distinctions are that burlesque is more general than parody, and that travesty takes a more serious (or satirical) view of its subject. If a travesty is humorous, its humor is likely to be in deadly earnest, and to call accepted idols in question. An example of a parody is Elinor Goulding Smith's "Story for the Slicks," in Part Four.
See also *Humor* and *Satire.*

PASTORAL
The depiction in literature of rural persons, scenes, and atmosphere, usually with a view to extoling the simplicity of country life. The *lyric, comedy,* and even a form of the *novel* have all been frequent vehicles for the pastoral convention. In particular, the *ode* and the *elegy* are especially well suited for conveying pastoral attitudes and feelings. In modern literary criticism, the term has been widely expanded by William Empson (in *Some Versions of*

Pastoral, 1938), who uses the term to designate any literature that treats a complicated subject in simplified terms. Examples of the pastoral convention in different genres are Spenser's *The Shepheardes Calender;* William Collins's "Ode to Simplicity"; Gray's "Elegy Written in a Country Churchyard"; Shakespeare's *As You Like It* and Fletcher's *The Faithful Shepherdess;* and Thomas Lodge's *Rosalynde.*

PERSONIFICATION

Figurative language in which an author attributes human qualities to what is not human. In fanciful poetry, the personified being is often addressed by the poet. Thus, in Keats's "Bright Star" and "Ode on a Grecian Urn," and in Shelley's "To a Skylark," the poet typically addresses the star, the urn, and the skylark, as if these things were human. The following stanzas from "The Rose," by Richard Lovelace, illustrate how far the tradition was carried in the seventeenth-century lyric:

> Sweet serene sky-like flower,
> Haste to adorn her bower:
> > From thy long cloudy bed
> > Shoot forth thy damask head. . . .
>
> Dear offspring of pleased Venus
> And jolly, plump Silenus:
> > Haste, haste to deck the hair
> > Of the only sweetly fair.

Personification has been an extremely popular device, and through the ages, it has been used with the widest range of subject matter. A final example is the following *tercet,* "Upon Nothing," the first of seventeen stanzas by the seventeenth-century Earl of Rochester.

> Nothing! Thou elder brother ev'n to shade,
> Thou hadst a being ere the world was made,
> And well-fixed art alone of ending not afraid.

PLOT

In general, the pattern of behavior and circumstance in a work of
literature. To ask "what happens" in a piece of literature is to
stress the term *plot,* which is usually a <u>coherent combination of
events or acts.</u> Thus, the term designates the *structure* of a literary
work, as distinct from its characters, setting, style, and moral. As
Aristotle implied, the key to the understanding of plot is the term
act, which may retain its everyday meanings—a division of a play,
further divided into scenes, or simply a segment of human behavior. Act is the master term, since not only the characters but
the other elements also may play active or functional parts in the
plot.

Nevertheless, in studying the plot of a specific work, one usually
finds himself focusing upon human behavior. In analyzing works
like the *Iliad* and the *Divine Comedy,* for instance, a student can
see that the plans of these poems are made up of connected structures of human and superhuman acts. There are, of course, scenes,
moral purposes, and situations also, but these elements are not in
the foreground. The reader is most interested in what Zeus, Athena,
Achilles, Hector; Dante, Virgil, Beatrice, and the other characters
do—for example, their acts—and these acts taken together form
the plots or structures of the poems. Thus, the term may be used
readily to analyze plays, novels, and even essays and lyric poems.
Wherever narrative conflict is present, as in fiction, the term *act*
has immediate use to designate the forces in conflict. When these
forces form a pattern, the result is called a *plot.*

Even when narrative conflict is not on the surface, one may
discover a kind of "plot" in literature, since the essayist and the
lyric poet both act to recommend or to express their views of their
topics. It is true that such lyric "acts" are not always obvious, and
even that the more obvious they are, the less effective they may be
as literature. But an act may exist as an important, unifying element without being obvious, just as the girders in a building hold

it together without being seen. In the lyric, for instance, an attitude or a frame of mind may be all there is to the "plot" of the poem, but one may say that the major human aspect of any act is precisely its attitude or frame of mind.

See also *Narration* and *Suspense*.

POETRY

A general term for all literature, and a specific term to distinguish particular poems. The word is a convenient label for high quality in literature, and is used in this general meaning through the whole history of critical practice and theory. In its particular meaning, the term *poetry* helps to distinguish poems from prose works; moreover, the term *verse* (see *Prosody*), which designates the mechanical form of a poem, should not be confused with *poetry*. A work lacking the mechanical appearance of a poem may have the high quality denoted by the general term *poetry*. On the contrary, a work in verse—using meter and/or rhyme—may lack this high quality and therefore not be a true poem. The point is that of the criteria implied by the term *poetry,* quality of utterance takes precedence over outward appearance. As Coleridge says in *Biographia Literaria* (Part Four), such a limerick as "Thirty days hath September . . ." is not fully a poem even though it is written with rhythm and rhyme.

POINT OF VIEW

The set of attitudes from which a work of literature is written. The narrator's position in a novel, a short story, or a fictional poem, as indicated under *Omniscient observer,* reveals his point of view. Also, the moral or *purpose* behind the plot of a drama, as revealed in the topic and style helps to determine dramatic point of view. In an essay, the manner and angle of approach, as well as the style, may also express point of view. Broadly, the term implies the frame of mind embodied in the work, which may be discovered partly according to rule and partly by analysis of small elements of style, characterization, scenic ingredients, and *form*.

To be esthetically satisfying, a consistent point of view should normally inform every part of a literary work. This is another way of saying that most good literature strives for unity of effect. On the other hand, the attitudes behind a given work may be extremely complex, and even apparently self-contradictory as long as literary integrity is not violated. Such complexity is found in novels like *The Sound and the Fury,* by Faulkner, and in *Finnegans Wake,* by Joyce. But even in these books, a shift in point of view is likely to be marked by a shift to a new chapter or section.

Point of view may both conform to a literary tradition and follow the dictates of the individual author. For example, since Shakespeare's *As You Like It* is a pastoral *comedy,* the student may assume the point of view to be consistent with other works in both the pastoral and the comic traditions. It may make a good study to see how thoroughly such a work belongs to these traditions and hence exemplifies the genre itself. The basic plan behind this type of study would be to compare the work at hand with others in the same class, to specify elements comprising a single point of view for all of them. One could also study the work in relative isolation, and his analysis in this second type of study would focus upon ways in which the point of view is unique, or typical only of the author at hand. For a third idea, a contrast between a work and its source or sources—for example, between *As You Like It* and Thomas Lodge's novel, *Rosalynde*—may enable the student to discover clearly the original elements in an author's point of view, and to extract these elements from the derivative ones. Such a discovery would be deeply valuable in the student's progress toward understanding the author's whole output.

In brief: Intellectually, an author's point of view is his informing ideology, the system of ideas by means of which he selects and presents his subject matter. Emotionally, his point of view is the set of feelings he has expressed, in his own person and in his fictional characters, that infuse the literature with its own special tone and flavor. Thus, both thoughts and feelings contribute to the attitudes which, summed up, constitute a literary point of view.

PRÉCIS

See Chapter 10.

PROSE

Expression that uses no strict regularity of meter or rhyme; also, ordinary written and spoken discussion and conversation. (A character in Molière expressed surprise that he had been speaking prose all his life without knowing it.) As an honorific term, *prose* refers to composition, usually written, that is acceptable as literature. This use of the word would rule out random, haphazard conversation, and would imply the guidance of a *style*. Like *free verse,* some prose may be consciously contrived to emphasize rhythm; but unlike free verse, the paragraph, and not the line, is a basic compositional unit. An exception is some work of Faulkner and others using the *stream of consciousness technique*. Examples are the first and second sections of *The Sound and the Fury,* in which separate lines may reflect separate, disjointed thoughts. In the last analysis, some isolated passages of prose may be difficult to distinguish from free verse. Rarely, however, would a student confuse a metrical poem with a work of prose.

See also *Narration, Rhetoric, Style, Meter.*

PROSODY

The study of poetic meter and rhyme. Applied to specific poems prosody is ordinarily one part of the study of poetic form, with the goal of understanding how the sounds are fitted to and reinforce the meanings. If correctly approached, prosody can be much more than a rote exercise, and even rudimentary work here can teach the student some of the poet's basic problems. No poet can ever disregard the sounds of his words, and a "tin ear" would therefore handicap a reader of poetry almost as seriously as it would a listener to music. To improve one's poetic ear requires only that he learn a few terms and practice applying them to some poems.

The main branch of prosody is metrics, the study of poetic rhythm. The basic metrical unit is the foot, which is marked ˘ if unaccented and ´ if accented. There are four basic feet, named for the position of the accented syllable:

> *Iamb:* accent on last of two syllables: *tŏdáy*
> *Trochee:* accent on first of two syllables: *Móndăy*
> *Dactyl:* accent on first of three syllables: *Sátŭrdăy*
> *Anapest:* accent on last of three syllables: *ĭntĕrrúpt*

In English the iamb is the most common foot, and the normal rhythm of even a prose sentence is roughly iambic.

Because phrases in English are often expressed in five accents, the most common length of poetic line is pentameter (*pent* meaning five). The number of feet in a line is indicated by Latin prefixes:

monometer	one foot
dimeter	two feet
trimeter	three feet
tetrameter	four feet
pentameter	five feet
sextameter	six feet
heptameter	seven feet
octameter	eight feet

A line of six feet or more would be extremely rare.

When the names of feet are combined with names for length of line, the lines themselves can be named:

My love is like a red red rose

could be labeled iambic tetrameter because at first glance there seem to be four iambs in the line. An important caution, which makes the difference between a mechanical and a perceptive reading, is now in order: *The poem must be read in a natural rhythm and tone of voice.* For this reason, there is more than one way of scanning even such a simple line as that of Robert Burns above. To read it with absolutely equal stress on every other syllable is not natural. Therefore, it is convenient to have a mark for a secondary accent, and a centered dot is used for this purpose. Also, the feet should be separated by vertical lines:

My love / is like / a red / red rose

When marking poems for scansion, where these vertical lines are placed is extremely important: putting the divisions in the wrong places can cause the student to misname both the foot and the length of line. As a matter of fact, deciding on these divisions is usually the first real problem encountered in learning how to scan. Such problems occur because no poem is absolutely regular: any single poem worthy of the name uses different kinds of feet, so that iambs may be mingled with dactyls, anapests, and spondees. In this profusion and variety of rhythms, it usually seems to the beginning student that the poet is really careless, or that he lacks the ability to make his poem metrically regular. However, control over all aspects of his diction—especially its sounds—is the poet's greatest pride. It is therefore the rare poem indeed that has achieved greatness by a metrical accident.

PROTAGONIST

The central character of a fiction, usually the hero. The term is best used to denote the character at the center of the *plot,* the individual whose motives and behavior the reader is invited to contem-

plate most thoroughly. If the fiction has dramatic or narrative conflict, the person or force opposing the protagonist is called the
antagonist.

PURPOSE

Purpose in a work of literature may be discussed either as intention
or as goal, and it may be approached either from the point of view
of the author or from that of the *audience*. Wimsatt and Beardsley,
in "The Intentional Fallacy," show that it is pointless for the student to dispute questions about an author's intentions (see page
61). Goals expressed or implied in the literature may therefore
present better subject matter to write about.

A good analysis of purpose in a work of literature may be
written on a simple plan. The student may pose a question like the
following without committing the intentional fallacy: "If the author
uses *X* as a goal, how clearly and in what ways does he reach this
goal?" An important part of such a study would be to outline the
X clearly as a goal; later the student would show how this goal is
more plausible than some alternative. There need be no assertion
that a given statement of *X* would coincide with that of the author;
the study would rest, finally, upon a hypothesis. For instance, the
most consistent meaning in the following lines from John Keats's
"Ode on a Grecian Urn" has been debated by the best critics:

> "Beauty is truth, truth beauty,"—that is all
> Ye know on earth, and all ye need to know.

The kind of paper suggested here could isolate one of the debatable meanings—or a group of them—and show how other lines in
the poem serve this meaning as its goal, as the central purpose
around which the rest of the poem is written.

The term *purpose* is more useful and more important than it
may appear at first. The literary student would therefore do well to

be aware of the purposefulness of each literary work he studies. Since meaning itself is bound up with purpose, to explain the meaning of a work is to enable an explanation of its purpose. In this continuing study, the student should find that literary purpose varies from explicit *didacticism* to sheer enjoyment for its own sake.

Very rich material for specific study may be found in the relationships between purpose and the other elements of the literature. For instance, passages or aspects of a given work could be isolated, and the student could write a specific critique to answer one of the questions on pages 19 to 27, under "Purpose"; or one of the following: How does a given scene advance the work one or more steps toward a completion of the plot? How does the purpose, as hinted or stated in the introduction or in the conclusion, determine the tone, the devices of style, the *point of view?* What over-all purpose in the literature is served by conflict of purposes in the characters? In such projects, the student is warned to limit his topic, to avoid undue generalities, and to make his examples relevant and cogent.

QUATRAIN

See *Sonnet* and *Stanza.*

QUESTION BEGGING

In *rhetoric,* the assumption of rightness without appeal to facts or logic. Since literature is rarely based on formal logic, and is always connotative, unobjectionable elements of question begging may be present even in the most nonrhetorical forms, like the informal *essay* or the *lyric* poem. It is in literature for propaganda, which may utilize the style of *argumentation,* that one may expose violations of logic as flaws. An example is the legal chestnut: "When did you stop beating your wife?" This begs the question, since in order to answer, a respondent must admit (1) that he has a wife, and (2) that he has been beating her.

Question begging in literature may be less specific than in law, however: if the subject matter and the attitudes underlying the work are suited for debate but treated as matters of accepted fact, and if the reader is exhorted to concur, then the author may be begging the question. In this case, the literature masquerades as statement of fact. To be effective, the question-begging device must be buried deeply beneath the surface of the literature. Finally, the essential elements of verbal combat that distinguish rhetoric from other types of composition may also be found in company with this device. Good places to look for question begging are political and ecclestiastical debates, like those of the seventeenth century.

REALISM

The attempt at reflection of reality in literature. William Dean Howells, Henry James, and George Eliot are good exemplars of realism, which is found in both British and American literature, but primarily in the *novel* of the late nineteenth century. The use of exact detail, the portrayal of specific situations that express human values, and the appearance of a lack of design or plot in the episodes—all may be characteristic of realistic fiction. Also, the typical realist may react against *romanticism,* which he may deem excessively emotional, and attempt to write from a more impersonal *point of view. Realism,* which is as much a stylistic word as a name for a literary philosophy, should be distinguished from *naturalism.* Although there is an overlap between the two terms, the careful student would rarely confuse a work of naturalistic fiction with one of realism.

See *Naturalism.*

RHETORIC

The art of persuasion. Every kind of literature uses rhetorical devices for many reasons—for example, to show characters influencing one another, to enable *identification* of the reader with a character, to set off a cause or an idea in its best or worst light. Early in its career, the term *rhetoric* was associated with speech making and has never completely lost its oratorical overtones, though today the word is frequently used to mean any written composition. In its older meanings, because the aim of rhetoric was always to influence an audience, the term was and still is associated with propaganda, advertising, and special interest.

One definition of "literature" itself is the combination of rhetoric with information and entertainment. To emphasize the latter two elements may result in providing information or enjoyment, but to stress its rhetorical aspect is to attempt to persuade. The three components are never found in isolation or in purity, and interesting analyses may be made to show how one of these elements in a given work may do service for the other two. For instance, in Andrew Marvell's "To His Coy Mistress" (quoted in part under *Hyperbole* in this list), the fact of life's brevity and the consequent need for enjoyment assist rhetorically in the aims of courtship.

RHYME

See *Assonance* and *Stanza*.

RHYME ROYAL

See *Stanza*.

RHYTHM

See *Cadence, Meter,* and *Prosody*.

ROMANTICISM

A literary philosophy, which, in contrast with *classicism,* holds that man's primitive impulses are benign. Romanticism flourished in the poetry of early nineteenth-century poets like Wordsworth, Coleridge, Shelley, and Keats, who vary in their individual attitudes but who agree that tragedy results from man's divorcing himself from his natural setting. Two consequences of this belief are that evil accompanies the shift of population from the countryside to the city, and that, in a life of dignity, *nature* should be respected, not warred upon. Several lines of poems in the eighteenth and nineteenth centuries—for example, those of Gray, Wordsworth, Tennyson, Arnold, and Carlyle in England; Thoreau, Emerson, and Whitman in America—exemplify these aspects of romanticism. Such writers help to bring western attitudes toward nature closer to those of India and the Far East.

Any brief study of romanticism in literature should limit this broad topic to manageable proportions. Since romanticists are individualists par excellence, a contrast between two authors in this school would be a practical starting idea. The plan should be unified around a concept like the authors' respective positions on acquisitiveness or simplicity, and it should result in a paper that clearly delineates one or both positions. Other ideas are to analyze a work for its contribution to or deviation from romanticism as an ideology, or to illustrate how a particular strand of romanticism is woven into the work.

SATIRE

A form of *rhetoric* in *prose* or *verse* in which the author ridicules the evils, vices, or foibles of the world. The motives of the satirist are usually higher, and his composition more purely literary, than those of a writer who merely indulges in sarcasm. Like *irony,* satire may achieve its effect by *figurative language,* but the satirist may or may not express the literal opposite of what is meant. Moreover, a satire may be more or less intense and more or less specific. Elinor Goulding Smith's "Story for the Slicks" (pages 358 to 363) and Ring Lardner's "How to Write Short Stories" (pages 354 to 358) are pronounced examples of satire—one a *parody* and the other a *burlesque*. Especially in Miss Smith's story, the tone is astringent, and the targets for the humor in both Smith and Lardner are relatively specific. In contrast, the satirical essay by Joseph Wood Krutch, "No Essays, Please!" (pages 379 to 385) pokes more gentle fun at a less definite objective—the modern-day impersonal scientific habit of mind. In all these examples, irony is a potent ingredient.

In the following short poem by Arthur Hugh Clough, a still different shading of the satirical tone is achieved. The poem is extremely ironic, but one should notice also how the light, flippant attitude expressed in some lines contrasts with the serious subject matter and with the intent:

> Thou shalt have one God only; who
> Would be at the expense of two?
> No graven images may be
> Worshipped, except the currency.
> Swear not at all; for, for thy curse
> Thine enemy is none the worse.
> At church on Sunday to attend
> Will serve to keep the world thy friend.
> Honor thy parents; that is, all
> From whom advancement may befall.
> Thou shalt not kill; but need'st not strive
> Officiously to keep alive.
> Do not adultery commit;
> Advantage rarely comes of it.
> Thou shalt not steal: an empty feat,
> When it's so lucrative to cheat.
> Bear not false witness; let the lie
> Have time on its own wings to fly.

> Thou shalt not covet, but tradition
> Approves all forms of competition.

See also *Parody, Burlesque, Humor,* and *Irony*.

SCENE

The setting for action. Broadly, *scene* in literature is atmosphere, setting, milieu, context. Scenes, which are both physical places and nonphysical environments, can lend meaning and tone to a work, and can even indicate *point of view*. Ordinarily, a scene is simply a context for action, but a scene may contain other scenes.

For instance, most of Thomas Hardy's novels use the general setting of the English heath country; the specific scenes in villages and cottages take much of their flavor from the heath—a rich growth that covers the area like hair on a head. As the heath changes colors with the seasons, as Hardy's characters hide, get lost, find terror, solitude, or comfort in it, the heath gradually acquires a personality and the setting almost shifts its nature from that of a scene to that of a character.

Not only may a scene thus change its own character, but it may also transform the other elements of a literary work. For instance, in the first part of Shakespeare's *Henry IV,* Prince Hal is one person among his jovial friends of the tavern, another person with his father in the palace, and quite another on the battlefield duelling with Hotspur. Thus his surroundings help to comprise much of his character as an agent at given times. For another example, Shakespeare's Macbeth must use darkness and solitude as the scene for the murders of Duncan and others, and must conceal his motives (though his madness partly gives them away), when he is in the light, among the personages of the court. Here, scene or setting determines the methods employed by Macbeth.

Studies of *scene* could thus focus upon how it is interrelated with other literary elements. To avoid excessive complexity, the student should discover the physical properties of a setting and then show how these properties have psychological or other overtones. He should not choose all of the other elements, but only one or two of them, and should explain, as deeply and thoroughly as he can, how the mixture affects the components themselves. The concept that one element determines the nature of another would be the controlling idea of his analysis.

SENTIMENTALITY

A literary trait prominent in *romanticism,* by which emotion receives the emphasis—sometimes to the detriment of intellectual content. The term is often used to disparage a piece of literature that invites the reader to experience unwarranted emotion. Works that call on the reader to pity a downtrodden *protagonist* have one common symptom of sentimentality. Most genres of literature include examples of the trait: *comedy*—Richard Steele's *The Conscious Lovers; tragedy*—Arthur Miller's *The Death of a Salesman;* the *novel*—Richardson's *Pamela;* the *lyric*—Gray's "Elegy Written in a Country Churchyard."
See also *Decadence* and *Romanticism.*

SESTET
See *Sonnet.*

SHORT STORY

A brief fictional work in *prose,* varying in length from about 500 to 20,000 words. The short story has had a long history, dating from Greek episodes; through such Biblical passages as the "Story of Ruth"; into medieval times, with Boccaccio's *Decameron* and Chaucer's *Canterbury Tales;* and the eighteenth-century character sketch. The short story as a consciously practiced genre, however, begins in the nineteenth century. Poe, Hawthorne, Balzac,

DeMaupassant, Chekov, and Sherwood Anderson each contributed a new aspect to the form, which proliferated together with the growth of the nineteenth- and twentieth-century periodical. Elinor Goulding Smith's "Story for the Slicks" (pages 358 to 363) is a *parody* of the short story as it conforms to the demands of one contemporary popular magazine formula.

See section on "Short Story," in Part Four.

SIMILE

An expressed comparison, often in fanciful terms, between two similar things. The simile usually employs comparatives: *as if, like, than,* or *similar to.* The following complete poem by Robert Herrick is an example:

> Her pretty feet
> Like snails did creep
> A little out, and then,
> As if they started at bo-peep,
> Did soon draw in again.

See also *Analogy, Figurative language, Metaphor.*

SOLILOQUY

A speech in a play by a character who is alone on the stage. The soliloquy is sometimes spoken directly to the audience, but more often the character, in bemusement, simply "thinks out loud," so that the audience may know his state of mind. The playwright may also indicate offstage or backstage information in the soliloquy. Shakespeare, especially in *Hamlet* and *Macbeth,* used the device frequently.

SONNET

A *lyric* poem usually of fourteen lines and usually rhymed. Most sonnets are independent poems, but in the *sonnet sequence,* they may form *stanzas* in a more or less connected story. Although there are many experimental variants, two main branches of the form should be distinguished: (1) The Shakespearean or English sonnet is in four parts, with three quatrains (four-line stanzas) and a *couplet*. The quatrains are interlinked with rhyme, usually in the following scheme: *abab, cdcd, efef, gg.* (2) The Petrarchan or Italian sonnet is composed of two parts, an octave (an eight-line stanza) and a sestet. Though rhyme schemes vary widely, the octave is often rhymed *abba, abba;* and the sestet *cde, cde.* Rhyme in the sestet may, however, be of nearly any arrangement.

Though it is essential to know about these mechanical characteristics, the spirit of the sonnet is its most important aspect. One statement of what a sonnet should be is in the following example, by Dante Gabriel Rossetti:

> A Sonnet is a moment's monument—
> Memorial from the Soul's eternity
> To one dead deathless hour. Look that it be,
> Whether for lustral rite or dire portent,
> Of its own arduous fullness reverent;
> Carve it in ivory or in ebony,
> As Day or Night may rule; and let Time see
> Its flowering crest impearled and orient.
>
> A Sonnet is a coin: its face reveals
> The soul—its converse, to what Power 'tis due—
> Whether for tribute to the august appeals
> Of Life, or dower in Love's high retinue,
> It serve; or, mid the dark wharf's cavernous breath,
> In Charon's palm it pay the toll to Death.

Some of the best practitioners of the sonnet are named in the following example, by Wordsworth:

> Scorn not the Sonnet; Critic, you have frown'd,
> Mindless of its just honours; with this key
> Shakespeare unlock'd his heart; the melody

Of this small lute gave ease to Petrarch's wound;
A thousand times this pipe did Tasso sound;
With it Camōens sooth'd an exile's grief;
The Sonnet glitter'd a gay myrtle leaf
Amid the cypress with which Dante crown'd
His visionary brow: a glowworm lamp,
It cheer'd mild Spenser, call'd from Faeryland
To struggle through dark ways; and when a damp
Fell round the path of Milton, in his hand
The Thing became a trumpet; whence he blew
Soul-animating strains—alas, too few!

SPECTACLE

The scenic element in *drama*. The *masque* depends almost wholly on spectacle, as does present-day musical comedy. The term *spectacle* may thus refer not only to visual but also to auditory appeal. Many current motion pictures and television shows, called *spectaculars*, illustrate the extent to which spectacle may invade the drama. In modern parlance, the term "legitimate theater" is an attempt to denote dramatic productions with less emphasis on spectacle than on acting. The commentary by Eric Bentley, "Broadway—and the Alternative" (pages 320 to 326) gives one explanation of why many critics believe such elements as spectacle have damaged contemporary drama almost beyond repair.
See also *Scene*.

SPENSERIAN STANZA

See *Stanza*.

SPONDEE

A foot of *verse* in which two syllables are accented. Compound nouns, expletives, and juxtaposed monosyllables may be spondaic. The first two or the last two syllables of a line or the syllables just before or just after a *caesura* may be placed so as to be spondaic. See also *Prosody*.

STANZA

A unit of two or more lines of *verse* corresponding roughly to the paragraph in prose. The stanza may be ordered by a regular pattern of rhyme, or it may include rhymes that form no consistent pattern, or it may lack rhyme altogether. If rhyme is inconsistent or absent, the stanzas in a poem of metrical verse may be ordered merely by the units of thought. In this case, the stanzaic divisions, which may be called *verse paragraphs,* may differ in number of lines but are consistent in length of line. For instance, the *blank verse* of *Paradise Lost* is divided into verse paragraphs. By contrast, *free verse,* besides lacking rhyme, may have different lengths and numbers of lines in its larger units. Subdivisions in free verse, consequently, may appear to be as little restricted as are the paragraph divisions in prose.

In many cases the poet invents his own stanzaic patterns, but even so, there are varying degrees of freedom possible to him. In the *ode* the poet uses his own stanza forms, but, as in the Pindaric ode, he may decide to repeat these stanzas in conformity to a larger, conventional pattern. Moreover, he may or may not decide to use different kinds of stanzas in the same poem or to use a refrain that repeats an identical or similar stanza at regular or irregular intervals. A discussion of the stanza in English should include a number of structures that have been adopted as conventional. Some frequently used stanzas in English rhymed metrical verse are the *couplet;* in sonnet sequences, the *sonnet;* and the examples illustrated below:

Ottava rima: Eight lines rhyming *a b a b a b c c,* used by Milton, Spenser, Byron, and Keats. The sample is the first stanza of Keats's "Isabella":

Fair Isabel, poor simple Isabel!	*a*
Lorenzo, a young palmer in Love's eye!	*b*
They could not in the self-same mansion dwell	*a*
Without some stir of heart, some malady;	*b*
They could not sit at meals but feel how well	*a*
It soothed each to be the other by;	*b*
They could not, sure, beneath the same roof sleep	*c*
But to each other dream, and nightly weep.	*c*

Quatrain: A four-line unit using one, two, or three rhymes in any combination. Second and third rhymes are often used to link quatrains together; rhyming lines are usually of the same length. Quatrains may also be unrhymed, but are rarely so. The example is the first stanza of Wordsworth's "Strange Fits of Passion":

> Strange fits of passion have I known:
> And I will dare to tell,
> But in the Lover's ear alone,
> What once to me befell.

Rhyme royal: A seven-line stanza in *iambic pentameter* (see *Prosody*), rhyming *a b a b b c c*. Rhyme royal was used frequently by Chaucer and during the sixteenth and seventeenth centuries by Wyatt and Shakespeare. The example is from William Morris's *The Earthly Paradise:*

Of Heaven or Hell I have no power to sing;	*a*
I cannot ease the burden of your fears,	*b*
Or make quick-becoming death a little thing,	*a*
Or bring again the pleasure of past years;	*b*
Nor for my words shall ye forget your tears,	*b*
Or hope again for aught that I can say—	*c*
The idle singer of an empty day.	*c*

Spenserian stanza: A highly unified nine-line stanza in *iambic pentameter,* except for the last line, which is an *alexandrine.* The rhyme scheme is *a b a b b c b c c*. Named for its creator, Edmund Spenser, the Spenserian stanza has been used by Burns, Shelley,

Keats, and Byron. The example is from Byron's *Childe Harold's Pilgrimage:*

There was a sound of revelry by night,	*a*
And Belgium's capital had gathered then	*b*
Her beauty and her chivalry, and bright	*a*
The lamps shone o'er fair women and brave men:	*b*
A thousand hearts beat happily; and when	*b*
Music arose with its voluptuous swell,	*c*
Soft eyes looked love to eyes which spake again,	*b*
And all went merry as a marriage bell—	*c*
But hush! hark! a deep sound strikes like a rising knell!	*c*

Tercet: Three lines in sequence, all rhyming; or, one-half of the sestet of a *sonnet;* or the unit of *terza rima,* which rhymes *aba, cbc, ded,* etc. In English poetry, *terza rima* has been used infrequently, except for such translations of Dante's *Divine Comedy* as that of John Ciardi. Tercets used without interlinking rhyme are more frequent; in such examples, length of lines may vary. The following is from Alice Meynell's "A Letter from a Girl to Her Own Old Age":

Listen, and when thy hand this paper presses,
O time-worn woman, think of her who blesses
What thy thin fingers touch, with her caresses.

STREAM OF CONSCIOUSNESS TECHNIQUE

The method of telling a story by narrating whatever goes through the mind of a chief character. An author may also be using this device when he makes a selection of the thoughts of a character; the vital ingredient in the technique is the objectification of the mental events. That is, not only is the story told from the *point of view* of the narrator, but the story *is* what the narrator *thinks* (as in T. S. Eliot's "The Love Song of J. Alfred Prufrock"); or daydreams (as in a large part of James Thurber's "The Catbird Seat"); or even dreams in sleep (as in James Joyce's *Ulysses*). Often, a *flashback* is depicted by this device, as in the scenes of Arthur Miller's *Death of a Salesman* in which Willy Loman remembers his relationships with his sons and his shabby love affair. The technique is also used in the extraordinary first section of Faulkner's *The Sound and the Fury,* which is told as the stream of consciousness of an idiot, Benjy Compson. Faulkner makes Benjy's story at the same time rich and artistic; for this reason, critics have called this part of his novel one of the astonishing accomplishments of modern fiction.

STRUCTURE

The outline or plan of a work of literature, which, taken together with *texture* comprises its *form.* In fiction, *plot* is structure; in nonfiction, the plan—or the arrangement of the blocks of thought, indicated by paragraph divisions and section breaks—is the basic structural makeup. In some instances, the structure of a literary work is taken from the subject matter; in others, the author largely superimposes an order on his material; but in most cases, partly the subject matter and partly the author's individual *point of view* determine what the structure will be.

Moreover, even in fiction the author must cooperate with his reader in determining the order, the relative emphases, the arrangement of the parts of his plot. The author appeals to his reader through assumed agreements about what in life is valuable and what is not. These agreements help to make for interest and *suspense,* the primary structural components of fiction. In nonfiction, suspense also plays a part, since the author may select and arrange the details of his material so as to follow a line of increasing interest that is similar to a fictional plot.

One may conceive of literary structure either as temporal or as spatial, just as a person may make a plan for his future or a plan for his house. In a plan for the future, the flow of events forms a structure that fulfills the plan; and in the plan for a house, concrete things—boards, bricks, shingles—are the materials. In literature, words must do service both in time and in space. In its temporal aspect, literary structure is like music: only one note (with its chord) at a time may be played, and only one word at a time (with its cluster of associations) may be written. Spatially, literature may be compared with architecture: As different purposes determine the size and shape—the structure—of a building and its rooms, so different motives determine the length and complexity of a literary work and its parts.

Studies of literary structure may be made most profitably in connection with such terms as *texture, form, suspense,* described in this Glossary. To isolate the main lines of a literary structure from the rest of the work is simply to render a plot summary or a précis (see Chapter 10). Though such a summary may be useful, it is not, by itself, a literary study. Therefore, the student should combine his structural analysis, for example, with a study of *texture,* to arrive at a description of form. Another idea may be to distinguish the different kinds of *suspense* that make up the structure and to illustrate these kinds by examples from the literature itself.

STYLE

In literature, an author's way of writing. Literary style varies not only from one author to another, but is determined according to the subject matter to be treated, the *point of view* and attitude to be expressed, the type of literature to be produced, and the *audience* addressed. Notwithstanding the fact that a writer's style may be as individual as his fingerprints, one mark of an accomplished author is his versatility and flexibility of style. Thus, the same author may use widely different styles for different purposes and still maintain his individuality. For instance, Samuel Johnson wrote nearly all kinds of poetry, criticism, prose fiction, drama, many

personal letters, and even a dictionary; moreover, much of his conversation was recorded (in Boswell's *Life of Johnson*). Yet, even
though Johnson's style touched most of the notes in a very wide
scale, the well-read student should have little difficulty in identifying the Johnsonian style as it appears in any genre. Thus, to study
the style of a work is to study also some of the indelible traits of
its author.

See also *Texture*.

SUSPENSE

The interest that holds the *structure* of literature together. Suspense
may be broken down into two types: suspense by expectation and
suspense by eloquence. Both types depend on a feeling of interest,
or audience-*identification,* so that the reader is absorbed with the
issues of the work. For suspense to occur, at least a temporary
belief must be granted, and the reader lives for the moment in the
author's world, which may be as fanciful as that of *Alice in
Wonderland* or as grimly realistic as that of Defoe's *Journal of the
Plague Year.* In constructing his work, the author appeals to his
reader's sensibilities and arranges his materials to follow the principle of climax. Even in nonfiction, but especially in fiction, he
makes use of feelings, emotions, and ideas to create a pattern that
catches up the reader's attention and sympathy in a line of increasing intensity. In style, the periodic sentence is the basic suspense
pattern.

Suspense by expectation depends upon mechanical arrangement
of facts or details. The modern mystery story, in which the reader
must put events and circumstances together like a puzzle, represents one verson of this kind of suspense. In another, the author
keeps the reader partly in the dark and stimulates his appetite to
know more of the story by presenting its parts bit by bit. In
Macbeth, Shakespeare employs this second method most effec-

tively. O. Henry typifies a third version in his short stories, which often conclude with a shock that makes clear all that has been obscure.

Suspense by eloquence is a matter of style. The skill required to be eloquent is not necessary if the author wishes merely to stimulate his readers' expectations. Nevertheless, where the student discovers excellence of style, he may also find the pronounced plot lines of the more mechanical type of suspense. The interest of *Oedipus Rex,* for instance, seems to depend largely upon expectations in the mechanics of its plot, but the Greek audiences knew this plot well and returned time and again to see the play. The same has always been true with most audiences of Shakespeare. Arguing from these facts, one may say that suspense by eloquence exists when the reader returns to the literature for his own satisfaction, even though he knows "what will happen." Further, one may advance the idea that suspense by eloquence makes a literary work more valuable, more refined. It appeals to the reader's sense of style rather than to his gross appetite for facts.

SYMBOL

In literature, anything that represents or stands for something other than itself. Broadly, one may say that all language is symbolic in much the same way that it depends upon *metaphor*. Specifically, the white whale in Melville's *Moby Dick* is used to symbolize the whole complex of good and evil; the green hair ribbon is a symbol for hope, and the letter A, for adultery in Hawthorne's "Young Goodman Brown" and *The Scarlet Letter;* the lamb stands for innocence and the lion for experience in the poems of William Blake.

In literature, symbols can form a network to catch up the significance that would be lost if single words and objects could carry only single meanings. A specific symbol may thus be part of a metaphor, the part that aids the metaphorical expression to have meaning on more than one level. The term *metaphor,* moreover, may denote a figure of speech to be used for the nonce and then dropped; such a meaning is not common for the term *symbol,* which identifies one of the mechanical objects in a system or in a literary structure.

Good ground for the study of symbols in literature is the *allegory,* but in many other genres also, broad issues are simplified by the use of symbols, and are seen to be more complicated when analyzed in depth. The goal of most studies of specific symbols is to discover meanings and to unearth the complexity that lies beneath simplicity. Besides the works of Hawthorne, Melville, and Blake, interesting embodiments of symbols are found in works like Donne's "The Flea," Swift's *A Tale of a Tub,* Pope's *The Rape of the Lock,* Dante's *La Vita Nuova.* The student should be alert for symbols in the work of each author he reads. In this study, he should scrutinize each repetition of a suspected symbol and note how it summarizes meanings and ties together otherwise unrelated parts of the literature. If he observes these uses and relationships carefully, he may find—and should report in his paper—deep waters where there had seemed only shallows, richness where there appeared only superficiality.

SYNECDOCHE

A figure of speech whereby a part is used to designate or connote the whole, as a *sail* for a *ship;* or the whole for a part, as the *navy* for a *sailor.*
See also *Figurative language.*

TERCET

See *Stanza.*

TEXTURE

The quality of style in a literary work. *Texture,* a term adopted by John Crowe Ransom from textiles, is best used together with *structure* to comprise literary *form.* Style, manner, and tone are components of texture.

In specific literature, fineness of texture results from economy of expression, so that in a closely woven work the author has made every word count. Just as in textiles, however, at least the appearance of coarseness of texture is sometimes desirable; and the student should not discount a work because it does not seem to pack ideas or images closely together.

The texture of a literary work is determined partly by an author's *point of view,* and partly by his individual genius for adjusting the tone and style of his work to its subject matter. As De Goncourt said, "Style is the man"; and when the object of study is to understand the author, textural analysis is a valuable tool to discover the depth and quality of his mental equipment.

Textural study would also reveal the subject matter itself in the varied lights that the author throws upon it. As against the scientific position that one must have no attitude about an object of study, must be "objective" about it, the literary position, by analysis of texture, would study both the object and a set of possible human attitudes about it. *Texture* is thus defined as the quality of literature, and as attitude toward the world depicted in literature.

To study the texture of a specific work one's knowledge about it should be as thorough as possible. Ransom himself shows that one good approach is first to place the literature as dealing primarily with things and images, or with ideas. The value of literature as art which deals with things would be based upon the arrangement and choice of expression—upon texture, judged effective if it achieves the attitude aimed at. Literature as *rhetoric,* which deals with ideas, must be approached not for its esthetic satisfaction but for its persuasive efficiency, as revealed primarily in its texture.

TONE

The aspect of *style* that reveals the attitude or *point of view* of the author or of a character.

TRAGEDY

The major form of the drama, often contrasted with *comedy*. Aristotle, who specified that tragedy must effect a *catharsis* of pity and fear, described the ideal tragedy, using Sophocles's *Oedipus Rex* as his model. A simplification of this definition is that a tragedy is a drama which ends in catastrophe for the hero. As distinguished from comedy, tragedy employs noble characters, usually follows the unities of time, place, and action, and is concerned basically with the good of the whole state. Writers through history have observed Aristotle's requirements in varying degrees, from purists, like Corneille and Racine, to those like Shakespeare, who break the Aristotelian rules when they find good reason to do so.

As a genre, tragedy has close ties with the philosophy of *classicism,* just as *comedy* is linked, in attitude, with *romanticism.* Much is claimed for tragedy as an *archetype,* because it presents both life and death in a strong, revealing light. As a clarification of the meaning of death, tragedy helps its audience toward true solace by its forceful illustration that even kings must die. As a source of a deeper or more thorough understanding of life, tragedy may contain the insight that what is true and noble lives on despite human frailty. An overemphasis on tragic death would result in unenlightened pessimism. And since, in tragedy, the understanding of life seems to go deeper than that of death, one could argue that the basic attitude of tragedy is enlightened optimism.

TRAVESTY

A work of literature that satirizes or mocks a serious or dignified subject or *tone.* The travesty, which is likely to be humorous or witty, may also be disrespectful of convention or authority.
See also *Satire* and *Parody.*

TROCHEE
See *Prosody*.

UNITIES
See the passage from Dryden's "Essay of Dramtic Poesy," pages 308 to 311.

VERSE
Metrical discourse; also, a line of poetry. The term *verse* does not necessarily imply the high quality that is connoted by the term *poetry;* its use may be a conscious attempt to avoid such evaluation. For an excellent discussion of the distinctions between verse and poetry, see Coleridge's *Biographia Literaria,* pages 291 to 295.

VERSE PARAGRAPH
See *Stanza*.

WIT
As a literary term, *wit* can embrace the whole complex of mental power and activity (with emphasis on *style*), or it can denote, more narrowly, the quick or sharp perception and juxtaposition of different meanings. One of its broader senses is implied in a designation like "University Wits," to identify a group of Elizabethan poets including Lodge, Nash, Greene, and Lyly; the term is also related to stylistic terms like *irony, humor, satire*. Its narrower meaning is an important aspect of Coleridge's definition of *fancy:* ". . . the parts of the meaning are apprehended as though independent of their fellow members (as they would be if they belonged to quite other wholes). . . ." Incongruity, perceived and expressed, may thus be a vital element in the literary application of the term.

part four

Points
of
departure

IN THE FOLLOWING five sections are some important statements by critics and authors concerning the nature and functions of the different kinds of literature—poetry, drama, novel, short story, and essay. Each selection has been chosen because it throws the searching light of a professional mind upon literary meaning and value within these genres. There are several ways you can approach these statements; perhaps the most valuable way is to study them for a critical background and a perspective that helps you see what a given kind of literature is and what it does. The selections are not designed to make you a creative author, but they may help you see how the different kinds of literature are produced. You are thus taken behind the scenes, where you may see some examples of literature itself and of deeply considered commentary about literature. For instance, the selection from Charles Lamb both concerns the drama and is a familiar essay. The insights you gain should enhance your appreciation of literature; one consequence of this appreciation should be an improvement in your own specific interpretative writing.

284

poetry

THE SELECTIONS presented here attempt to achieve two common goals—a definition of poetry and a description of what it is supposed to accomplish. Moreover, most of these essays make a distinction between poetry and science. As Sir Philip Sidney had been before, Wordsworth is concerned to show that poetry is at once greater than philosophy, history, and science: because it is limited neither to theory, nor to fact, nor to a narrow logic, poetry may yield deeper satisfaction (which Wordsworth calls "pleasure") than any of these disciplines. Coleridge begins by distinguishing poetry from verse; then, like Wordsworth, he takes up the term "pleasure" as the characteristic that distinguishes poetry from all other kinds of discourse. Finally, Coleridge describes two further criteria by which to measure a poem: harmony between the part and the whole, and a quality he calls the "soul" of poetry—imagination. Like Coleridge, Matthew Arnold sets a high destiny for poetry: because it encompasses both thought and emotion, poetry (not merely specific poems) may both interpret and order our world. Where science and religion have failed, poetry may succeed. Finally, in our own century, T. S. Eliot describes several functions of poetry that help to answer the questions, "What are the practical values of literature?" and "What can literature do for us today, for a society whose members are necessarily preoccupied with their individual problems of making their separate ways in the world?"

285

from Preface to the Lyrical Ballads (*1800*)
by William Wordsworth

Taking up the subject, then, upon general grounds, let me ask, what is meant by the word *Poet?* What is a poet? To whom does he address himself? And what language is to be expected from him?—He is a man speaking to men: a man, it is true, endowed with more lively sensibility, more enthusiasm and tenderness, who has a greater knowledge of human nature, and a more comprehensive soul, than are supposed to be common among mankind; a man pleased with his own passions and volitions, and who rejoices more than other men in the spirit of life that is in him; delighting to contemplate similar volitions and passions as manifested in the goings-on of the universe, and habitually impelled to create them where he does not find them. To these qualities he has added a disposition to be affected more than other men by absent things as if they were present; an ability of conjuring up in himself passions which are indeed far from being the same as those produced by real events, yet (especially in those parts of the general sympathy which are pleasing and delightful) do more nearly resemble the passions produced by real events than anything which, from the motions of their own minds merely, other men are accustomed to feel in themselves:—whence, and from practice, he has acquired a greater readiness and power in expressing what he thinks and feels, and especially those thoughts and feelings which, by his own choice, or from the structure of his own mind, arise in him without immediate external excitement.

But whatever portion of this faculty we may suppose even the greatest poet to possess, there cannot be a doubt that the language which it will suggest to him must often, in liveliness and truth, fall short of that which is uttered by men in real life under the actual pressure of those passions, certain shadows of which the poet thus produces, or feels to be produced, in himself.

However exalted a notion we would wish to cherish of the character of a poet, it is obvious that while he describes and imitates
passions, his employment is in some degree mechanical, compared
with the freedom and power of real and substantial action and
suffering. So that it will be the wish of the poet to bring his feelings
near to those of the persons whose feelings he describes,—nay, for
short spaces of time, perhaps, to let himself slip into an entire
delusion, and even confound and identify his own feelings with
theirs; modifying only the language which is thus suggested to him
by a consideration that he describes for a particular purpose, that
of giving pleasure. Here, then, he will apply the principle of selection which has been already insisted upon. He will depend upon
this for removing what would otherwise be painful or disgusting in
the passion; he will feel that there is no necessity to trick out or to
elevate nature: and, the more industriously he applies this principle,
the deeper will be his faith that no words which *his* fancy or
imagination can suggest will be compared with those which are the
emanations of reality and truth.

But it may be said by those who do not object to the general
spirit of these remarks, that, as it is impossible for the poet to
produce upon all occasions language as exquisitely fitted for the
passion as that which the real passion itself suggests, it is proper
that he should consider himself as in the situation of a translator,
who does not scruple to substitute excellencies of another kind for
those which are unattainable by him, and endeavors occasionally to
surpass his original, in order to make some amends for the general
inferiority to which he feels that he must submit. But this would be
to encourage idleness and unmanly despair. Further, it is the
language of men who speak of what they do not understand; who
talk of poetry as of a matter of amusement and idle pleasure; who
will converse with us as gravely about a *taste* for poetry, as they
express it, as if it were a thing as indifferent as a taste for rope-
dancing, or Frontiniac or Sherry.[1] Aristotle, I have been told, has

---

[1] Kinds of wine.

said that poetry is the most philosophic of all writing: it is so: its object is truth, not individual and local, but general, and operative; not standing upon external testimony, but carried alive into the heart by passion; truth which is its own testimony, which gives competence and confidence to the tribunal to which it appeals, and receives them from the same tribunal. Poetry is the image of man and nature. The obstacles which stand in the way of the fidelity of the biographer and historian, and of their consequent utility, are incalculably greater than those which are to be encountered by the poet who comprehends the dignity of his art. The poet writes under one restriction only, namely, the necessity of giving immediate pleasure to a human being possessed of that information which may be expected from him, not as a lawyer, a physician, a mariner, an astronomer, or a natural philosopher, but as a man. Except this one restriction, there is no object standing between the poet and the image of things; between this, and the biographer and historian, there are a thousand.

Nor let this necessity of producing immediate pleasure be considered as a degradation of the poet's art. It is far otherwise. It is an acknowledgment of the beauty of the universe, an acknowledgment the more sincere, because not formal, but indirect; it is a task light and easy to him who looks at the world in the spirit of love: further, it is a homage paid to the native and naked dignity of man, to the grand elementary principle of pleasure, by which he knows, and feels, and lives, and moves. We have no sympathy but what is propagated by pleasure: I would not be misunderstood; but wherever we sympathize with pain, it will be found that the sympathy is produced and carried on by subtle combinations with pleasure. We have no knowledge, that is, no general principles drawn from the contemplation of particular facts, but what has been built up by pleasure, and exists in us by pleasure alone. The man of science, the chemist and mathematician, whatever difficulties and disgusts they may have had to struggle with, know and feel this. However painful may be the objects with which the anatomist's knowledge is connected, he feels that his knowledge is pleasure; and where he has no pleasure he has no knowledge. What then does the poet? He considers man and the objects that surround him as acting and reacting upon each other, so as to produce an infinite complexity of pain and pleasure; he considers man in his own nature and in his ordinary life as contemplating this with a certain quantity of immediate knowledge, with certain convictions, intuitions, and deductions, which from habit acquire the quality of intuitions; he considers him as looking upon this complex scene of ideas and sensations, and finding everywhere objects that immediately excite in him sympathies which, from the necessities of his nature, are accompanied by an over-balance of enjoyment.

To this knowledge which all men carry about with them, and to these sympathies in which, without any other discipline than that of our daily life, we are fitted to take delight, the poet principally directs his attention. He considers man and nature as essentially adapted to each other, and the mind of man as naturally the mirror of the fairest and most interesting properties of nature. And thus the poet, prompted by this feeling of pleasure, which accompanies him through the whole course of his studies, converses with general nature, with affections akin to those which, through labor and length of time, the man of science has raised up in himself, by conversing with those particular parts of nature which are the objects of his studies. The knowledge both of the poet and the man of science is pleasure; but the knowledge of the one cleaves to us as a necessary part of our existence, our natural and unalienable inheritance; the other is a personal and individual acquisition, slow to come to us, and by no habitual and direct sympathy connecting us with our fellow-beings. The man of science seeks truth as a remote and unknown benefactor; he cherishes and loves it in his solitude: the poet, singing a song in which all human beings join with him, rejoices in the presence of truth as our visible friend and hourly companion. Poetry is the breath and finer spirit of all knowledge; it is the impassioned expression which is in the countenance of all science. Emphatically may it be said of the poet, as Shakespeare hath said of man, that "he looks before and after." He is the rock of defence for human nature; an upholder and preserver, carrying everywhere with him relationship and love. In spite of difference of soil and climate, of language and manners, of laws and customs: in spite of things silently gone out of mind, and things violently destroyed; the poet binds together by passion and knowledge the vast empire of human society, as it is spread over the whole earth, and over all time. The objects of the poet's thoughts are everywhere; though the eyes and senses of man are, it is true, his favorite guides, yet he will follow wheresoever he can find an atmosphere of sensation in which to move his wings. Poetry is the first and last of all knowledge—it is as immortal as the heart of man. If the labors of men of science should ever create any material revolution, direct or indirect, in our condition, and in the impressions which we habitually receive, the poet will sleep then no more than at present; he will be ready to follow the steps of the man of science, not only in those general indirect effects, but he will be at his side, carrying sensation into the midst of the objects of the science itself. The remotest discoveries of the chemist, the botanist, or mineralogist, will be as proper objects of the poet's art as any upon which it can be employed, if the time should ever come when these things shall be familiar to us, and the relations under which they are contemplated by the followers of these respective sciences shall be manifestly and palpably material to us as enjoying and suffering beings. If the time should ever come when what is now called science, thus familiarized to men, shall be ready to put on, as it were, a form of flesh and blood, the poet will end his divine spirit to aid the transfiguration, and will welcome the being thus produced, as a dear and genuine inmate of the household of man.—It is not, then, to be supposed that any one who holds that sublime notion of poetry which I have attempted to convey, will break in upon the sanctity and truth of his pictures by transitory and accidental ornaments, and endeavor to excite admiration of himself by arts, the necessity of which must manifestly depend upon the assumed meanness of his subject. . . .

from Biographia Literaria
by Samuel Taylor Coleridge

A poem contains the same elements as a prose composition; the difference therefore must consist in a different combination of them, in consequence of a different object being proposed. According to the difference of the object will be the difference of the combination. It is possible, that the object may be merely to facilitate the recollection of any given facts or observations by artificial arrangement; and the composition will be a poem, merely because it is distinguished from prose by metre, or by rhyme, or by both conjointly. In this, the lowest sense, a man might attribute the name of a poem to the well-known enumeration of the days in the several months:

> Thirty days hath September,
> April, June, and November, &c.

and others of the same class and purpose. And as a particular pleasure is found in anticipating the recurrence of sounds and quantities, all compositions that have this charm super-added, whatever be their contents, *may* be entitled poems.

So much for the superficial *form*. A difference of object and contents supplies an additional ground of distinction. The immediate purpose may be the communication of truths; either of truth absolute and demonstrable, as in works of science; or of facts experienced and recorded, as in history. Pleasure, and that of the highest and most permanent kind, may *result* from the *attainment* of the end; but it is not itself the immediate end. In other works the communication of pleasure may be the immediate purpose; and though truth, either moral or intellectual, ought to be the *ultimate* end, yet this will distinguish the character of the author, not the class to which the work belongs. Blest indeed is that state of society, in which the immediate purpose would be baffled by the perversion of the proper ultimate end; in which no charm of diction or imagery could exempt the Bathyllus even of an Anacreon, or the Alexis of Virgil, from disgust and aversion!

But the communication of pleasure may be the immediate object of a work not metrically composed and that object may have been in a high degree attained, as in novels and romances. Would then the mere superaddition of metre, with or without rhyme, entitle *these* to the name of poems? The answer is, that nothing can permanently please which does not contain in itself the reason why it is so, and not otherwise. If metre be superadded, all other parts must be made consonant with it. They must be such, as to justify the perpetual and distinct attention to each part, which an exact correspondent recurrence of accent and sound are calculated to excite. The final definition then, so deduced, may be thus worded. A poem is that species of composition, which is opposed to works of science, by proposing for its *immediate* object pleasure, not truth; and from all other species (having *this* object in common with it) it is discriminated by proposing to itself such delight from the *whole,* as is compatible with a distinct gratification from each component *part*.

Controversy is not seldom excited in consequence of the disputants attaching each a different meaning to the same word; and in few instances has this been more striking, than in disputes concerning the present subject. If a man chooses to call every composition a poem, which is rhyme, or measure, or both, I must leave his opinion uncontroverted. The distinction is at least competent to characterize the writer's intention. If it were subjoined, that the whole is likewise entertaining or affecting, as a tale, or as a series of interesting reflections, I of course admit this as another fit ingredient of a poem, and an additional merit. But if the definition sought for be that of a *legitimate* poem, I answer, it must be one, the parts of which mutually support and explain each other; all in their proportion harmonizing with, and supporting the purpose and known influences of metrical arrangement. The philosophic critics of all ages coincide with the ultimate judgement of all countries, in equally denying the praises of a just poem, on the one hand, to a series of striking lines or distiches, each of which, absorbing the whole attention of the reader to itself, disjoins it from its context, and makes it a separate whole, instead of an harmonizing part; and on the other hand, to an unsustained composition, from which the reader collects rapidly the general result, unattracted by the component parts. The reader should be carried forward, not merely or chiefly by the mechanical impulse of curiosity, or by a restless desire to arrive at the final solution; but by the pleasurable activity of mind excited by the attractions of the journey itself. Like the motion of a serpent, which the Egyptians made the emblem of intellectual power; or like the path of sound through the air; at every step he pauses and half recedes, and from the retrogressive movement collects the force which again carries him onward. "Praecipitandus est *liber* spiritus [a free spirit ought to be hurled along]," says Petronius Arbiter most happily. The epithet, *liber,* here balances the preceding verb; and it is not easy to conceive more meaning condensed in fewer words.

But if this should be admitted as a satisfactory character of a poem, we have still to seek for a definition of poetry. The writings of Plato, and Bishop Taylor, and the "Theoria Sacra" of Burnet, furnish undeniable proofs that poetry of the highest kind may exist without metre, and even without the contradistinguishing objects of a poem. The first chapter of Isaiah (indeed a very large portion of the whole book) is poetry in the most emphatic sense; yet it would be not less irrational than strange to assert, that pleasure, and not truth, was the immediate object of the prophet. In short, whatever *specific* import we attach to the word, poetry, there will be found involved in it, as a necessary consequence, that a poem of any length neither can be, or ought to be, all poetry. Yet if an harmonious whole is to be produced, the remaining parts must be preserved *in keeping* with the poetry; and this can be no otherwise effected than by such a studied selection and artificial arrangement, as will partake of *one,* though not a *peculiar* property of poetry. And this again can be no other than the property of exciting a more continuous and equal attention than the language of prose aims at, whether colloquial or written.

My own conclusions on the nature of poetry, in the strictest use of the word, have been in part anticipated in the preceding disquisition on the fancy and imagination. What is poetry? is so nearly the same question with, what is a poet? that the answer to the one is involved in the solution of the other. For it is a distinction resulting from the poetic genius itself, which sustains and modifies the images, thoughts, and emotions of the poet's own mind.

The poet, described in *ideal* perfection, brings the whole soul of man into activity, with the subordination of its faculties to each other, according to their relative worth and dignity. He diffuses a tone and spirit of unity, that blends, and (as it were) *fuses,* each into each, by that synthetic and magical power, to which I would exclusively appropriate the name of imagination. This power, first put in action by the will and understanding, and retained under their irremissive, though gentle and unnoticed, control (*laxis effertur habenis*),[1] reveals itself in the balance or reconciliation of opposite or discordant qualities: of sameness, with difference; of the general, with the concrete; the idea, with the image; the individual, with the representative; the sense of novelty and freshness, with old and familiar objects; a more than usual state of emotion, with more than usual order; judgement ever awake and steady self-

---

[1] [*laxis effertur habenis:* is born onward with loose reins.]

possession, with enthusiasm and feeling profound or vehement; and while it blends and harmonizes the natural and the artificial, still subordinates art to nature; the manner to the matter; and our admiration of the poet to our sympathy with the poetry. Doubtless, as Sir John Davies observes of the soul (and his words may with slight alteration be applied, and even more appropriately, to the poetic IMAGINATION)

> Doubtless this could not be, but that she turns
>   Bodies to spirit by sublimation strange,
> As fire converts to fire the things it burns,
>   As we our food into our nature change.
>
> From their gross matter she abstracts their forms,
>   And draws a kind of quintessence from things;
> Which to her proper nature she transforms
>   To bear them light on her celestial wings.
>
> Thus does she, when from individual states
>   She doth abstract the universal kinds;
> Which then re-clothed in divers names and fates
>   Steal access through our senses to our minds.

Finally, GOOD SENSE is the BODY of poetic genius, FANCY its DRAPERY, MOTION its LIFE, and IMAGINATION the SOUL that is everywhere, and in each; and forms all into one graceful and intelligent whole. . . .

from "The Study of Poetry"
by Matthew Arnold

"The future of poetry is immense, because in poetry, where it is worthy of its high destinies, our race, as time goes on, will find an ever surer and surer stay. There is not a creed which is not shaken, not an accredited dogma which is not shown to be questionable, not a received tradition which does not threaten to dissolve. Our religion has materialized itself in the fact, in the supposed fact; it has attached its emotion to the fact, and now the fact is failing it. But for poetry the idea is everything; the rest is a world of illusion, of divine illusion. Poetry attaches its emotion to the idea; the idea *is* the fact. The strongest part of our religion today is its unconscious poetry."

Let me be permitted to quote these words of my own, as uttering the thought which should, in my opinion, go with us and govern us in all our study of poetry. In the present work it is the course of one great contributory stream to the world-river of poetry that we are invited to follow. We are here invited to trace the stream of English poetry. But whether we set ourselves, as here, to follow only one of the several streams that make the mighty river of poetry, or whether we seek to know them all, our governing thought should be the same. We should conceive of poetry worthily, and more highly than it has been the custom to conceive of it. We should conceive of it as capable of higher uses, and called to higher destinies, than those which in general men have assigned to it hitherto. More and more mankind will discover that we have to turn to poetry to interpret life for us, to console us, to sustain us. Without poetry, our science will appear incomplete; and most of what now passes with us for religion and philosophy will be replaced by poetry. Science, I say, will appear incomplete without it. For finely and truly does Wordsworth call poetry "the impassioned expression which is in the countenance of all science"; and what is a countenance without its expression? Again, Wordsworth finely and truly calls poetry "the breath and finer spirit of all knowledge"; our religion, parading evidences such as those on which the popular mind relies now; our philosophy, pluming itself on its reasonings about causation and finite and infinite being; what are they but the shadows and dreams and false shows of knowledge? The day will come when we shall wonder at ourselves for having trusted to them, for having taken them seriously; and the more we perceive their hollowness, the more we shall prize "the breath and finer spirit of knowledge" offered to us by poetry.

But if we conceive thus highly of the destinies of poetry, we must also set our standard for poetry high, since poetry, to be capable of fulfilling such high destinies, must be poetry of a high order of excellence. We must accustom ourselves to a high standard and to a strict judgment. Sainte-Beuve[1] relates that Napoleon one day said, when somebody was spoken of in his presence as a charlatan: "Charlatan as much as you please; but where is there *not* charlatanism?"—"Yes," answers Sainte-Beuve, "in politics, in the art of governing mankind, that is perhaps true. But in the order of thought, in art, the glory, the eternal honor is that charlatanism shall find no entrance; herein lies the inviolableness of that noble portion of man's being." It is admirably said, and let us hold fast to it. In poetry, which is thought and art in one, it is the glory, the eternal honor, that charlatanism shall find no entrance; that this noble sphere be kept inviolate and inviolable. Charlatanism is for confusing or obliterating the distinctions between excellent and inferior, sound and unsound or only half-sound, true and untrue or only half-true. It is charlatanism, conscious or unconscious, whenever we confuse or obliterate these. And in poetry, more than anywhere else, it is unpermissible to confuse or obliterate them. For in poetry the distinction between excellent and inferior, sound and unsound or only half-sound, true and untrue or only half-true, is of paramount importance. It is of paramount importance because of the high destinies of poetry. In poetry, as a criticism of life under the conditions fixed for such a criticism by the laws of poetic truth and poetic beauty, the spirit of our race will find, we have said, as time goes on and as other helps fail, its consolation and

[1] Sainte-Beuve: A French critic (1804–1869), in Arnold's opinion "the master of us all in criticism."

stay. But the consolation and stay will be of power in proportion to the power of the criticism of life. And the criticism of life will be of power in proportion as the poetry conveying it is excellent rather than inferior, sound rather than unsound or half-sound, true rather than untrue or half-true.

The best poetry is what we want; the best poetry will be found to have a power of forming, sustaining, and delighting us, as nothing else can. A clearer, deeper sense of the best in poetry, and of the strength and joy to be drawn from it, is the most precious benefit which we can gather from a poetical collection such as the present. And yet in the very nature and conduct of such a collection there is inevitably something which tends to obscure in us the consciousness of what our benefit should be, and to distract us from the pursuit of it. We should therefore steadily set it before our minds at the outset, and should compel ourselves to revert constantly to the thought of it as we proceed.

Yes; constantly in reading poetry, a sense for the best, the really excellent, and of the strength and joy to be drawn from it, should be present in our minds and should govern our estimate of what we read. But this real estimate, the only true one, is liable to be superseded, if we are not watchful, by two other kinds of estimate, the historic estimate and the personal estimate, both of which are fallacious. A poet or a poem may count to us historically, they may count to us on grounds personal to ourselves, and they may count to us really. They may count to us historically. The course of development of a nation's language, thought, and poetry, is profoundly interesting; and by regarding a poet's work as a stage in this course of development we may easily bring ourselves to make it of more importance as poetry than in itself it really is, we may come to use a language of quite exaggerated praise in criticizing it; in short, to over-rate it. So arises in our poetic judgments the fallacy caused by the estimate which we may call historic. Then, again, a poet or a poem may count to us on grounds personal to ourselves. Our personal affinities, likings, and circumstances, have great power to sway our estimate of this or that poet's work, and to make us attach more importance to it as poetry than in itself it really possesses, because to us it is, or has been, of high importance. Here also we over-rate the object of our interest, and apply to it a language of praise which is quite exaggerated. And thus we get the source of a second fallacy in our poetic judgments —the fallacy caused by an estimate which we may call personal. . . .

Only one thing we may add as to the substance and matter of poetry, guiding ourselves by Aristotle's profound observation that the superiority of poetry over history consists in its possessing a higher truth and a higher seriousness. . . . Let us add, therefore, to what we have said, this: that the substance and matter of the best poetry acquire their special character from possessing, in an eminent degree, truth and seriousness. We may add yet further, what is in itself evident, that to the style and manner of the best poetry their special character, their accent, is given by their diction, and, even yet more, by their movement. And though we distinguish between the two characters, the two accents, of superiority, yet they are nevertheless vitally connected one with the other. The superior character of truth and seriousness, in the matter and substance of the best poetry, is inseparable from the superiority of diction and movement marking its style and manner. The two superiorities are closely related, and are in steadfast proportion one to the other. So far as high poetic truth and seriousness are wanting to a poet's matter and substance, so far also, we may be sure, will a high poetic stamp of diction and movement be wanting to his style and manner. In proportion as this high stamp of diction and movement, again, is absent from a poet's style and manner, we shall find, also, that high poetic truth and seriousness are absent from his substance and matter.

So stated, these are but dry generalities; their whole force lies in their application. And I could wish every student of poetry to make the application of them for himself. Made by himself, the application would impress itself upon his mind far more deeply than made by me. Neither will my limits allow me to make any full application of the generalities above propounded; . . . We are often told that an era is opening in which we are to see multitudes of a common sort of readers, and masses of a common sort of literature; that such readers do not want and could not relish anything better than such literature, and that to provide it is becoming a vast and profitable industry. Even if good literature entirely lost currency with the world, it would still be abundantly worth while to continue to enjoy it by oneself. But it never will lose currency with the world, in spite of momentary appearances; it never will lose supremacy. Currency and supremacy are insured to it, not indeed by the world's deliberate and conscious choice, but by something far deeper,—by the instinct of self-preservation in humanity.

from "The Social Function of Poetry"
by T. S. Eliot

The title of this essay is so likely to suggest different things to different people, that I may be excused for explaining first what I do not mean by it before going on to try to explain what I do mean. When we speak of the "function" of anything we are likely to be thinking of what that thing *ought* to do rather than of what it does do or has done. That is an important distinction, because I do not intend to talk about what I think poetry *ought* to do. People who tell us what poetry ought to do, especially if they are poets

Reprinted from *On Poetry and Poets,* by T. S. Eliot. © 1943, 1945, 1957 by T. S. Eliot. By permission of Farrar, Straus & Company, Inc. and Faber and Faber Ltd.

themselves, usually have in mind the particular kind of poetry that they would like to write. It is always possible, of course, that poetry may have a different task in the future from what it has had in the past; but even if that is so, it is worth while to decide first what function it has had in the past, both at one time or another in one language or another, and universally. I could easily write about what I do with poetry myself, or what I should like to do, and then try to persuade you that this is exactly what all good poets have tried to do, or ought to have done, in the past—only they have not succeeded completely, but perhaps that is not their fault. But it seems to me probable that if poetry—and I mean *all* great poetry— has had no social function in the past, it is not likely to have any in the future.

When I say *all* great poetry I mean to avoid another way in which I might treat the subject. One might take up the various kinds of poetry, one after another, and discuss the social function of each kind in turn without reaching the general question of what is the function of poetry as poetry. I want to distinguish between the general and particular functions, so that we shall know what we are not talking about. Poetry may have a deliberate, conscious social purpose. In its more primitive forms this purpose is often quite clear. There are, for example, early runes and chants, some of which had very practical magical purposes—to avert the evil eye, to cure some disease, or to propitiate some demon. Poetry is early used in religious ritual, and when we sing a hymn we are still using poetry for a particular social purpose. The early forms of epic and saga may have transmitted what was held to be history before surviving for communal entertainment only; and before the use of written language a regular verse form must have been ex- tremely helpful to the memory—and the memory of primitive bards, story-tellers and scholars must have been prodigious. In more advanced societies, such as that of ancient Greece, the recog- nized social functions of poetry are also very conspicuous. The

Greek drama develops out of religious rites, and remains a formal public ceremony associated with traditional religious celebrations; the pindaric ode develops in relation to a particular social occasion. Certainly, these definite uses of poetry gave poetry a framework which made possible the attainment of perfection in particular kinds.

In more modern poetry some of these forms remain, such as that of the religious hymn which I have mentioned. The meaning of the term *didactic* poetry has undergone some change. *Didactic* may mean "conveying information," or it may mean "giving moral instruction," or it may mean something which comprehends both. Virgil's *Georgics,* for instance, are very beautiful poetry, and contain some very sound information about good farming. But it would seem impossible, at the present day, to write an up-to-date book about farming which should also be fine poetry: for one thing the subject itself has become much more complicated and scientific; and for another, it can be handled more readily in prose. Nor should we, as the Romans did, write astronomical and cosmological treatises in verse. The poem, the ostensible aim of which is to convey information, has been superseded by prose. Didactic poetry has gradually become limited to poetry of moral exhortation, or poetry which aims to *persuade* the reader to the author's point of view about something. It therefore includes a great deal of what can be called *satire,* though satire overlaps with burlesque and parody, the purpose of which is primarily to cause mirth. Some of Dryden's poems, in the seventeenth century, are satires in the sense that they aim to ridicule the objects against which they are directed, and also didactic in the aim to persuade the reader to a particular political or religious point of view; and in doing this they also make use of the allegorical method of disguising reality as fiction: *The Hind and the Panther,* which aims to persuade the reader that right was on the side of the Church of Rome against the Church of England, is his most remarkable poem in this kind.

In the nineteenth century a good deal of the poetry of Shelley is inspired by a zeal for social and political reforms.

As for *dramatic* poetry, that has a social function of a kind now peculiar to itself. For whereas most poetry to-day is written to be read in solitude, or to be read aloud in a small company, dramatic verse alone has as its function the making an immediate, collective impression upon a large number of people gathered together to look at an imaginary episode acted upon a stage. Dramatic poetry is different from any other, but as its special laws are those of the drama its function is merged into that of the drama in general, and I am not here concerned with the special social function of the drama.

As for the special function of philosophical poetry, that would involve an analysis and an historical account of some length. I have, I think, already mentioned enough kinds of poetry to make clear that the special function of each is related to some other function: of dramatic poetry to drama, of didactic poetry of information to the function of its subject-matter, of didactic poetry of philosophy or religion or politics or morals to the function of these subjects. We might consider the function of any of these kinds of poetry and still leave untouched the question of the function of *poetry*. For all these things can be dealt with in prose.

But before proceeding I want to dismiss one objection that may be raised. People sometimes are suspicious of any poetry that has a particular purpose: poetry in which the poet is advocating social, moral, political or religious views. And they are much more inclined to say that it isn't poetry when they dislike the particular views; just as other people often think that something is real poetry because it happens to express a point of view which they like. I should say that the question of whether the poet is using his poetry to advocate or attack a social attitude does not matter. Bad verse may have a transient vogue when the poet is reflecting a popular attitude of the moment; but real poetry survives not only a change of popular opinion but the complete extinction of interest in the issues with which the poet was passionately concerned. Lucretius' poem remains a great poem, though his notions of physics and astronomy are discredited; Dryden's, though the political quarrels of the seventeenth century no longer concern us; just as a great poem of the past may still give great pleasure, though its subject-matter is one which we should now treat in prose.

Now if we are to find the essential social function of poetry we must look first at its more obvious functions, those which it must perform if it is to perform any. The first, I think, that we can be sure about is that poetry has to give pleasure. If you ask what kind of pleasure then I can only answer, the kind of pleasure that poetry gives: simply because any other answer would take us far afield into aesthetics, and the general question of the nature of art.

I suppose it will be agreed that every good poet, whether he be a great poet or not, has something to give us besides pleasure: for if it were only pleasure, the pleasure itself could not be of the highest kind. Beyond any specific intention which poetry may have, such as I have already instanced in the various kinds of poetry, there is always the communication of some new experience, or some fresh understanding of the familiar, or the expression of something we have experienced but have no words for, which enlarges our consciousness or refines our sensibility. But it is not with such individual benefit from poetry, any more than it is with the quality of individual pleasure, that this paper is concerned. We all understand, I think, both the kind of pleasure which poetry can give, and the kind of difference, beyond the pleasure, which it makes to our lives. Without producing these two effects it simply is not poetry. We may acknowledge this, but at the same time overlook something which it does for us collectively, as a society. And I mean that in the widest sense. For I think it is important that every people should have its own poetry, not simply for those who enjoy poetry—such people could always learn other languages and enjoy their poetry—but because it actually makes a difference to the society as a whole, and that means to people who do not enjoy poetry. I include even those who do not know the names of their own national poets. That is the real subject of this paper.

We observe that poetry differs from every other art in having a value for the people of the poet's race and language, which it can have for no other. It is true that even music and painting have a local and racial character: but certainly the difficulties of appreciation in these arts, for a foreigner, are much less. It is true on the other hand that prose writings have significance in their own language which is lost in translation; but we all feel that we lose much less in reading a novel in translation than in reading a poem; and in a translation of some kinds of scientific work the loss may be virtually nil. That poetry is much more local than prose can be seen in the history of European languages. Through the Middle Ages to within a few hundred years ago Latin remained the language for philosophy, theology, and science. The impulse towards the literary use of the languages of the peoples began with poetry. And this appears perfectly natural when we realize that poetry has primarily to do with the expression of feeling and emotion; and that feeling and emotion are particular, whereas thought is general. It is easier to think in a foreign language than it is to feel in it. Therefore no art is more stubbornly national than poetry. A people may have its language taken away from it, suppressed, and another language compelled upon the schools; but unless you teach that people to *feel* in a new language, you have not eradicated the old one, and it will reappear in poetry, which is the vehicle of feeling. I have just said "feel in a new language," and I mean something more than merely "express their feelings in a new language." A thought expressed in a different language may be practically the same thought, but a feeling or emotion expressed in a different language is not the same feeling or emotion. One of the reasons for learning at least one foreign language well is that we acquire a kind of supplementary personality; one of the reasons for not acquiring a new language *instead* of our own is that most of us do not want to become a different person. A superior language can seldom be exterminated except by the extermination of the people who speak it. When one language supersedes another it is usually because that language has advantages which commend it, and which offer not merely a difference but a wider and more refined range, not only for thinking but for feeling, than the more primitive language.

Emotion and feeling, then, are best expressed in the common language of the people—that is, in the language common to all classes: the structure, the rhythm, the sound, the idiom of a language, express the personality of the people which speaks it. When I say that it is poetry rather than prose that is concerned with the expression of emotion and feeling, I do not mean that poetry need have no intellectual content or meaning, or that great poetry does not contain more of such meaning than lesser poetry. But to develop this investigation would take me away from my immediate purpose. I will take it as agreed that people find the most conscious expression of their deepest feelings in the poetry of their own language rather than in any other art or in the poetry of other languages. This does not mean, of course, that true poetry is limited to feelings which everyone can recognize and understand; we must not limit poetry to *popular* poetry. It is enough that in a homogeneous people the feelings of the most refined and complex have something in common with those of the most crude and simple, which they have not in common with those of people of their own level speaking another language. And, when a civilization is healthy, the great poet will have something to say to his fellow countrymen at every level of education. . . .

drama

THIS SECTION includes selections from representative critics of the last four centuries. In Dryden's "An Essay of Dramatic Poesy," four disputants argue the question of whether a playwright should follow a set of rules. After agreeing upon a definition of a play, one of the characters (Crites) explains and defends these rules as the unities of time, place, and action. In the next century, Samuel Johnson takes up the argument. Showing how and why Shakespeare did not observe the unities except when it suited his purpose, Johnson argues persuasively against Crites's position and defends only the unity of action. Johnson's stand is taken upon interesting ground— the psychology of the audience. Upon this premise, much later dramatic criticism is based. In 1822, Charles Lamb objects to the drama of his own day because it is not artificial enough: the audience, he claims, wish to escape their humdrum lives, to avoid having to make moral choices while seeing a play. In the final selection, Eric Bentley, in 1946, attempts to explain why the theater is again "in trouble." Agreeing in one particular with Johnson, Bentley places the blame upon the audience. Our society, he says, has a middle-class taste that can only support inferior dramatic art. Through all four selections in this chapter runs the question, "What fosters the highest quality in the drama—observing the rules, following nature, satisfying an audience, or a special combination of these solutions?"

from "An Essay of Dramatic Poesy"
by John Dryden

. . . Eugenius was going to continue this discourse, when Lisideius told him that it was necessary, before they proceeded further, to take a standing measure of their controversy; for how was it possible to be decided who writ the best plays before we know what a play should be? But this once agreed on by both parties, each might have recourse to it, either to prove his own advantages or to discover the failings of his adversary.

He had no sooner said this, but all desired the favor of him to give the definition of a play; and they were the more importunate, because neither Aristotle nor Horace nor any other who had writ of that subject, had ever done it.

Lisideius, after some modest denials, at last confessed he had a rude notion of it; indeed, rather a description than a definition; but which served to guide him in his private thoughts, when he was to make a judgment of what others writ: that he conceived a play ought to be a *just and lively image of human nature, representing its passions and humors, and the changes of fortune to which it is subject, for the delight and instruction of mankind.*

This definition (though Crites raised a logical objection against it, that it was only *a genere et fine,* and so not altogether perfect) was yet well received by the rest; and after they had given order to the watermen to turn their barge and row softly, that they might take the cool of the evening in their return, Crites, being desired by the company to begin, spoke on behalf of the ancients, in this manner:

. . . "Out of these two [Aristotle's *Poetics* and Horace's *Art of Poetry*] have been extracted the famous rules, which the French call *Des Trois Unités,* or the Three Unities, which ought to be observed in every regular play; namely, of time, place, and action.

"The unity of time they comprehend in twenty-four hours, the compass of a natural day, or as near as it can be contrived; and the reason of it is obvious to everyone—that the time of the feigned action, or fable of the play, should be proportioned as near as can be to the duration of that time in which it is represented; since, therefore, all plays are acted on the theater in the space of time much within the compass of twenty-four hours, that play is to be thought the nearest imitation of nature, whose plot or action is confined within that time. And by the same rule which concludes this general proportion of time, it follows that all the parts of it are (as near as may be) to be equally subdivided; namely, that one act take not up the supposed time of half a day, which is out of proportion to the rest; since the other four are then to be straitened within the compass of the remaining half; for it is unnatural that one act which being spoke or written is not longer than the rest should be supposed longer by the audience; 'tis therefore the poet's duty to take care that no act should be imagined to exceed the time in which it is represented on the stage; and that the intervals and inequalities of time be supposed to fall out between the acts. . . .

"This rule of time, how well it has been observed by the ancients, most of their plays will witness. You see them in their tragedies (wherein to follow this rule, is certainly most difficult) from the very beginning of their plays falling close into that part of the story which they intend for the action or principal object of it, leaving the former part to be delivered by narration; so that they set the audience, as it were, at the post where the race is to be concluded; and saving them the tedious expectation of seeing the poet set out and ride the beginning of the course, they suffer you not to behold him till he is in sight of the goal and just upon you.

"For the second unity, which is that of place, the ancients meant by it that the scene ought to be continued through the play in the same place where it was laid in the beginning; for the stage on which it is represented being but one and the same place it is unnatural to conceive it many, and those far distant from one another. I will not deny but by the variation of painted scenes the fancy, which in these cases will contribute to its own deceit, may sometimes imagine it several places with some appearance of probability; yet it still carries the greater likelihood of truth, if those places be supposed so near each other as in the same town or city, which may all be comprehended under the larger denomination of one place; for a greater distance will bear no proportion to the shortness of time which is allotted, in the acting, to pass from one of them to another. For the observation of this, next to the ancients, the French are to be most commended. They tie themselves so strictly to the unity of place that you never see in any of their plays a scene changed in the middle of an act; if the act begins in a garden, a street, or chamber, 'tis ended in the same place; and that you may know it to be the same, the stage is so supplied with persons that it is never empty all the time; he who enters second has business with him who was on before; and before the second quits the stage, a third appears who has business with him. This Corneille calls *la liaison des scènes,* the continuity or joining of the scenes; and 'tis a good mark of a well-contrived play when all the persons are known to each other and every one of them has some affairs with all the rest.

"As for the third unity, which is that of action, the ancients meant no other by it than what the logicians do by their *finis,* the end or scope of any action—that which is the first in intention, and last in execution. Now the poet is to aim at one great and complete action, to the carrying on of which all things in his play, even the very obstacles, are to be subservient; and the reason of this is as evident as any of the former. For two actions, equally labored and driven on by the writer, would destroy the unity of the poem; it would be no longer one play, but two; not but that there may be many actions in a play, as Ben Jonson has observed in his *Discoveries;* but they must be all subservient to the great one (which our language happily expresses in the name of *under-plots*); such as in Terence's *Eunuch* is the difference and reconcilement of Thais and Phaedria, which is not the chief business of the play but promotes the marriage of Chaerea and Chremes's sister, principally intended by the poet. There ought to be but one action, says Corneille, that is, one complete action, which leaves the mind of the audience in a full repose; but this cannot be brought to pass but by many other imperfect actions which conduce to it and hold the audience in a delightful suspense of what will be.

"If by these rules (to omit many other drawn from the precepts and practice of the ancients) we should judge our modern plays, 'tis probable that few of them would endure the trial; that which should be the business of a day takes up in some of them an age; instead of one action, they are the epitomes of a man's life; and for one spot of ground which the stage should represent we are sometimes in more countries than the map can show us. . . ."

from *"Preface to Shakespeare"*
by Samuel Johnson

[Shakespeare's] histories, being neither tragedies nor comedies, are not subject to any of their laws. Nothing more is necessary to all the praise which they expect than that the changes of action be so prepared as to be understood; that the incidents be various and affecting, and the characters consistent, natural, and distinct. No other unity is intended, and therefore none is to be sought.

In his other works he has well enough preserved the unity of action. He has not, indeed, an intrigue regularly perplexed and regularly unraveled; he does not endeavor to hide his design only to discover it, for this is seldom the order of real events, and

Shakespeare is the poet of nature. But his plan has commonly what Aristotle requires, a beginning, a middle, and an end; one event is concatenated with another and the conclusion follows by easy consequence. There are perhaps some incidents that might be spared, as in other poets there is much talk that only fills up time upon the stage; but the general system makes gradual advances and the end of the play is the end of expectation.

To the unities of time and place he has shown no regard; and perhaps a nearer view of the principles on which they stand will diminish their value and withdraw from them the veneration which, from the time of Corneille, they have generally received, by discovering that they have given more trouble to the poet than pleasure to the auditor.

The necessity of observing the unities of time and place arises from the supposed necessity of making the drama credible. The critics hold it impossible that an action of months or years can be possibly believed to pass in three hours; or that the spectator can suppose himself to sit in the theater while ambassadors go and return between distant kings, while armies are levied and towns besieged, while an exile wanders and returns, or till he whom they saw courting his mistress shall lament the untimely fall of his son. The mind revolts from evident falsehood, and fiction loses its force when it departs from the resemblance of reality.

From the narrow limitation of time necessarily arises the contraction of place. The spectator who knows that he saw the first act at Alexandria cannot suppose that he sees the next at Rome, at a distance to which not the dragons of Medea could in so short a time have transported him. He knows with certainty that he has not changed his place, and he knows that place cannot change itself—that what was a house cannot become a plain; that what was Thebes can never be Persepolis.

Such is the triumphant language with which a critic exults over the misery of an irregular poet and exults commonly without resistance or reply. It is time, therefore, to tell him by the authority of Shakespeare that he assumes as an unquestionable principle a position which, while his breath is forming it into words, his understanding pronounces to be false. It is false that any representation is mistaken for reality; that any dramatic fable in its materiality was ever credible, or for a single moment was ever credited.

The objection arising from the impossibility of passing the first hour at Alexandra, and the next at Rome, supposes that when the play opens the spectator really imagines himself at Alexandria and believes that his walk to the theater has been a voyage to Egypt and that he lives in the days of Antony and Cleopatra. Surely he that imagines this may imagine more. He that can take the stage at one time for the palace of the Ptolemies may take it in half an hour for the promontory of Actium. Delusion, if delusion be admitted, has no certain limitation. If the spectator can be once persuaded that his old acquaintance are Alexander and Caesar, that a room illuminated with candles is the plain of Pharsalia, or the bank of Granicus, he is in a state of elevation above the reach of reason or of truth, and from the heights of empyrean poetry may despise the circumscriptions of terrestrial nature. There is no reason why a mind thus wandering in ecstasy should count the clock, or why an hour should not be a century in that calenture of the brains that can make the stage a field.

The truth is that the spectators are always in their senses, and know, from the first act to the last, that the stage is only a stage and that the players are only players. They come to hear a certain number of lines recited with just gesture and elegant modulation. The lines relate to some action, and an action must be in some place; but the different actions that complete a story may be in places very remote from each other; and where is the absurdity of allowing that space to represent first Athens and then Sicily, which was always known to be neither Sicily nor Athens but a modern theater? . . .

Whether Shakespeare knew the unities and rejected them by design, or deviated from them by happy ignorance, it is, I think, impossible to decide and useless to inquire. We may reasonably suppose that, when he rose to notice, he did not want the counsels and admonitions of scholars and critics, and that he at last deliberately persisted in a practice which he might have begun by chance. As nothing is essential to the fable but unity of action, and as the unities of time and place arise evidently from false assumptions and by circumscribing the extent of the drama lessen its variety, I cannot think it much to be lamented that they were not known by him or not observed. Nor, if such another poet could arise, should I very vehemently reproach him that his first act passed at Venice and his next in Cyprus. Such violations of rules merely positive become the comprehensive genius of Shakespeare, and such censures are suitable to the minute and slender criticism of Voltaire.

> *Non usque adeo permiscuit imis*
> *Longus summa dies, ut non, si voce Metelli*
> *Serventur leges, malint a Caesare tolli.*[1]

Yet when I speak thus slightly of dramatic rules, I cannot but recollect how much wit and learning may be produced against me. Before such authorities I am afraid to stand; not that I think the present question one of those that are to be decided by mere authority, but because it is to be suspected that these precepts have not been so easily received, but for better reasons than I have yet been able to find. The result of my inquiries, in which it would be ludicrous to boast of impartiality, is that the unities of time and place are not essential to a just drama; that, though they may sometimes conduce to pleasure, they are always to be sacrificed to

---

[1] "The long day has not so far confused the highest with the lowest that it is not preferable to have laws set aside by Caesar rather than have them preserved by the voice of Metellus" (Lucan, *Pharsalia*, III, 138–140).

the nobler beauties of variety and instruction; and that a play written with nice observation of critical rules is to be contemplated as an elaborate curiosity, as the product of superfluous and ostentatious art, by which is shown rather what is possible than what is necessary.

He that without diminution of any other excellence shall preserve all the unities unbroken, deserves the like applause with the architect who shall display all the orders of architecture in a citadel without any deduction from its strength. But the principal beauty of a citadel is to exclude the enemy, and the greatest graces of a play are to copy nature and instruct life.

Perhaps what I have here not dogmatically but deliberately written may recall the principles of the drama to a new examination. I am almost frighted at my own temerity; and, when I estimate the fame and the strength of those that maintain the contrary opinion, am ready to sink down in reverential silence, as Aeneas withdrew from the defense of Troy when he saw Neptune shaking the wall and Juno heading the besiegers. . . .

from "On the Artificial Comedy of the Last Century" by Charles Lamb

The artificial comedy, or comedy of manners, is quite extinct on our stage. Congreve and Farquhar show their heads once in seven years only, to be exploded and put down instantly. The times cannot bear them. Is it for a few wild speeches, an occasional license of dialogue? I think not altogether. The business of their dramatic

The second of three essays on "The Old Actors," published in the *London Magazine* (April, 1822).

characters will not stand the moral test. We screw everything up to that. Idle gallantry in a fiction, a dream, the passing pageant of an evening, startles us in the same way as the alarming indications of profligacy in a son or ward in real life should startle a parent or guardian. We have no such middle emotions as dramatic interests left. We see a stage libertine playing his loose pranks of two hours' duration, and of no after consequence, with the severe eyes which inspect real vices with their bearings upon two worlds. We are spectators to a plot or intrigue (not reducible in life to the point of strict morality), and take it all for truth. We substitute a real for a dramatic person, and judge him accordingly. We try him in our courts, from which there is no appeal to the *dramatis personae,* his peers. We have been spoiled with—not sentimental comedy—but a tyrant far more pernicious to our pleasures which has succeeded to it, the exclusive and all-devouring drama of common life; where the moral point is everything; where, instead of the fictitious half-believed personages of the stage (the phantoms of old comedy), we recognize ourselves, our brothers, aunts, kinsfolk, allies, patrons, enemies—the same as in life—with an interest in what is going on so hearty and substantial that we cannot afford our moral judgment, in its deepest and most vital results, to compromise or slumber for a moment. What is *there* transacting, by no modification is made to affect us in any other manner than the same events or characters would do in our relationships of life. We carry our fireside concerns to the theater with us. We do not go thither like our ancestors, to escape from the pressure of reality so much as to confirm our experience of it; to make assurance double, and take a bond of fate. We must live our toilsome lives twice over, as it was the mournful privilege of Ulysses to descend twice to the shades. All that neutral ground of character which stood between vice and virtue, or which in fact was indifferent to neither, where neither properly was called in question, that happy breathing-place from the burden of a perpetual moral questioning—the sanctuary and quiet Alsatia of hunted casuistry—is broken up and defranchised, as injurious to the interests of society. The privileges of the place are taken away by law. We dare not dally with images, or names, of wrong. We bark like foolish dogs at shadows. We dread infection from the scenic representation of disorder, and fear a painted pustule. In our anxiety that our morality should not take cold, we wrap it up in a great blanket surtout of precaution against the breeze and sunshine.

I confess for myself that (with no great delinquencies to answer for) I am glad for a season to take an airing beyond the diocese of the strict conscience—not to live always in the precincts of the law courts—but now and then, for a dream-while or so, to imagine a world with no meddling restrictions—to get into recesses, whither the hunter cannot follow me—

> —Secret shades
> Of woody Ida's inmost grove,
> While yet there was no fear of Jove.[1]

I come back to my cage and my restraint the fresher and more healthy for it. I wear my shackles more contentedly for having respired the breath of an imaginary freedom. I do not know how it is with others, but I feel the better always for the perusal of one of Congreve's—nay, why should I not add even of Wycherley's?—comedies. I am the gayer at least for it; and I could never connect those sports of a witty fancy in any shape with any result to be drawn from them to imitation in real life. They are a world of themselves almost as much as fairyland. Take one of their characters, male or female (with few exceptions they are alike), and place it in a modern play, and my virtuous indignation shall rise against the profligate wretch as warmly as the Catos of the pit could desire; because in a modern play I am to judge of the right and the wrong. The standard of *police* is the measure of *political justice*. The atmosphere will blight it; it cannot live here. It has got

[1] Milton, "Il Penseroso," ll. 28–30.

into a moral world, where it has no business, from which it must needs fall headlong; as dizzy and incapable of making a stand as a Swedenborgian bad spirit that has wandered unawares into the sphere of one of his Good Men or Angels. But in its own world do we feel the creature is so very bad?—The Fainalls, and the Mirabels,[2] the Dorimants[3] and the Lady Touchwoods,[4] in their own sphere, do not offend my moral sense; in fact, they do not appeal to it at all. They seem engaged in their proper element. They break through no laws of conscious restraints. They know of none. They have got out of Christendom into the land—what shall I call it?—of cuckoldry—the Utopia of gallantry, where pleasure is duty, and the manners perfect freedom. It is altogether a speculative scene of things, which has no reference whatever to the world that is. No good person can be justly offended as a spectator, because no good person suffers on the stage. Judged morally, every character in these plays—the few exceptions only are *mistakes*—is alike essentially vain and worthless. The great art of Congreve is especially shown in this, that he has entirely excluded from his scenes—some little generosities in the part of Angelica[5] perhaps excepted—not only anything like a faultless character, but any pretensions to goodness or good feelings whatsoever. Whether he did this designedly, or instinctively, the effect is as happy as the design (if design) was bold. I used to wonder at the strange power which his *Way of the World* in particular possesses of interesting you all along in the pursuits of characters for whom you absolutely care nothing—for you neither hate nor love his personages—and I think it is owing to this very indifference for any that you endure the whole. He has spread a privation of moral light, I will call it, rather than by the ugly name of palpable darkness, over his crea-

[2] Characters in Congreve's *Way of the World*.
[3] Character in Etherege's *Man of Mode*.
[4] Character in Congreve's *Double Dealer*.
[5] Character in Congreve's *Love for Love*.

tions; and his shadows flit before you without distinction or preference. Had he introduced a good character, a single gush of moral feeling, a revulsion of the judgment to actual life and duties, the impertinent Goshen would have only lighted to the discovery of deformities, which now are none because we think them none.

Translated into real life, the characters of his and his friend Wycherley's dramas, are profligates and strumpets—the business of their brief existence, the undivided pursuit of lawless gallantry. No other spring of action, or possible motive of conduct, is recognized; principles which, universally acted upon, must reduce this frame of things to a chaos. But we do them wrong in so translating them. No such effects are produced in *their* world. When we are among them, we are amongst a chaotic people. We are not to judge them by our usages. No reverend institutions are insulted by their proceedings—for they have none among them. No peace of families is violated—for no family ties exist among them. No purity of the marriage bed is stained—for none is supposed to have a being. No deep affections are disquieted, no holy wedlock bands are snapped asunder—for affection's depth and wedded faith are not of the growth of that soil. There is neither right nor wrong— gratitude or its opposite—claim or duty—paternity or sonship. Of what consequence is it to Virtue, or how is she at all concerned about it, whether Sir Simon or Dapperwit steal away Miss Martha; or who is the father of Lord Froth's or Sir Paul Pliant's children?

The whole is a passing pageant, where we should sit as unconcerned at the issues, for life or death, as at the battle of the frogs and mice. But, like Don Quixote, we take part against the puppets, and quite as impertinently. We dare not contemplate an Atlantis, a scheme, out of which our coxcombical moral sense is for a little transitory ease excluded. We have not the courage to imagine a state of things for which there is neither reward nor punishment. We cling to the painful necessities of shame and blame. We would indict our very dreams. . . .

from "Broadway—and the Alternative"
by Eric Bentley

Probably not many would join Mr. Bennett Cerf in denying that
the situation of the theater is today very problematic. Most discussions of the problem, however, go wrong—not in denying its existence but in regarding it as new and peculiar to our generation, and
thus in attributing it to some localized cause, such as the rise of
movies or the high Manhattan rents. It should be recognized that
the theater is almost always a problem. Over a century ago Carlyle
wrote: "Nay, do not we English hear daily for the last twenty
years, that the Drama is dead, or in a state of suspended anima-
tion: and are not medical men sitting on the case, and propounding
their remedial appliances, weekly, monthly, quarterly, to no manner
of purpose?" Such statements are to be found not only in times of
dramatic drought but also in the harvest seasons. Looking back on
the eighteen-nineties today, we regard them as years of considerable
dramatic achievement; Bernard Shaw's *Dramatic Opinions,* written
at the time, tell another story. We think of the Restoration as the
age of Congreve, yet the great comedian was very inconspicuous
in his own day, and his now acknowledged masterpiece was a total
failure on the stage. Shakespeare, the most read and the most performed of all dramatists, was probably best known in his lifetime
for his cheapest and rawest plays, and a contemporary editor boasts
that one of his best plays was "never clapper-clawed by the hands
of the vulgar."

The theater is always in trouble because its success depends
upon too rare a set of coincidences. A poem needs only an author
and a reader. A sonata needs a composer, a performer, and a

listener. Closer to the drama is the symphony, which requires team-work, co-ordination at the hands of a conductor, a large audience, and a heap of money. The drama, however, boasting of being a meeting place of all the arts, requires a too rare conjunction of economic, social, and artistic elements. Especially in its synthetic manifestations, which include everything in musical-choreographic-spectacular-mimetic-rhetorical theater from the Greeks to *Tann-häuser* and beyond, drama is the most impossible of the arts.

Yet the very citation of titles reminds us of its possibility. The fact is that, while high theater has a harder time than any other high art, the popular theater, dedicated to entertainment, and today functioning chiefly on the screen and over the air, is perpetually the most flourishing of the arts. It is the art which most excites children, savages, and all who are least conscious of artistic leanings. It seems to be an inextinguishable and indispensable art, an addiction more universal than smoking. It followed the doughboys to foxholes on tropical islands. It followed the dehumanized, doubly "mechanized" divisions of the Third Reich. It lures the schoolboy twice a week to the movies; it entices the student to turn on the radio while supposedly studying.

Entertainment means the redemption of leisure time by a pleasing titillation of the senses and of that small part of the brain which the simplest jokes call into play. Entertainment is an infinitely complex industry devoted to the evocation of the crudest responses. In its modern form it presupposes an audience that is already tired, inclined to be bored, probably not educated and certainly not cultured, yet not totally illiterate, but acquainted with that segment of knowledge and sensibility provided by the radio and the press. The power of entertainment in modern life is shown by the fact that even the knowledge presupposed in entertainment is acquired through entertainment, for what is modern reporting and propaganda if not a cunning use of histrionic method in the commercial, political, and educational spheres? All information is nowadays supposed to be "entertainingly" presented, and the results are evident in radio news reports and radio advertising, in the screen popularization of musical and literary classics, and in schools where the pupils expect to be entertained by the teacher. The founders of democracy hoped and expected that universal suffrage would mean a sober presentation of issues to a people which would soberly weigh them. A recent development, however, is the setting of political slogans to hot jazz choral music and the staging of vast political pageants that would be the envy of a Roman emperor. At the center of these entertainments is the very symbol of entertainment itself, the man-god, hero, and totem animal of modern civilization, the film star.

The techniques of the theater, run wild, have taken over every other branch of public communication, especially in countries where industrialism and mechanization have gone furthest. The Salvation Army began the application of the methods of mass entertainment to religion, and visitors to Aimee Semple MacPherson's Los Angeles Temple know how far the idea has been carried since the days of General Booth. Northcliffe and Hearst pursued the same art in politics, and Goebbels turned their skill into an industry. A Nazi rally, where masses of soldiers saluted and applauded and sang at given signals, where music, spectacle, and oratory combined in a macabre *gesamtkunstwerk,*[1] and where the master tragicomedian himself played systematically upon every group prejudice and stock response—this was at once the apotheosis and the nemesis of entertainment.

Entertainment has almost been the death of all the arts. How could music hope to survive the onslaughts of the popularizers? What room is there for Beethoven in a world where a hundred hacks make his music "more entertaining" by removing his individuality? How could literature survive the *Saturday Evening Post?*

[1] [Mass spectacle. Literally, "combined work of art."]

Recently a writer in that journal defended himself with the argument that Shakespeare also was a popular writer, not afraid to use as material the cliché absurdities of current convention. Great writers, he argued, come out of the hard school of commercial writing, not out of coteries. The hard-headedness of the remark and its one per cent of truth give it the color of plausibility, and while criticism remains unhistorical the argument is not easily disposed of. But history supplies the answers, and they are germane to our theme. To be popular in an aristocratic culture, like ancient Greece or Elizabethan England, is quite a different manner from being popular in a middle-class culture. Like Dr. Johnson, our critic is suspicious of those who do not write for money. And there is nothing wrong with money. It all depends on what is demanded of you in return. To earn his living Shakespeare had, for example, to acquire a highly complex literary language, far above the usage of his native Stratford; to earn his, the modern *Post* writer has to unlearn anything he might have learned from acknowledged classics, or from the depths of personal experience, and acquire the crude, vacuum-concealing lingo which titillates the miseducated sensibility.

That is only one factor among many, but it permits us to glimpse the difference between Elizabethan and modern culture. Industrialism, capitalism, and the democratic movement created an unprecedented cultural situation; its problems are the subject of all the anti-industrialist, anticapitalist, and antidemocratic literature which lovers of the arts have written in the past hundred and fifty years. The essence of the matter is that the extension of literacy to the previously illiterate majority created, not a nation of philosophers, but a nation of newspaper readers. In this context popularity takes on a new meaning.

Popularity is a very flexible term and an impossible criterion. Medieval and Chinese drama are "popular" in that they appeal to a totally illiterate populace; the "popular" *Post* is read by many college graduates and, perhaps, hardly at all by the least educated classes for whom the funnies and the pulps suffice. The pulps are "popular"; so is Somerset Maugham. The difference can be appreciated only by those who recognize the cultural stratification which has taken place in recent generations. While changes in the mechanics of communication and the promotion of democratic and religious ideas have in modern times brought men closer together, other forces have wrenched them apart. One need hardly mention nationalist politics, imperialist economics, and racial ideology. The same technology which brought men closer through mechanized transport and telegraphy kept them apart by the mention of their manufacture, mass production. The kind of man they created was portrayed by Charlie Chaplin in *Modern Times*.

There is no need to linger over the general matter of middle-class culture. The point is that if the new conditions have significance for the culture as a whole, they have all the more significance for the drama, which has had the closest link with the people, possibly, of all the arts. In the days before general literacy, the drama was, with the sermon, the great bond between verbal culture and the people; in books on the drama one constantly reads that drama is the least esoteric, the most democratic of the arts. Drama critics are indeed never tired of asserting that great drama belongs to the people, and that obscurity and "rareness" are out of place on the stage; theorists of the drama insist on the communal character of theatrical experience and cite LeBon on the psychology of the crowd. Well and good. But what becomes of the drama in an age like ours when popular taste is debauched, when "entertainment" has a monopoly of public attention, when greedy capital controls production and consumption alike? Lowbrow writers will repeat their argument that art, particularly dramatic art, is always an adjustment of an artist's purpose to public demand. But, as I have said, it all depends on what is demanded: if the public's demands, or the plutocrat's demands, are degrading, we shall not have dramatic art at all; which is the situation on Broadway today.

To be sure, drama depends on an audience, upon common human experience, upon crowd psychology; but there are crowds and crowds. There is a difference between an audience of Athenians at a time when the Athenian citizenry represented, so we are told, one of the peaks of human and social development, an audience for whom a play was also an important rite, and a crowd of oddly miseducated twentieth-century folk who for years have been subjected to half-baked ideas and cheap sensations.

At this point someone will say that, at times when drama flourished, audiences were not always Periclean. They were often illiterate or frivolous or both. When Stanislavsky audiences changed from the sophisticated upper classes of Tsarism to the ignorant peasantry and proletariat of the early Soviet years, this very aristocratic director was, after initial apprehension, delighted by the spontaneity and keenness of the latter, even when the play performed was *The Cherry Orchard*. Such facts prove that an ignorant audience can enjoy a great play. They do not prove that all ignorant audiences would enjoy that play or that even the same ignorant audience would enjoy every great play. They do not reveal how far such an audience understands the play, nor do they help us to settle what for us is the great problem, the problem not of the ignorant and illiterate but that of the half-literate, the possessors of the little knowledge which is a dangerous thing, the readers of the pulps and the Hearst press, and even the comparative high-brows who read *Collier's* and the *Saturday Evening Post*. Today it is almost inconceivable that any drama would satisfy the canons of the most exacting criticism and also be popular. Already in the nineteenth century, Matthew Arnold wondered whether drama had become an impossibility. The vulgarization and consequent social stratification of culture had gone too far, he seems to have thought, and modern British society in particular lacked the homogeneity which drama requires. Some critics have met the situation by lowering their standards. They consider the exacting critics *too* exacting, and erupt occasionally in jibes against high-brows, aesthetes, sophisticates, and coteries. More disconcerting are the arguments of those who are distressed by mediocrity yet who are reluctant to draw revolutionary conclusions.

Theatre Arts, the only theatrical magazine of repute in the English-speaking world, frequently publishes such arguments. One of its most intelligent writers, Mr. George Beiswanger, has gone so far as to discourage us from even *trying* to make a home for drama in America. The drama, he observes, has little past and little present here, and there is no reason to suppose that it will have a future—"which may or may not be too bad," he adds; "after all, there is no moral compulsion, is there, for any one type or branch of art to continue in existence?" Mr. Beiswanger thinks that vaudeville will do instead of drama. "Such a masterpiece" as *Oklahoma!* possesses a "perfection" which has "deep subconscious roots." At last the Composite Art Work has triumphed:

> There is one stage today on which all the theater arts unite in happy combination to produce theater that is sheer, ample, and without inner tension or quarrel. I refer again to the musical stage, to such natural triumphs of the American theater imagination as *Lady in the Dark* and *Oklahoma!* Grant that these are not Shakespeare nor Euripides nor Dante. But they come close to being Aristophanes or Moliere. Increasingly they approach opera. And they are our own, genuine outpourings of American temperament, honest mirrorings of what we are. An age cannot fight itself. It has to make what theater it can. . . .

Here is a revived and jazzified Wagnerism which does not omit Wagner's nationalism and praise of the soil nor his belief in the historical inevitability of his success. One is tempted to meet assertion with assertion by retorting bluntly: *Oklahoma!* is *not* in the same class as *Tartuffe,* commercial musical comedy does *not* approach great opera. . . . And what can an age do except fight itself? The great minds of the modern age are the great fighters against the modern age. An age can and must fight itself. . . .

the novel

IN THE FOLLOWING selections on the novel, each of the four critics is concerned with the definition of a novel; also, the selections attempt to describe a novelist's proper subject matter. In the first selection, Hawthorne calls one of his own works a romance, in order to distinguish it from the novel. He asks to be allowed a freedom of fancy that a novelist could not claim. In this passage, Hawthorne is one of the first writers of fiction to describe the novel as a reflection of reality. For Henry James, a novel is defined by its structure; he asserts that the novel is an art form, that the novelist is an artist whose duty is to create an illusion, a "sense of reality." As long as the novelist accomplishes this goal, James would allow him to deal with any subject matter. Émile Zola disagrees; he is not basically concerned with illusion but with what he calls a scientific process. In this process he believes the novelist can explain man to himself completely. Zola's was a revolutionary idea, and it resulted in a whole school of writers who tried to practice it. (See *Naturalism* in the "Glossary of Literary Terms.") Finally, Lionel Trilling makes an interesting distinction that may account for many differences between British and American novels—the difference between novels written with a social theme and those lacking such a theme.

327

Preface to The House of Seven Gables
by Nathaniel Hawthorne

When a writer calls his work a Romance, it need hardly be observed that he wishes to claim a certain latitude, both as to its fashion and material, which he would not have felt himself entitled to assume had he professed to be writing a Novel. The latter form of composition is presumed to aim at a very minute fidelity, not merely to the possible, but to the probable and ordinary course of man's experience. The former—while, as a work of art, it must rigidly subject itself to laws, and while it sins unpardonably so far as it may swerve aside from the truth of the human heart—has fairly a right to present that truth under circumstances, to a great extent, of the writer's own choosing or creation. If he think fit, also, he may so manage his atmospherical medium as to bring out or mellow the lights and deepen and enrich the shadows of the picture. He will be wise, no doubt, to make a very moderate use of the privileges here stated, and, especially, to mingle the Marvellous rather as a slight, delicate, and evanescent flavor, than as any portion of the actual substance of the dish offered to the public. He can hardly be said, however, to commit a literary crime even if he disregard this caution.

In the present work, the author has proposed to himself—but with what success, fortunately, it is not for him to judge—to keep undeviatingly within his immunities. The point of view in which this tale comes under the Romantic definition lies in the attempt to connect a bygone time with the very present that is flitting away from us. It is a legend prolonging itself, from an epoch now gray in the distance, down into our own broad daylight, and bringing along with it some of its legendary mist, which the reader, according to his pleasure, may either disregard, or allow it to float almost imperceptibly about the characters and events for the sake of a picturesque effect. The narrative, it may be, is woven of so humble a texture as to require this advantage, and, at the same time, to render it the more difficult of attainment.

Many writers lay very great stress upon some definite moral purpose, at which they profess to aim their works. Not to be deficient in this particular, the author has provided himself with a moral,—the truth, namely, that the wrong-doing of one generation lives into the successive ones, and, divesting itself of every temporary advantage, becomes a pure and uncontrollable mischief; and he would feel it a singular gratification if this romance might effectually convince mankind—or, indeed, any one man—of the folly of tumbling down an avalanche of ill-gotten gold, or real estate, on the heads of an unfortunate posterity, thereby to maim and crush them, until the accumulated mass shall be scattered abroad in its original atoms. In good faith, however, he is not sufficiently imaginative to flatter himself with the slightest hope of this kind. When romances do really teach anything, or produce any effective operation, it is usually through a far more subtle process than the ostensible one. The author has considered it hardly worth his while, therefore, relentlessly to impale the story with its moral as with an iron rod,—or, rather, as by sticking a pin through a butterfly,— thus at once depriving it of life, and causing it to stiffen in an ungainly and unnatural attitude. A high truth, indeed, fairly, finely, and skilfully wrought out, brightening at every step, and crowning the final development of a work of fiction, may add an artistic glory, but is never any truer, and seldom any more evident, at the last page than at the first.

The reader may perhaps choose to assign an actual locality to the imaginary events of this narrative. If permitted by the historical connection,—which, though slight, was essential to his plan,—the author would very willingly have avoided anything of this nature. Not to speak of other objections, it exposes the romance to an inflexible and exceedingly dangerous species of criticism, by bringing his fancy-pictures almost into positive contact with the realities of the moment. It has been no part of his object, however, to describe local manners, nor in any way to meddle with the characteristics of a community for whom he cherishes a proper respect and a natural regard. He trusts not to be considered as unpardonably offending by laying out a street that infringes upon nobody's private rights, and appropriating a lot of land which had no visible owner, and building a house of materials long in use for constructing castles in the air. The personages of the tale—though they give themselves out to be of ancient stability and considerable prominence—are really of the author's own making, or, at all events, of his own mixing; their virtues can shed no lustre, nor their defects redound, in the remotest degree, to the discredit of the venerable town of which they profess to be inhabitants. He would be glad, therefore, if—especially in the quarter to which he alludes—the book may be read strictly as a Romance, having a great deal more to do with the clouds overhead than with any portion of the actual soil of the County of Essex.

from "The Experimental Novel" by Émile Zola

[The late French scientist and author of *Introduction to the Study of Experimental Medicine*] Claude Bernard discusses observation and experiment at great length. There exists . . . a very clear line of demarcation, as follows: "The name of 'observer' is given to him who applies the simple or complex process of investigation in the study of phenomena which he does not vary, and which he gathers, consequently, as nature offers them to him; the name of 'experimentalist' is given to him who employs the simple and complex process of investigation to vary or modify, for an end of some kind, the natural phenomena, and to make them appear under circumstances and conditions in which they are not presented by nature." For instance, astronomy is a science of observation, because you cannot conceive of an astronomer acting upon the stars; while chemistry is an experimental science, as the chemist acts upon nature and modifies it. . . . I repeat [Bernard's] words: ". . . experiment is an observation instigated for the purpose of verification. . . . The observer relates purely and simply the phenomena which he has under his eyes. . . . He should be the photographer of phenomena, his observation should be an exact representation of nature . . . He listens to nature and he writes under its dictation. But once the fact is ascertained and the phenomenon observed, an idea or hypothesis comes into his mind, reason intervenes, and the experimentalist comes forward to interpret the phenomenon. . . ."

Now, to return to the novel, we can easily see that the novelist is equally an observer and an experimentalist. The observer in him gives the facts as he has observed them, suggests the point of departure, displays the solid earth on which his characters are to tread and the phenomena to develop. Then the experimentalist appears and introduces an experiment, . . . sets his characters going in a certain story so as to show that the succession of facts will be such as the requirement of the determination of the phenomena under examination call for. . . . I will take as an example the character of the Baron Hulot in "Cousine Bette," by Balzac. The general fact observed by Balzac is the ravages that the amorous temperament of a man makes in his home, in his family, and in society. As soon as he has chosen his subject, he starts from known facts; then he makes his experiment, and exposes Hulot to a series of trials, placing him amid certain surroundings in order to exhibit how the complicated machinery of his passions works. It is then evident that there is not only observation there, but that there is also experiment; as Balzac does not remain satisfied with photographing the facts collected by him, but interferes in a direct way to place his character in certain conditions, and of these he remains the master. The problem is to know what such a passion, acting in such a surrounding and under such circumstances, would produce from the point of view of an individual and of society; and an experimental novel, 'Cousine Bette,' for example, is simply the report of the experiment that the novelist conducts before the eyes of the public. In fact, the whole operation consists in taking facts in nature, then in studying the mechanism of these facts, acting upon them, by the modification of circumstances and surroundings, without deviating from the laws of nature. Finally, you possess knowledge of the man, scientific knowledge of him, in both his individual and social relations. . . .

A contemptible reproach which they heap upon us naturalistic writers is the desire to be solely photographers. We have in vain declared that we admit the necessity of an artist's possessing an individual temperament and a personal expression. . . . The idea of experiment carries with it the idea of modification. We start, indeed, from the true facts, which are our indestructible basis; but to show the mechanism of these facts it is necessary for us to produce and direct the phenomena; this is our share of invention, here is the genius in the book. . . .

[Bernard] makes doubt the great scientific lever. "The doubter is the true savant; he doubts only himself and his interpretations; he believes in science; he even admits in the experimental sciences a criterion or a positive principle, the determinism of phenomena, which is absolute in living beings as in inanimate bodies." Thus, instead of confining the novelist within narrow bounds, the experimental method gives full sway to his intelligence as a thinker, and to his genius as a creator. . . .

[If] the experimental method can be carried from chemistry and physics into physiology and medicine, it can also be carried from physiology into the naturalistic novel.

Cuvier . . . pretended that experiment as applied to inanimate bodies could not be used with living beings. . . . The vitalists even admit a vital force in unceasing battle with the physical and chemical forces neutralizing their action. Claude Bernard, on the contrary, denies all presence of a mysterious force, and affirms that experiment is applicable everywhere. "I propose," he says, "to establish the fact that the science of the phenomena of life can have no other basis than the science of the phenomena of inanimate bodies, and that there are, in this connection, no differences between the principles of biological science and those of physics and chemistry. In fact, the end the experimental method proposes is the same everywhere; it consists in connecting, by experiment, the natural phenomena to their conditions of existence or to their nearest causes. . . . [The vitalists] consider life as a mysterious and supernatural agent, which acts arbitrarily, free from all determinism, and they condemn as materialists all those who endeavor to trace vital phenomena to definite organic and physiochemical conditions. These are false ideas, which it is not easy to root out once they have become domiciled in the mind; only the progress of science can dissipate them." And he lays down this axiom: "With living beings as well as inanimate, the conditions of the existence of each phenomenon are determined in an absolute manner." . . .

Thus you see the progress which science has made. In the last century a more exact application of the experimental method creates physics and chemistry, which then are freed from the irrational and supernatural. Men discover that there are fixed laws, thanks to analysis, and make themselves masters of phenomena. Then . . . living beings, in which the vitalists still admitted a mysterious influence, are in their turn brought under and reduced to the general mechanism of matter. Science proves that the existing conditions of all phenomena are the same in living beings as in inanimate; and from that time on physiology assumes little by little the certainty of chemistry and medicine. But are we going to stop there? Evidently not. When it has been proved that the body of man is a machine, whose machinery can be taken apart and put together again at the will of the experimenter, then we can pass to the passionate and intellectual acts of man. Then we shall enter into the domain which up to the present has belonged to physiology and literature; it will be the decisive conquest by science of the hypotheses of philosophers and writers. We have experimental chemistry and medicine; we shall have an experimental physiology, and later on an experimental novel. It is an inevitable evolution, the goal of which it is easy to see today. All things hang together; it is necessary to start from the determinism of inanimate bodies in order to arrive at the determinism of living beings; and since savants like Claude Bernard demonstrate now that fixed laws govern the human body, we can easily proclaim . . . the hour in which the laws of thought and passion will be formulated in their turn. A like determinism will govern the stones of the roadway and the brain of man. . . .

I consider that the question of heredity has a great influence in the intellectual and passionate manifestations of man. I also attach considerable importance to the surroundings. I ought to touch upon Darwin's theories . . . but I will only say a word on the subject of surroundings. We have just seen the great importance given by Claude Bernard to the study of those inter-organic conditions which must be taken into account if we wish to find the determinism of phenomena in living beings. Well, then! in the study of a family, of a group of living beings, I think that the social condition is of equal importance. Some day the physiologist will explain to us the mechanism of the thoughts and the passions; we shall know how the individual machinery of each man works; how he thinks, how he loves, how he goes from reason to passion and folly; but these phenomena, resulting as they do from the mechanism of the organs, acting under the influence of an interior condition, are not produced in isolation or in the bare void. Man is not alone; he lives in society . . . and consequently, for us novelists, this social condition unceasingly modifies the phenomena. Indeed our great study is just there, in the reciprocal effect of society on the individual and the individual on society. For the physiologist, the exterior and interior conditions are purely chemical and physical, and this aids him in finding the laws which govern them easily. We are not yet able to prove that the social condition is also physical and chemical. It is that certainly, or rather it is the variable product of a group of living beings who themselves are absolutely submissive to the physical and chemical laws which govern alike living beings and inanimate. From this we shall see that we can act upon the social conditions, in acting upon the phenomena of which we have made ourselves master in man. And this is what constitutes the experimental novel: to possess a knowledge of the mechanism of the phenomena inherent in man, to show the machinery of his intellectual and sensory manifestations, under the influences of heredity and environment, such as physiology shall give them to us, and then finally to exhibit man living in social conditions produced by himself, which he modifies daily, and in the heart of which he himself experiences a continual transformation. . . .

[The] dream of the physiologist and the experimental doctor is also that of the novelist, who employs the experimental method in his study of man as a simple individual and as a social animal. Their object is ours; we also desire to master certain phenomena of an intellectual and personal order, to be able to direct them. We are, in a word, experimental moralists, showing by experiment in what way a passion acts in a certain social condition. The day in which we gain control of the mechanism of this passion we can treat it and reduce it, or at least make it as inoffensive as possible. And in this consists the practical utility and high morality of our naturalistic works, which experiment on man, and which dissect piece by piece this human machinery in order to set it going through the influence of the environment. When things have advanced further, when we are in possession of the different laws,

it will only be necessary to work upon the individuals and the surroundings if we wish to find the best social condition. In this way
we shall construct a practical sociology, and our work will be a
help to political and economical sciences. I do not know . . . of a
more noble work. . . . To be the master of good and evil, to regulate life, to regulate society, to solve in time all the problems of
socialism, above all, to give justice a solid foundation by solving
through experiment the questions of criminality—is not this being
the most useful and the most moral workers in the human work-
shop?

Claude Bernard says truly: "The intellectual conquest of man
consists in diminishing and driving back indeterminism, and so,
gradually, by the aid of experimental method, gaining ground for
determinism." . . . If our work, often cruel, if our terrible pictures
needed justification, I should find, indeed, with Claude Bernard this
argument conclusive: "You will never reach really fruitful and
luminous generalizations on the phenomena of life until you have
experimented yourself and stirred up in the hospital, the amphi-
theatre, and the laboratory the fetid or palpitating sources of life.
If it were necessary for me to give a comparison which would explain my sentiments on the science of life, I should say that it is a
superb salon, flooded with light, which you can only reach by passing through a long and nauseating kitchen." . . .

They think to crush the naturalistic novelists by treating them as
fatalists. How many times have they wished to prove to us that as
soon as we did not accept free will, that as soon as man was no
more to us than a living machine, acting under the influence of
heredity and surroundings, we should fall into gross fatalism, we
should debase humanity to the rank of a troop marching under
the baton of destiny. It is necessary to define our terms: we are
not fatalists, we are determinists, which is not at all the same thing.
Claude Bernard explains the two terms very plainly: "We have
given the name of determinism to the nearest or determining cause

of phenomena. We never act upon the essence of phenomena in nature, but only on their determinism, and by this very fact, that we act upon it, determinism differs from fatalism, upon which we could not act at all. Fatalism assumes that the appearance of any phenomenon is necessary apart from its conditions, while determinism is just the condition essential for the appearance of any phenomenon, and such appearance is never forced. . . ." All we do is to apply this method in our novels, and we are the determinists who experimentally try to determine the condition of the phenomena, without departing in our investigations from the laws of nature. As Claude Bernard very truly says, the moment that we can act, and that we do act, on the determining cause of phenomena—by modifying their surroundings, for example—we cease to be fatalists.

As our power [as novelists] is not the same as that of a savant, as we are experimentalists without being practitioners, we ought to content ourselves with searching out the determinism of social phenomena, and leaving to legislators and to men of affairs the care of controlling sooner or later these phenomena in such a way as to develop the good and reject the bad, from the point of view of their utility to man. . . . Compare with ours the work of the idealistic writers, who rely upon the irrational and the supernatural, and whose every flight upward is followed by a deeper fall into metaphysical chaos. We are the ones who possess strength and morality. . . .

Let it be well understood that I am speaking of the "how" of things and not of the "why." For an experimental savant, the ideal which he is endeavoring to reduce, the indeterminate, is always restricted to the "how." He leaves to philosophers the other ideal, that of the "why," which he despairs of determining. I think that the experimental novelists equally ought not to occupy themselves with this unknown quality, unless they wish to lose themselves in the follies of the poets and the philosophers. It is surely an object large enough to try to know the entire mechanism of nature, without troubling one's self for the time being with the origin of the mechanism.

from "The Art of Fiction"
by Henry James

. . . It is equally excellent and inconclusive to say that one must write from experience; to our suppositious aspirant such a declaration might savor of mockery. What kind of experience is intended, and where does it begin and end? Experience is never limited, and it is an immense sensibility, a kind of huge spider-web of the finest silken threads suspended in the chamber of consciousness, and catching every air-borne particle in its tissue. It is the very atmosphere of the mind; and when the mind is imaginative—much more when it happens to be that of a man of genius—it takes to itself the faintest hints of life, it converts the very pulses of the air into revelations. The young lady living in a village has only to be a damsel upon whom nothing is lost to make it quite unfair (as it seems to me) to declare to her that she shall have nothing to say about the military. Greater miracles have been seen than that, imagination assisting, she should speak the truth about some of these gentlemen. I remember an English novelist, a woman of genius, telling me that she was much commended for the impression she had managed to give in one of her tales of the nature and way of life of the French Protestant youth. She had been asked where she learned so much about this recondite being, she had been congratulated on her peculiar opportunities. These opportunities consisted in her having once, in Paris, as she ascended a staircase, passed an open door where, in the household of a *pasteur,* some of the young Protestants were seated at table round a finished meal. The glimpse made a picture; it lasted only a moment, but that moment was experience. She had got her direct personal impression, and she turned out her type. She knew what youth was, and what Protestantism; she also had the advantage of having seen what it was to be French, so that she converted these ideas into a concrete image and produced a reality. Above all, however, she was blessed with the faculty which when you give it an inch takes an ell, and which for the artist is a much greater source of strength than any accident of residence or of place in the social scale. The power to guess the unseen from the seen, to trace the implication of things, to judge the whole piece by the pattern, the condition of feeling life in general so completely that you are well on your way to knowing any particular corner of it—this cluster of gifts may almost be said to constitute experience, and they occur in country and in town, and in the most differing stages of education. If experience consists of impressions, it may be said that impressions are experience, just as (have we not seen it?) they are the very air we breathe. Therefore, if I should certainly say to a novice, "Write from experience and from experience only," I should feel that this was rather a tantalizing monition if I were not careful immediately to add, "Try to be one of the people on whom nothing is lost!"

I am far from intending by this to minimize the importance of exactness—of truth of detail. One can speak best from one's own taste, and I may therefore venture to say that the air of reality (solidity of specification) seems to me to be the supreme virtue of a novel—the merit on which all its other merits helplessly and submissively depend. If it be not there they are all as nothing, and if these be there, they owe their effect to the success with which the author has produced the illusion of life. The cultivation of this success, the study of this exquisite process, form, to my taste, the beginning and the end of the art of the novelist. They are his inspiration, his despair, his reward, his torment, his delight. It is here in very truth that he competes with life; it is here that he competes with his brother the painter in *his* attempts to render the look of things, the look that conveys their meaning, to catch the color, the relief, the expression, the surface, the substance of the human spectacle. He cannot possibly take too many [notes], he cannot possibly take enough. All life solicits him, and to "render" the simplest surface, to produce the most momentary illusion, is a very complicated business. But this, I fear, he can never learn in any manual; it is the business of his life. He has to take a great many [notes] in order to select a few, he has to work them up as he can, and even the guides and philosophers who might have most to say to him must leave him alone when it comes to the application of precepts, as we leave the painter in communion with his palette. That his characters "must be clear in outline"—he feels that down to his boots; but how he shall make them so is a secret between his good angel and himself. It would be absurdly simple if he could be taught that a great deal of "description" would make them so, or that on the contrary the absence of description and the cultivation of dialogue, or the absence of dialogue and the multiplication of "incident," would rescue him from his difficulties. Nothing, for instance, is more possible than that he be of a turn of mind for which this odd, literal opposition of description and dialogue, incident and description, has little meaning and light. People often talk of these things as if they had a kind of internecine distinctness, instead of melting into each other at every breath, and being intimately associated parts of one general effort of expression. I cannot imagine composition existing in a series of blocks, nor conceive, in any novel worth discussing at all, of a passage of description that is not in its intention narrative, a passage of dialogue that is not in its intention descriptive, a touch of truth of any sort that does not partake of the nature of incident, or an incident that derives its interest from any other source than the general and only source of the success of a work of art—that of being illustrative. A novel is a living thing, all one and continuous, like any other organism, and in proportion as it lives will it be found, I think, that in each of the parts there is something of each of the other parts. The critic who over the close texture of a finished work shall pretend to trace a geography of items will mark some frontiers as artificial, I fear, as any that have been known to history. There is an old-fashioned distinction between the novel of character and the novel of incident which must have cost many a smile to the intending fabulist who was keen about his work. It appears to me as little to the point as the equally celebrated distinction between the novel and the romance—to answer as little to any reality. There are bad novels and good novels, as there are bad pictures and good pictures; but that is the only distinction in which I see any meaning, and I can as little imagine speaking of a novel of character as I can imagine speaking of a picture of character. When one says picture one says of character, when one says novel one says of incident, and the terms may be transposed at will. What is character but the determination of incident? What is incident but the illustration of character? What is either a picture or a novel that is not of character? What else do we seek in it and find in it? It is an incident for a woman to stand up with her hand resting on a table and look at you in a certain way; or if it be not an incident I think it will be hard to say what it is. At the same time it is an expression of character. If you say you don't see it (character in *that—allons donc!*), this is exactly what the artist who has reasons of his own for thinking he does see it undertakes to show you. When a young man makes up his mind that he has not faith enough after all to enter the Church as he intended, that is an incident, though you may not hurry to the end of the chapter to see whether perhaps he doesn't change once more. I do not say that these are extraordinary or startling incidents. I do not pretend to estimate the degree of interest proceeding from them, for this will depend upon the skill of the painter. It sounds almost puerile to say that some incidents are intrinsically much more important that others, and I need not take this precaution after having professed my sympathy for the major ones in remarking that the only classification of the novel that I can understand is into that which has life and that which has it not.

Nothing, of course, will ever take the place of the good old fashion of "liking" a work of art or not liking it: the most improved criticism will not abolish that primitive, that ultimate test. . . . As people feel life, so they will feel the art that is most closely related to it. This closeness of relation is what we should never forget in talking of the effort of the novel. Many people speak of it as a factitious, artificial form, a product of ingenuity, the business of which it is to alter and arrange the things that surround us, to translate them into conventional, traditional moulds. This, however, is a view of the matter which carries us but a very short way, condemns the art to an eternal repetition of a few familiar clichés, cuts short its development, and leads us straight up to a dead wall. Catching the very note and trick, the strange irregular rhythm of life, that is the attempt whose strenuous force keeps Fiction upon her feet.

I cannot see what is meant by talking as if there were a part of a novel which is the story and part of it which for mystical reasons is not—unless indeed the distinction be made in a sense in which it is difficult to suppose that any one should attempt to convey anything. "The story," if it represents anything, represents the subject, the idea, the *donnée* of the novel; and there is surely no "school" which urges that a novel should be all treatment and no subject. There must assuredly be something to treat every school is intimately conscious of that. This sense of the story being the idea, the starting-point, of the novel, is the only one that I see in which it can be spoken of as something different from its organic whole; and since in proportion as the work is successful the idea permeates and penetrates it, informs and animates it, so that every word and every punctuation-point contribute directly to the expression, in that proportion do we lose our sense of the story being a blade which may be drawn more or less out of its sheath. The story and the novel, the idea and the form, are the needle and thread, and I never heard of a guild of tailors who recommended the use of the thread without the needle, or the needle without the thread.

I have left the question of the morality of the novel till the last, and at the last I find I have used up my space. It is a question surrounded with difficulties, as witness the very first that meets us, in the form of a definite question, on the threshold. Vagueness, in such a discussion, is fatal, and what is the meaning of your morality and your conscious moral purpose? Will you not define your terms and explain how (a novel being a picture) a picture can be either moral or immoral? You wish to paint a moral picture or carve a moral statue: will you not tell us how you would set about it? We are discussing the Art of Fiction; questions of art are questions (in the widest sense) of execution; questions of morality are quite another affair, and will you not let us see how it is that you find it so easy to mix them up? . . . There is one point at which the moral sense and the artistic sense lie very near together; that is in the light of the very obvious truth that the deepest quality of a work of art will always be the quality of the mind of the producer. In proportion as that intelligence is fine will the novel, the picture, the statue partake of the substance of beauty and truth. To be constituted of such elements is, to my vision, to have purpose enough. No good novel will ever proceed from a superficial mind; that seems to me an axiom which, for the artist in fiction, will cover all needful moral ground.

from "Manners, Morals, and the Novel"
by Lionel Trilling

. . . An English writer, recognizing the novel's central concern with snobbery, recently cried out half-ironically against it. "Who cares whether Pamela finally exasperates Mr. B. into marriage, whether Mr. Elton is more or less than moderately genteel, whether it is sinful for Pendennis nearly to kiss the porter's daughter, whether young men from Boston can ever be as truly refined as middle-aged women in Paris, whether the District Officer's fiancée ought to see so much of Dr. Aziz, whether Lady Chatterley ought to be made love to by the gamekeeper, even if he was an officer during the war? Who cares?"

The novel, of course, tells us much more about life than this. It tells us about the look and feel of things, how things are done and what things are worth and what they cost and what the odds are. If the English novel in its special concern with class does not, as the same writer says, explore the deeper layers of personality, then the French novel in exploring these layers must start and end in class, and the Russian novel, exploring the ultimate possibilities of spirit, does the same—every situation in Dostoevski, no matter how spiritual, starts with a point of social pride and a certain number of rubles. The great novelists knew that manners indicate the largest intentions of men's souls as well as the smallest and they are perpetually concerned to catch the meaning of every dim implicit hint.

The novel, then, is a perpetual quest for reality, the field of its research being always the social world, the material of its analysis being always manners as the indication of the direction of man's soul. When we understand this we can understand the pride of profession that moved D. H. Lawrence to say, "Being a novelist, I consider myself superior to the saint, the scientist, the philosopher and the poet. The novel is the one bright book of life."

Now the novel as I have described it has never really established itself in America. Not that we have not had very great novels but that the novel in America diverges from its classic intention, which, as I have said, is the investigation of the problem of reality beginning in the social field. The fact is that American writers of genius have not turned their minds to society. Poe and Melville were quite apart from it; the reality they sought was only tangential to society. Hawthorne was acute when he insisted that he did not write novels but romances—he thus expressed his awareness of the lack of social texture in his work. Howells never fulfilled himself because, although he saw the social subject clearly, he would never take it with full seriousness. In America in the nineteenth century, Henry James was alone in knowing that to scale the moral and aesthetic heights in the novel one had to use the ladder of social observation.

There is a famous passage in James's life of Hawthorne in which James enumerates the things which are lacking to give the American novel the thick social texture of the English novel—no state; barely a specific national name; no sovereign; no court; no aristocracy; no church; no clergy; no army; no diplomatic service; no country gentlemen; no palaces; no castles; no manors; no old country houses; no parsonages; no thatched cottages; no ivied ruins; no cathedrals; no great universities; no public schools; no political society; no sporting class—no Epsom, no Ascot! That is, no sufficiency of means for the display of a variety of manners, no opportunity for the novelist to do his job of searching out reality, not enough complication of appearance to make the job interesting. Another great American novelist of very different temperament had said much the same thing some decades before: James Fenimore Cooper found that American manners were too simple and dull to nourish the novelist.

This is cogent but it does not expain the condition of the American novel at the present moment. For life in America has increasingly thickened since the nineteenth century. It has not, to be sure, thickened so much as to permit our undergraduates to understand the characters of Balzac, to understand, that is, life in a crowded country where the competitive pressures are great, forcing intense passions to express themselves fiercely and yet within the limitations set by a strong and complicated tradition of manners. Still, life here has become more complex and more pressing. And even so we do not have the novel that touches significantly on society, on manners. Whatever the virtues of Dreiser may be, he could not report the social fact with the kind of accuracy it needs. Sinclair Lewis is shrewd, but no one, however charmed with him as a social satirist, can believe that he does more than a limited job of social understanding. John Dos Passos sees much, sees it often in the great way of Flaubert, but can never use social fact as more than either backdrop or "condition." Of our novelists today perhaps only William Faulkner deals with society as the field of tragic reality and he has the disadvantage of being limited to a provincial scene.

It would seem that Americans have a kind of resistance to looking closely at society. They appear to believe that to touch accurately on the matter of class, to take full note of snobbery, is somehow to demean themselves. It is as if we felt that one cannot touch pitch without being defiled—which, of course, may possibly be the case. Americans will not deny that we have classes and snobbery, but they seem to hold it to be indelicate to take precise cognizance of these phenomena. Consider that Henry James is, among a large part of our reading public, still held to be at fault for noticing society as much as he did. Consider the conversation that has, for some interesting reason, become a part of our literary folklore. Scott Fitzgerald said to Ernest Hemingway, "The very rich are different from us." Hemingway replied, "Yes, they have more money." I have seen the exchange quoted many times and always with the intention of suggesting that Fitzgerald was infatuated by wealth and had received a salutary rebuke from his democratic friend. But the truth is that after a certain point quantity of money does indeed change into quality of personality: in an important sense the very rich *are* different from us. So are the very powerful, the very gifted, the very poor. Fitzgerald was right, and almost for that remark alone he must surely have been received in Balzac's bosom in the heaven of novelists.

It is of course by no means true that the American reading class has no interest in society. Its interest fails only before society as it used to be represented by the novel. And if we look at the commercially successful serious novels of the last decade, we see that almost all of them have been written from an intense social awareness—it might be said that our present definition of a serious book is one which holds before us some image of society to consider and condemn. What is the situation of the dispossessed Oklahoma farmer and whose fault it is, what situation the Jew finds himself in, what it means to be a Negro, how one gets a bell for Adano, what is the advertising business really like, what it means to be insane and how society takes care of you or fails to do so—these are the matters which are believed to be most fertile for the novelist, and certainly they are the subjects most favored by our reading class.

The public is probably not deceived about the quality of most of these books. If the question of quality is brought up, the answer is likely to be: no, they are not great, they are not imaginative, they are not "literature." But there is an unexpressed addendum: and perhaps they are all the better for not being imaginative, for not being literature—they are not literature, they are reality, and *in a time like this* what we need is reality in large doses.

When, generations from now, the historian of our times undertakes to describe the assumptions of our culture, he will surely discover that the word *reality* is of central importance in his understanding of us. He will observe that for some of our philosophers the meaning of the word was a good deal in doubt, but that for our political writers, for many of our literary critics, and for most of our reading public, the word did not open discussion but, rather, closed it. Reality, as conceived by us, is whatever is external and hard, gross, unpleasant. Involved in its meaning is the idea of power conceived in a particular way. Some time ago I had occasion to remark how, in the critical estimates of Theodore Dreiser, it is always being said that Dreiser has many faults but that it cannot be denied that he has great power. No one ever says "a kind of power." Power is assumed to be always "brute" power, crude, ugly, and undiscriminating, the way an elephant appears to be. It is seldom understood to be the way an elephant actually is, precise and discriminating; or the way electricity is, swift and absolute and scarcely embodied.

The word *reality* is an honorific word and the future historian will naturally try to discover our notion of its pejorative opposite, appearance, mere appearance. He will find it in our feeling about the internal; whenever we detect evidences of style and thought we suspect that reality is being a little betrayed, that "mere subjectivity" is creeping in. There follows from this our feeling about complication, modulation, personal idiosyncrasy, and about social forms, both the great and the small.

Having gone so far, our historian is then likely to discover a puzzling contradiction. For we claim that the great advantage of reality is its hard, bedrock, concrete quality, yet everything we say about it tends toward the abstract and it almost seems that what we want to find in reality is abstraction itself. Thus we believe that one of the unpleasant bedrock facts is social class, but we become extremely impatient if ever we are told that social class is indeed so real that it produces actual differences of personality. The very people who talk most about class and its evils think that Fitzgerald was bedazzled and Hemingway right. Or again, it might be observed that in the degree that we speak in praise of the "individual" we have contrived that our literature should have no individuals in it—no people, that is, who are shaped by our liking for the interesting and memorable and special and precious.

Here, then, is our generalization: that in proportion as we have committed ourselves to our particular idea of reality we have lost our interest in manners. For the novel this is a definitive condition because it is inescapably true that in the novel manners make men. It does not matter in what sense the word manners is taken—it is equally true of the sense which so much interested Proust or of the sense which interested Dickens or, indeed, of the sense which interested Homer. The Duchesse de Guermantes unable to delay departure for the dinner party to receive properly from her friend Swann the news that he is dying but able to delay to change the black slippers her husband objects to; Mr. Pickwick and Sam Weller; Priam and Achilles—they exist by reason of their observed manners. . . .

the short story

THE SELECTIONS here present some fairly profound contrasts in humor and seriousness. All, however, are concerned with the short story as a form of art. In the first selection is Edgar Allan Poe's famous explanation of how a short story is created—not to follow a pattern of incident, but to achieve a preconceived effect. In the second essay, Ring Lardner writes a parody of the methods of writing the short story; his essay lampoons the outlandish irrelevance in many stories. Elinor Goulding Smith also writes in the satirical vein against the popular taste that demands and gets insipid stories written to follow a pattern. Finally, in Eudora Welty's "The Reading and Writing of Short Stories," is a serious and intense discussion of pattern and beauty and the interrelationships between these elements of the short story.

from Review of Hawthorne's Twice-Told Tales
by Edgar Allen Poe

. . . There has long existed in literature a fatal and unfounded prejudice, which it will be the office of this age to overthrow—the idea that the mere bulk of a work must enter largely into our estimate of its merit. I do not suppose even the weakest of the quarterly reviewers weak enough to maintain that in a book's size or mass, abstractly considered, there is anything which especially calls for our admiration. A mountain, simply through the sensation of physical magnitude which it conveys, does, indeed, affect us with a sense of the sublime, but we cannot admit any such influence in the contemplation even of "The Columbiad." The Quarterlies themselves will not admit it. And yet, what else are we to understand by their continual prating about "sustained effort?" Granted that this sustained effort has accomplished an epic—let us then admire the effort, (if this be a thing admirable,) but certainly not the epic on the effort's account. Common sense, in the time to come, may possibly insist upon measuring a work of art rather by the object it fulfils, by the impression it makes, than by the time it took to fulfil the object, or by the extent of "sustained effort" which became necessary to produce the impression. The fact is, that perseverance is one thing and genius quite another; nor can all the transcendentalists in Heathendom confound them.

Full of its bulky ideas, the last number of the "North American Review," in what it imagines a criticism on Simms, "honestly avows that it has little opinion of the mere tale;" and the honesty of the avowal is in no slight degree guaranteed by the fact that this Review has never yet been known to put forth an opinion which was *not* a very little one indeed.

The tale proper affords the fairest field which can be afforded by the wide domains of mere prose, for the exercise of the highest

genius. Were I bidden to say how this genius could be most ad-
vantageously employed for the best display of its powers, I should
answer, without hesitation, "in the composition of a rhymed poem
not to exceed in length what might be perused in an hour." Within
this limit alone can the noblest order of poetry exist. I have discussed this topic elsewhere, and need here repeat only that the
phrase "a long poem" embodies a paradox. A poem must intensely
excite. Excitement is its province, its essentiality. Its value is in the
ratio of its (elevating) excitement. But all excitement is, from a
psychal necessity, transient. It cannot be sustained through a poem
of great length. In the course of an hour's reading, at most, it flags,
fails; and then the poem is, in effect, no longer such. Men admire,
but are wearied with the "Paradise Lost;" for platitude follows
platitude, *inevitably,* at regular interspaces, (the depressions between the waves of excitement,) until the poem, (which, properly
considered, is but a succession of brief poems,) having been
brought to an end, we discover that the sums of our pleasure and
of displeasure have been very nearly equal. The absolute, ultimate
or aggregate effect of any epic under the sun is, for these reasons,
a nullity. "The Iliad," in its form of epic, has but an imaginary
existence; granting it real, however, I can only say of it that it is
based on a primitive sense of Art. Of the modern epic nothing can
be so well said as that it is a blindfold imitation of a "come-by-
chance." By and by these propositions will be understood as self-
evident, and in the meantime will not be essentially damaged as
truths by being generally condemned as falsities.

A poem *too brief,* on the other hand, may produce a sharp or
vivid, but never a profound or enduring impression. Without a
certain continuity, without a certain duration or repetition of the
cause, the soul is seldom moved to the effect. There must be the
dropping of the water on the rock. There must be the pressing
steadily down of the stamp upon the wax. De Béranger has
wrought brilliant things, pungent and spirit-stirring, but most of

them are too immassive to have *momentum,* and, as so many feathers of fancy, have been blown aloft only to be whistled down the wind. Brevity, indeed, may degenerate into epigrammatism, but this danger does not prevent extreme length from being the one unpardonable sin.

Were I called upon, however, to designate that class of composition which, next to such a poem as I have suggested, should best fulfil the demands and serve the purposes of ambitious genius, should offer it the most advantageous field of exertion, and afford it the fairest opportunity of display, I should speak at once of the brief prose tale. History, philosophy, and other matters of that kind, we leave out of the question, of course. *Of course,* I say, and in spite of the graybeards. These grave topics, to the end of time, will be best illustrated by what a discriminating world, turning up its nose at the drab pamphlets, has agreed to understand as *talent.* The ordinary novel is objectionable, from its length, for reasons analogous to those which render length objectionable in the poem. As the novel cannot be read at one sitting, it cannot avail itself of the immense benefit of *totality.* Worldly interest, intervening during the pauses of perusal, modify, counteract and annul the impressions intended. But simple cessation in reading would, of itself, be sufficient to destroy the true unity. In the brief tale, however, the author is enabled to carry out his full design without interruption. During the hour of perusal, the soul of the reader is at the writer's control.

A skilful artist has constructed a tale. He has not fashioned his thoughts to accommodate his incidents, but having deliberately conceived a certain *single effect* to be wrought, he then invents such incidents, he then combines such events, and discusses them in such tone as may best serve him in establishing this preconceived effect. If his very first sentence tend not to the outbringing of this effect, then in his very first step has he committed a blunder. In the whole composition there should be no word written of which the tendency, direct or indirect, is not to the one pre-established design. And by such means, with such care and skill, a picture is at length painted which leaves in the mind of him who contemplates it with a kindred art, a sense of the fullest satisfaction. The idea of the tale, its thesis, has been presented unblemished, because undisturbed—an end absolutely demanded, yet, in the novel, altogether unattainable. . . .

from "How to Write Short Stories"
by Ring Lardner

A glimpse at the advertising columns of our leading magazines shows that whatever else this country may be shy of, there is certainly no lack of correspondence schools that learns you the art of short-story writing. The most notorious of these schools makes the boast that one of their pupils cleaned up $5000.00 and no hundreds dollars writing short stories according to the system learnt in their course, though it don't say if that amount was cleaned up in one year or fifty.

However, for some reason another when you skin through the pages of high class periodicals, you don't very often find them cluttered up with stories that was written by boys or gals who had win their phi beta skeleton keys at this or that story-writing college. In fact, the most of the successful authors of the short fiction of to-day never went to no kind of a college, or if they did, they studied piano tuning or the barber trade. They could of got just as far in what I call the literary game if they had of stayed home those four years and helped mother carry out the empty bottles.

The answer is that you can't find no school in operation up to date, whether it be a general institution of learning or a school that specializes in story writing, which can make a great author out of a born druggist.

But a little group of our deeper drinkers has suggested that maybe boys and gals who wants to take up writing as their life work would be benefited if some person like I was to give them a few hints in regards to the technic of the short story, how to go about planning it and writing it, when and where to plant the love interest and climax, and finally how to market the finished product without leaving no bad taste in the mouth.

Well, then, it seems to me like the best method to use in giving out these hints is to try and describe my own personal procedure from the time I get inspired till the time the manuscript is loaded on to the trucks.

The first thing I generally always do is try and get hold of a catchy title, like for instance, "Basil Hargrave's Vermifuge," Or "Fun at the Incinerating Plant." Then I set down to a desk or flat table of any kind and lay out 3 or 4 sheets of paper with as many different colored pencils and look at them cock-eyed a few moments before making a selection.

How to begin—or, as we professionals would say, "how to commence"—is the next question. It must be admitted that the method of approach (*"l'approchement"*) differs even among first class fictionists. For example, Blasco Ibáñez usually starts his stories with a Spanish word, Jack Dempsey with an "I" and Charley Peterson with a couple of simple declarative sentences about his leading character, such as "Hazel Gooftree had just gone mah jong. She felt faint."

Personally it has been my observation that the reading public prefers short dialogue to any other kind of writing and I always aim to open my tale with two or three lines of conversation between characters—or, as I call them, my puppets—who are to play important rôles. I have often found that something one of these characters says, words I have perhaps unconsciously put into his or her mouth, directs my plot into channels deeper than I had planned and changes, for the better, the entire sense of my story.

To illustrate this, let us pretend that I have laid out a plot as follows: Two girls, Dorothy Abbott and Edith Quaver, are spending the heated term at a famous resort. The Prince of Wales visits the resort, but leaves on the next train. A day or two later, a Mexican reaches the place and looks for accommodations, but is unable to find a room without a bath. The two girls meet him at the public filling station and ask him for a contribution to their autograph album. To their amazement, he utters a terrible oath, spits in their general direction and hurries out of town. It is not until years later that the two girls learn he is a notorious forger and realize how lucky they were after all.

Let us pretend that the above is the original plot. Then let us begin the writing with haphazard dialogue and see whither it leads:

"Where was you?" asked Edith Quaver.

"To the taxidermist's," replied Dorothy Abbott.

The two girls were spending the heated term at a famous watering trough. They had just been bathing and were now engaged in sorting dental floss.

"I am getting sick in tired of this place," went on Miss Quaver.

"It is mutual," said Miss Abbott, shying a cucumber at a passing paper-hanger.

There was a rap at their door and the maid's voice announced that company was awaiting them downstairs. The two girls went down and entered the music room. Garnett Whaledriver was at the piano and the girls tiptoed to the lounge.

The big Nordic, oblivious of their presence, allowed his fingers to form weird, fantastic minors before they strayed unconsciously into the first tones of Chopin's 121st Fugue for the Bass Drum.

From this beginning, a skilled writer could go most anywheres, but it would be my tendency to drop these three characters and take up the life of a mule in the Grand Canyon. The mule watches the trains come in from the east, he watches the trains come in from the west, and keeps wondering who is going to ride him. But he never finds out.

The love interest and climax would come when a man and a lady, both strangers, got to talking together on the train going back east.

"Well," said Mrs. Croot, for it was she, "what did you think of the Canyon?"

"Some cave," replied her escort.

"What a funny way to put it!" replied Mrs. Croot. "And now play me something."

Without a word, Warren took his place on the piano bench and at first allowed his fingers to form weird, fantastic chords on the black keys. Suddenly and with no seeming intention, he was in the midst of the second movement of Chopin's Twelfth Sonata for Flute and Cuspidor. Mrs. Croot felt faint.

That will give young writers an idea of how an apparently trivial thing such as a line of dialogue will upset an entire plot and lead an author far from the path he had pointed for himself. It will also serve as a model for beginners to follow in regards to style and technic. I will not insult my readers by going on with the story to its obvious conclusion. That simple task they can do for themselves, and it will be good practice.

So much for the planning and writing. Now for the marketing of the completed work. A good many young writers make the mistake of enclosing a stamped, self-addressed envelope, big enough for the manuscript to come back in. This is too much of a temptation to the editor.

Personally I have found it a good scheme to not even sign my name to the story, and when I have got it sealed up in its envelope and stamped and addressed, I take it to some town where I don't live and mail it from there. The editor has no idea who wrote the story, so how can he send it back? He is in a quandary.

In conclusion let me warn my pupils never to write their stories —or, as we professionals call them, "yarns"—on used paper. And never to write them on a post-card. And never to send them by telegraph (Morse code).

"Story for the Slicks"
by Elinor Goulding Smith

Carol Saunders brushed her thick mop of chestnut hair off her forehead with long, nervous white fingers. *How am I going to tell Jim?* she thought. *How can I tell him?* She thought of Jim's long, lean jaw, his dark tousled hair, and his crooked grin. *Oh, Jim, Jim* —(Opening paragraph plunges you right into the story with all its intense passion and suspense.)

But I mustn't think about that now. I'm so tired, she thought wearily, and the thin fingers twined nervously in the thick hair. She stood up suddenly and went into the bathroom, and she noticed dully that the faucet was still dripping. *I'll have to get Jim to fix it,* she thought automatically. (The homey touch.)

Determinedly, she turned on the cold water full force and let its clean sparkling freshness flow over her thin white wrists, and then she leaned over and dipped up the water with her slim hands and felt the sharp cold on her hot face. She dipped pads of absorbent cotton in the water and bathed her burning eyes, and she brushed out her hair with long, soothing rhythmic strokes, away from her forehead. (Beauty hints.)

She surveyed herself in the mirror. She saw the white, pointed face and the hair that seemed almost too heavy for the slim neck. It hung round her shoulders in a thick mass. "It's as soft to touch as a spaniel's ears," Jim always said. The lashes around the wide gray eyes were stuck together in dark points with little beads of the cold water still clinging to them. And the lower lip of the full crimson mouth was quivering. (Important that heroine be described, but not too specifically. Sprinkle liberally with "slim" wherever possible. Helpful if heroine can be made to whip in and out of tight sweaters.)

Tomorrow, she thought wearily, twisting and untwisting the long, nervous fingers. *Let tomorrow be time enough to tell him. I'm so tired today.* (There has to be as least one sentence starting with "let.")

She moved swiftly, with the easy flowing walk that Jim loved, and stood awkwardly for a moment in the living room. The late afternoon sun made a brilliant, warm golden splash on the center of the soft green carpet. *It's so quiet,* she thought, *and it seems almost strange to be here, in this house, now.* (This doesn't mean a thing, but it almost sounds as though it does, doesn't it?)

She thought suddenly that it was getting late, and Jim would be home soon. She went into the kitchen and leaned on the cool enamel table. The kitchen was bright and sunny with yellow walls and crisp curtains with appliquéd tulips. (Interior decorating hints are absolutely necessary.)

She caught herself humming a tune—"Star Dust," she realized suddenly. Their song. *Oh, Jim, Jim,* she thought, *remember how it was that night on the top of the bus, and it was so cold and clear, and I could feel the roughness of your coat against my cheek!* (Stir in a little nostalgia.)

And you were laughing because the clean cold wind kept whipping my hair across your face. Ah, we had fun. (Always change paragraphs at every possible opportunity, regardless of the meaning. Be sure heroine talks and thinks like a heroine, as opposed to a human being.)

And suddenly the small white face was down on the cold enamel table and bitter sobs shook the slim shoulders. (Got another "slim" in. Good!)

Then she straightened up with determination. *That's enough of that, Carol Saunders,* she thought, and she threw back the slim shoulders and lifted the little pointed chin. (A little pointed chin is always good too—tears at the heartstrings.)

I think I'll make some blueberry torte, she decided, and she glanced at the clock to see if there would be enough time before dinner. There would be, and she started working swiftly; she thought happily, *Jim always loves blueberry torte.* (Always be specific about food. A good recipe never hurts either.)

She deftly creamed a quarter of a cup of rich yellow butter and a tablespoon of sugar in the blue bowl, and added one egg yolk and a little salt and flour. (This is the most complicated recipe I could find in the Settlement Cook Book—it ought to be a killer.) She patted and pressed the dough in the shining greased pan (or spring form) with her slim quick fingers till it was a quarter of an inch thick, and placed it in the gleaming refrigerator overnight. Then she filled it with any desired Fruit Mixture, and baked.

Then, still humming to herself, having lined the bottom and sides of a spring form with Muerbe Teig No. 1, page 377, she sprinkled it with bread crumbs, added one quart of blueberries (*How ripe the berries are!* she thought, and she ate one, slowly savoring its sweetness), sprinkled it with one quarter of a cup of sugar (*How white the sugar is!* she thought unexpectedly), and cinnamon and two tablespoons of lemon juice. Over all she dripped the yolk of an egg beaten with three tablespoons of rich yellow cream. She baked it in the hot oven for fifteen minutes, then reduced the heat to three hundred and twenty-five degrees Fahrenheit.

This time she baked it till the crust was golden brown. *Jim loves it with the crust nice and brown,* she thought.

She sniffed the heavenly smell of the Muerbe Teig No. 1, page 377, and her face was flushed from the heat of the stove and her eyes were shining. She beat four egg whites until they were stiff and stood up in little white crusty peaks, and added powdered sugar. When the torte was ready, crust nicely browned, she spread the beaten eggs and sugar over it, returned it quickly to the oven, and baked it fifteen minutes more at three hundred degrees Fahrenheit. (I wonder if anybody ever tried this.)

While she was waiting for it to be ready, she realized suddenly that she was famished, and she thought, *I'll make pickled herring with lots of sour cream, just the way Jim loves it, and chicken soup with matzos balls, and creplach. And pot roast with potato latkes.* (Always give menus. Memo: Remember to get other cook book. Feel certain this is not the right cook book for magazine fiction writer.)

Carol didn't hear Jim's key turning in the lock, and he strode in and stood for a moment in the kitchen doorway, looking at her. Her face was flushed, and one tendril of hair had separated from the chestnut mass and curled over one cheek. (A loose tendril is always good.)

Suddenly she felt his presence, and she turned quickly. He was standing there, grinning that crooked grin that always made her heart turn over. (Crooked grin absolutely essential.) He was at her side with one step, and then he was crushing her to him, and her little white face was pressed tight against the warm roughness of his tweed shoulder. He buried his hands in the thick mass of her hair, and then he lifted her face up to kiss her. *She's so little,* he thought. He was always surprised at how little she was. (This establishes that he is of the necessary height and breadth for a proper hero.)

"Jim, darling," Carol said, "let me get my breath." (*He mustn't suspect,* she thought. *I'll tell him tomorrow.*) "And darling," she said, "you'd better hurry and wash—dinner's ready."

When they sat down to dinner, she was quite composed again. The tall glasses sparkled against the deep-blue linen table mats that she had made from that old blue linen dress, and trimmed with the oyster-white cotton fringe that made a happy design against the polished mahogany. (More housekeeping hints.) The lovely old silver that she had got from Grandmother Stanford on her wedding day gleamed softly. She kept the silver polished with reverent care, and its soft sheen never failed to remind her of Grandmother Stanford's shining white hair that she had carried bravely, like a banner. (Bravely, like a banner—isn't that *good?*) If only she could be as brave, if only she could have the strength that Grandmother had had.

Not that Carol Saunders hadn't been brave. She'd been brave the day that Jim had come home from the Army induction center, rejected. She had been strong then. She remembered how he had come home that day, his shoulders bent, his gray eyes smouldering with helpless rage. "It's no good," he had said, "they won't have me—that ankle—" Carol had known about his ankle—that time it had been broken, but he'd fought on to make his touchdown before he collapsed and was carried from the field. That ankle would never be right—she had known that. And she had been strong. (Naturally, there has to be a football injury.)

But this—this was different.

They finished dinner, and Jim helped her to clear away the dishes.

"Darling," she said, blinking back the tears, "I don't feel like washing the dishes tonight—let's just stack them in the sink, and I'll do them in the morning." She pushed her hair back from her forehead with the funny little gesture that Jim loved.

"Sure, honey," he said, "if you say so. It's certainly no hardship for me."

Carol laughed uncertainly. And then suddenly she knew that she had to tell him. Now.

"Come in the living room," she said. Her heart pounded painfully, and she could feel the pulse beating in the soft part of her neck. "I want to talk to you."

Jim looked puzzled, but he followed Carol into the living room. He sank down on the big soft couch covered with deep red frieze and trimmed with a looped woolen fringe of the palest gray. Carol came and sat close to him. She linked her thin fingers, and sat there a moment, looking down at her hands. *I have to tell him now,* she thought. But still she sat there, silently, twining and untwining the long, thin fingers.

Jim sat as still as death, waiting. Suddenly he leaned forward and caught both her hands in his big ones. "What is it, Carol?" he said, his deep voice vibrant with sympathy. "What is it?" he said again. "Darling," he added softly, "remember that I love you."

Carol looked up gratefully, and her wide gray eyes filled with tears.

She felt fear, like a cold hand laid across her heart.

And then suddenly she thought of Grandmother Stanford. And she knew then, deep within her, that she could be strong too. She held her little head high, and the gray eyes were shining.

"Jim," she said, "I'm going to tell you straight. I—I—" Her voice broke, but she swallowed and went on bravely in a clear voice. (Now, I believe, if I have learned the method properly, we are at the crux of the story. It just so happens I don't have a good crux on hand at the moment, but I can think one up later. It hardly matters, for the denouement is the same in any case.)

Jim stared at her a moment, unbelief in his honest eyes, his long jaw rigid. She saw a tiny muscle quivering in his temple. The room was very still, and somewhere off in the distance they heard the plaintive cry of a train rushing through the night.

Finally Jim spoke. "Carol," he said, and his voice shook a little. "Carol—we'll be all right. We'll start over, you and I, together."

"Jim!" Carol cried. "Oh, Jim!" She started to cry, and he wrapped her in his strong arms till she was quiet again. "Oh, darling," she said then. "Darling."

Suddenly she sat up straight. "Jim," she said. "Let's wash the dishes *now.*"

from "The Reading and Writing of Short Stories" by Eudora Welty

. . . In Katherine Mansfield's "Miss Brill," there are only one character and only one situation. The narrative is simple, Miss Brill's action consists nearly altogether in sitting down; she does nothing but go and sit in the park, return home and sit on her bed in her little room. Yet considerably more of a story is attempted by this lesser to-do than Crane attempted in "Yellow Sky"; its plot is all implication.

"Miss Brill" is set on a stage of delight. "Although it was so brilliantly fine—the blue sky powdered with gold, and great spots of light like white wine splashed over the *Jardins Publiques*—Miss Brill was glad that she had decided on her fur. . . . [She] put up her hand and touched her fur. Dear little thing!" We see right off that for Miss Brill delight is a kind of coziness. She sits listening to the band, her Sunday habit, and "Now there came a little flutey bit —very pretty!—a little chain of bright drops. She was sure it would be repeated. It was; she lifted her head and smiled."

Miss Brill has confidence in her world—anticipation: what will happen next? Ah, but she knows. She's delighted but safe. She sees the others from her little perch, her distance—the gay ones and then those on benches: "Miss Brill had often noticed there was something funny about nearly all of *them*. They were odd, silent, nearly all old, and from the way they stared they looked as though they'd just come from dark little rooms or even—even cupboards!" For she hasn't identified herself at all.

The drama is light in this story. There is no collision. Rather the forces meeting in the *Jardins Publiques* have, at the story's end, passed through each other and come out the other side; there has not been a collision, but a change—something much more significant. This is because, though there is one small situation going on, a very large and complex one is implied—the outside world, in fact.

One of the forces in the story is life itself, corresponding to the part of Scratchy Wilson, so to speak. Not violent life—like in the setting of a park on Sunday afternoon in Paris. All it usually does for Miss Brill is promenade stylishly while the band plays, form little tableaux, separate momently into minor, rather darker encounters, and keep in general motion with bright colors and light touches—there are no waving pistols at all, to storm and threaten.

Yet, being life, it does threaten. In what way, at last? Well, how much more deadly to Miss Brill than a flourished pistol is an overheard remark—about *her*. Miss Brill's vision—a vision of love—is brought abruptly face to face with another, ruder vision of love. The boy and girl in love sit down on her bench, but they cannot go on with what they have been saying because of her, though "still soundlessly singing, still with that trembling smile, Miss Brill prepared to listen.

" 'No, not now,' said the girl. 'Not here, I can't.'

" 'But why? Because of that stupid old thing at the end there? . . . Why does she come here at all—who wants her? Why doesn't she keep her silly old mug at home?'

" 'It's her fur which is so funny,' giggled the girl. 'It's exactly like a fried whiting.'

" 'Ah be off with you!' said the boy in an angry whisper."

So Miss Brill, she who could spare even pity for this world, in her innocence—pity, the spectator's emotion—is defeated. She had allowed herself occasional glimpses of lives not too happy, here in the park, which had moved her to little flutters of sadness. But that too had been coziness—coziness, a remedy visitors seek to take the chill off a strange place with. She hadn't known it wasn't good enough. All through the story she has sat in her "special seat"

—another little prop to endurance—and all unknown to her she sat in mortal danger. This is the story. The danger near, a word is spoken, the blow falls—and Miss Brill retires, ridiculously easy to mow down, as the man with the pistols was easy to stare down in "Yellow Sky," for comedy's sake. But Miss Brill was from the first defenseless and on the losing side, and her defeat is the deeper for it, and one feels sure it is for ever.

The plot of a short story in many instances is quite openly a projection of character. In a highly specialized instance, but a good example, the whole series of ghostly events in *The Turn of the Screw* may obviously be taken as a vision—a set of hallucinations of the governess who tells us the story. The story is a manufactured evidence against the leading character, in effect.

Not always does plot project character, even primarily. William Sansom, a young English writer, might be mentioned as one new writer who pays his highest respect to pure idea. Virginia Woolf too was at least as interested in a beam of light as she was in a tantrum.

In outward semblance, many stories have plots in common— which is of no more account than that many people have blue eyes. Plots are, indeed, what we see with. What's seen is what we're interested in.

On some level all stories are stories of search—which isn't surprising at all. From the intense wild penetration of the hunter in "The Bear" by William Faulkner to the gentle Sunday excursion of Katherine Mansfield's "Miss Brill"; from the cruel errand of Nick's father to the Indian camp in Ernest Hemingway's story to the fantasy of soaring into the realm of the poetic imagination in E. M. Forster's "Celestial Omnibus"; from the fireman seeking the seat of the fire in William Sansom's "Fireman Flower" to the Henry James man in "The Jolly Corner" seeking, with infinite pains and wanderings, the image of himself and what he might have been, through the corridors of a haunted house—in any group of stories we might name as they occur to us, the plot is search. It is the ancient Odyssey and the thing that was ancient when first the Odyssey was sung. Joyce's *Ulysses* is the titan modern work on the specific subject, but when Miss Brill sits in the park, we feel an old key try at an old lock again—she too is looking. Our most ancient dreams help to convince us that her timid Sunday afternoon is the adventure of her life, and measure for us her defeat.

Corresponding to the search involved is always the other side of the coin. On one side of James's coin is search, on the other side is blight. Faulkner is concerned with doom and history, Hemingway with career, ritual, and fate—and so on. Along with search go the rise and fall of life, pride and the dust. And Virginia Woolf sees errand and all alike dissolving in a surpassing mystery.

When plot, whatever it does or however it goes, becomes the outward manifestation of the very germ of the story, then it is purest—then the narrative thread is least objectionable, then it is not in the way. When it is identifiable in every motion and progression of its own with the motions and progression of simple revelation, then it is at its highest use. Plot can be made so beautifully to reveal character, reveal atmosphere and the breathing of it, reveal the secrets of hidden, inner (that is, "real") life, that its very unfolding is a joy. It is a subtle satisfaction—that comes from where? Probably it comes from a deep-seated perception we all carry in us of the beauty of organization—of that less strictly definable thing, of form.

Where does form come from—how do you "get it"? My guess is that form is evolved. It is the residue, the thrown-off shape, of the very act of writing, as I look at it. It is the work, its manifestation in addition to the characters, the plot, the sensory impressions—it is the result of these, which comes to more than their mathematical total. It is these plus something more. This something more springs from the whole. It pertains to the essence of the story. From the

writer's point of view, we might say that form is somehow connected with the process of the story's work—that form *is* the work.
From the reader's point of view, we might say that form is connected with recognition; it is what makes us know, in a story, what
we are looking at, what unique thing we are for a length of time
intensely contemplating. It does seem that the part of the mind
which form speaks to and reaches is the memory.

In stories today, form, however acutely and definitely it may be
felt, does not necessarily imply a formal structure. It is not ac-
counted for by structure, rather. A story with a "pattern," an exact
kind of design, may lack a more compelling over-all quality which
we call form. Edgar Allan Poe and other writers whose ultimate
aim depended on pattern, on a perfect and dovetailing structure
(note the relation to puzzles and to detection and mystery here),
might have felt real horror at a story by D. H. Lawrence first of all
because of the unmitigated shapelessness of Lawrence's narrative.
Lawrence's world of action and conversation is as far from the
frozen perfection, the marblelike situations, of Poe as we can
imagine; Lawrence's story world is a shambles—a world just let
go, like a sketchy housekeeper's un-straightened-up room. More
things are important than this dust! Lawrence would say, and he
would be as right as the crier of that cry always is.

And what about his characters? Are they real, recognizable, neat
men and women? Would you know them if you saw them? Not
even, I think, if they began to speak on the street as they speak in
the stories, in the very words—they would only appear as deranged
people. For the truth seems to be that Lawrence's characters don't
really speak their words—not conversationally, not to one another;
they are *not* speaking on the street, but are playing like fountains
or radiating like the moon or storming like the sea, or their silence
is the silence of wicked rocks. It is borne home to us that Lawrence
is writing of our human relationships on earth in terms of eternity,
and these terms set Lawrence's form. . . .

A story's major emphasis may fall on the things that make it up —on character, on plot, on its physical or moral world, in sensory or symbolic form, And perhaps the way this emphasis is let fall may determine the value of the story; may determine not how well it is written, but the worth of its being written.

Of course fashion and the habits of understanding stories at given periods in history may play their parts, unconsciously or willfully. But mainly, I venture to think, the way emphasis falls, the value of a story, is the thing nearest dependent upon the individual and personal factor involved, the writer behind the writing.

The fine story writers seem to be in a sense obstructionists. As if they hold back their own best interests. It's a strange illusion. For if we look to the source of the deepest pleasure we receive from a writer, how surprising it seems that this very source is the quondam obstruction. The fact is, in seeking our source of pleasure we have entered another world again. We are speaking of beauty.

And beauty is not a blatant or promiscuous or obvious quality; indeed at her finest she is somehow associated with obstruction— with reticence of a number of kinds. The beauty of "The Bear" seems tied up intimately with the reluctance to confine the story to its proper time sequence and space measurements; Faulkner makes fantastic difficulty about time and place both, and the result is beauty. Time after time Lawrence refuses to get his story told, to let his characters talk in any natural way; the story is held up forever, and through so delaying and through such refusal on the author's part, we enter the magical world of pure sense, of evocation—the shortest cut known through the woods.

Could it be that one who carps at difficulties in a writer ("Why didn't he write it like this? Why didn't he write another story?"), at infringements of the rules and lack of performance of duty, fails to take note of beauty? And fails to see straight off that beauty springs from deviation, from desire not to comply but to act inevitably, as long as truth is in sight, whatever that inevitability may mean?

Where does beauty come from, in the short story? Beauty comes from form, from development of idea, from after-effect. It often comes from carefulness, lack of confusion, elimination of waste— and yes, those are the rules. But that can be on occasion a cold kind of beauty, when there are warm kinds. And beware of tidiness. Sometimes spontaneity is the most sparkling kind of beauty— Katherine Mansfield had it. It is a fortuitous circumstance attending the birth of some stories, like a fairy godmother that has—this time—accepted the standing invitation and come smiling in.

Beauty may be missed or forgotten sometimes by the analyzers because it is not a means, not a way of getting the story along, or furthering a thing in the world. For beauty is a result—as form is a result. It *comes*. We are lucky when beauty comes, for often we try, but then when the virtues of our story are counted, beauty is standing behind the door. I think it may be wrong to try for beauty; we should try for other things, and then hope.

Intensity and beauty are qualities that will come out of man's imagination and out of his passion—which use sensitivity for their finding and focusing power. (This can't beg the question quite so hopelessly as assigning the best stories to genius.) It seems to be true that for practical purposes, in writing a story, beauty is in greatest accord with sensitivity.

The two things that cannot be imitated, beauty and sensitivity, are or may be kin to each other. But there is only one of them we can strive for. Sensitivity in ourselves. It is our technique. In the end, our technique is sensitivity, and beauty may be our reward.

A short-story writer can try anything. He has tried anything— but presumably not everything. Variety is, has been, and no doubt will remain endless in possibilities, because the power and stirring of the mind never rests. It is what this power will try that will most pertinently define the short story. Not rules, not aesthetics, not problems and their solution. It is not rules as long as there is imagination; not aesthetics as long as there is passion; not success as long as there is intensity behind the effort that calls forth and communicates, that will try and try again.

And at the other end of the stories is the reader. There is no use really to fear "the reader." The surly old bugaboo who wants his money's worth out of a magazine—yes, he is there (or I suspect it is a she, still wanting her money's worth and having yet to be convinced she's got it); but there is another reader too, perhaps with more at stake.

Inescapably, this reader exists—the same as ourselves; the reader who is also a user of imagination and thought. This reader picks up a story, maybe our new story, and behold, sees it fresh, and meets it with a storehouse of hope and interest.

And, reader and writer, we can wish each other well. Don't we after all want the same thing? A story of beauty and passion and truth?

the essay

THE FOUR SELECTIONS in this section may be read in any order, but they are placed here to show a historical progression. This is the phenomenon of increasing depersonalization in modern society. The first selection, by F. H. Pritchard, explains what a familiar essay is: a thoughtful expression of protest or of personal taste that is un-hurried, gentle, and not limited by strict rules. The second selection, from "Editor's Easy Chair," *Harper's Magazine*, observes the early symptoms of our modern disease: the clearly structured, factual "article" is gaining ground, and spoiling the popular taste for more leisurely, thoughtful types of literature, like the lyric and the essay. The third selection is a fine example of the essay itself; in "No Essays Please!" Joseph Wood Krutch, a sensitive contemporary, writes a biting satire on what modern literary taste has done to the essay. Finally, Russell Nye attempts the difficult task of pinning down a definition of the essay by dividing it into two types. Nye again classes the essay with the lyric, as the *Harper's* editor has done. Some of his concluding remarks on style would be appropriate for any literary genre.

from Introduction to Essays of Today
by F. H. Pritchard

That divine discontent which has been called "the secret spur of all our enterprises" is certainly the mainspring of our literature. And the milder form of it which gently laments instead of shrieking, shrugging its shoulders good-humouredly rather than trying to smash the furniture, finds its most natural means of expression in the essay. The man who is violently discontented with things as he finds them may preach stirring sermons, write exquisite sonnets, deliver inflammatory harangues, or turn pamphleteer; he will assuredly not write good essays.

Addison and his friends were dissatisfied with the state of society in their day, cleft as it was by reason of conflicting aims and lack of understanding, but with them dissatisfaction, however deep-rooted, never overcame good-humour. The result is seen in those suave and genial essays that, more effectually than sermon or pamphlet, moulded opinion, mended manners, and brought about a peaceful revolution. Charles Lamb, irked by the drudgery of ledger-entries and invoices, lamented that the noble fir-trees of the forest should, as he put it, "die into desks" similar to the one at which he sat daily expediting mercantile transactions. So his soul in gentle rebellion was moved to express itself in terms of "Old China" and "Roast Pig." The essay, then, perhaps more than any other literary form, is the outcome of a nice equipoise. A mild discontent; a wistful longing for that which is not, but which has been or might be; an attempt, brief and fragmentary but always sincere, to express a problem in terms of one's personality—these are the essentials of the true essay.

The limitations of length and scope that condition all essay-

Essays of Today, edited by F. H. Pritchard, 1923. Reprinted by permission of George G. Harrap & Co., Ltd.

writing are obvious enough. Brevity and informality are character-istics that all may behold. The essay is modest in its range, and it makes no pretensions. Just a little plot of ground is cultivated, and that after no set fashion. But more important than these obvious limitations is the fact that the essay is primarily an expression of personality. It must be, as Montaigne says, "consubstantial" with its author. By means of it one is placed on terms of close intimacy with the writer; not hectored from a platform, nor exhorted from a pulpit, but admitted to the familiarity of the fireside. And the style of a good essay reflects this. As Mr. Gosse says, that style must be "confidential," as well as "a model of current cultivated ease of expression and a mirror of the best conversation." It is in this personal trait that the essay corresponds most nearly to the lyric. They are both the most intimate revelations of personality that we have in literature. They are both valuable because by means of them we are able to get into close touch with some of the finest and noblest spirits of all time. And unlike as essay and lyric are superficially, there is in this fundamental respect no difference between them.

A man, calmly observant and with a sense of humour withal, muses on things as they are. The most trivial occurrences will serve to set him a-dreaming—the crowing of a cock, the books on his shelves gleaming in the firelight, a scent wafted in through the open window, the patter of raindrops on the leaves—and as gently and equably as he muses, so he writes. Thoughts, irresponsible and unbidden, come straying into his consciousness, and he dreams, perhaps, of what has been in some Golden Age of the past, or, in a glowing vision of the future, of what may be. With a sure but light touch he sets down these fancies in gentle prose, to soothe, to charm, and to encourage his fellows. And as they read, the gentle poignancy and subtle humour of these essays steal upon their consciousness, catching them unawares, and moving them where the strident tones of grand passion or high tragedy would probably fail.

But thoughts do not always pass with such calm ease through the writer's mind. Sometimes they burn with a white and passionate heat that, by reason of its very intensity, makes expression more difficult. We are all conscious of such thoughts, but with most of us they are accompanied by a feeling of utter incompetence and incoherence. The commonplaces of life we can utter, but these rare and burning ideas find us dumb. We cannot express them even to ourselves, and so they pass. But here and there is one to whom is given the incommunicable gift of controlling and marshalling such thoughts so as to give them coherent and glorious expression in measured speech. Ordered by the strict limitations of rhythm, and obedient to the recurrences of rime and metre, the unruly ideas are fashioned into a lyric, just as scattered particles, straying here and there, are drawn together and fused into crystalline beauty. The difference, indeed, is one of temperature. The metal bar, cold or lukewarm, will do anywhere, but heat it to melting-point and you must confine it within the rigid limits of the mould or see it at length but an amorphous splash at your feet.

So lyric and essay are both pre-eminently expressions of personality, but whereas one is the embodiment of rare moments of passion and exaltation, the other is the expression of those quiet everyday moods when one is at leisure and peace, yet not all at ease. The mind, vaguely seeking for better things, unfolds and particularizes its own most intimate longings. Just because it is so apt an expression of everyday personality the essay is one of the most elusive of literary forms. Its easy, unobtrusive rhythm, its subtle recurrences, its quiet humour, are not obvious to the casual beholder as are the corresponding traits in drama, novel, or sonnet. But they are there nevertheless, and well repay the search. It would be wrong, too, to imagine that the essay is merely a tepid affair subsisting solely on the dead level of the commonplace. If it keeps largely to the commonplace, it is only that it may reveal its beauty, as when Mrs. Rhys directs our admiring gaze to the pig-sty. The essay has, it should be remembered, its own sublimities; as when Leigh Hunt muses upon the deaths of little children, or Edward Thomas conjures up the spirit that dwells in a neglected London garden.

When we come to look at the essays of today we find, in the wealth of material at our disposal, all those characteristics that we have been noticing clearly set forth. There is the gentle dissatisfaction with things as they are; the quiet determination to depose existing idols. Mr. J. Middleton Murry, in an acute piece of criticism, has pointed out that each generation lives by slaughtering the ideals of its parents. Thus we move—whether by way of progress or not we cannot here argue. At all events, the revolt against what is conveniently labelled Victorianism, a revolt of which we shall find many evidences in these essays, is not a mere whim, but an expression of the instinct for self-preservation. We must show that we are alive and different. The man who will judge decisively between our parents and ourselves will come in a later age, when the heat of the struggle will have cooled. Meanwhile, without attempting to anticipate that judgment, we may notice one or two unmistakable features. The ideals of one age always seem topsy-turvy to the next. And each will take a boyish delight in overturning the older notions, discarding them altogether or setting them, as it thinks, right way up. Dixon Scott pillories the early-riser as an immoral person; Mr. G. K. Chesterton holds up detective stories as a branch of literature worthy of our highest admiration; Vernon Lee shows how much may be gained by losing a train; and Roger Wray replaces the old autumn legend by one more virile and pleasing to youth.

This basic dissatisfaction with existing ideals shows itself in various guises other than the boyish way of turning them upside down. Just as Montaigne had his tower of refuge, so every essayist finds a means of occasional escape from the exigent "here and now." Some shrink into themselves and give us intimate bits of self-revelation, or retire to the library, to finger lovingly their favourite volumes. We see this exemplified in much of the work of Edward Thomas and in that of George Gissing writing as "Henry Ryecroft." Others look for romance and, finding it not, seek places that are more promising. Mr. Belloc, for instance, takes us to Delft and shows us its beauty, characteristically adding, "And to think that you can get to a place like that for less than a pound!" . . .

from "Editor's Easy Chair" by the Editors of Harper's Magazine

The old-fashioned essay, as we had it in Montaigne, and almost as we had it in Bacon, obeyed a law as subjective as that of the gypsy music which the Hungarian bands made so popular with us ten or fifteen years ago. Wandering airs of thought strayed through it, owning no allegiance stricter than that which bound the wild chords to a central motive. Often there was apparently no central motive in the essay; it seemed to begin where it would, and end where it liked. The author was bound to give it a name, but it did not hold him bound otherwise. It could not very well take for title a first line, or part of a first line, like those poems, now rarely written, which opened with some such phrase as, When those bright eyes; or, Had I the wings; or, If yon sweet star. If it could, that would have been the right way of naming most of the essays which have loitered down to us from antiquity, as well as those which help to date the revival of polite learning. Such a custom would have befitted nearly all the papers in the *Spectator* and the *Tatler* and the *Rambler,* and the other periodicals illustrating the

From "Editor's Easy Chair," *Harper's Magazine,* October, 1902.

heyday of the English essay. These, indeed, preserved an essential liberty by setting out from no subject more severely ascertained than that which lurked in some quotation from the classics, and unless there was an allegory or an apologue in hand, gadded about at their pleasure, and stopped as far from it as they chose. That gave them their charm, and kept them lyrical, far from the dread perhaps of turning out a sermon, when the only duty they had was to turn out a song.

Just how or why the essay should have departed from this elder ideal, and begun to have a conscience about having a beginning, a middle and an ending, like a drama, or a firstly, secondly, and thirdly, like a homily, it would not be easy to say, though we feel pretty sure that it was not from any occasion of Charles Lamb's, or Leigh Hunt's, or William Hazlitt's, or their compeers, in bearing down to our day the graceful tradition which seems now to have been lost. We suspect that the change may have happened through the greater length to which the essay has run in modern times. You may sing a song for a certain period, but if you keep on you have an opera, which you are bound to give obvious form. At any rate, the moment came when the essay began to confuse itself with the article, and to assume an obligation of constancy to premises and conclusions, with the effect of so depraving the general taste that the article is now desired more and more, and the essay less and less. It is doubtful, the corruption has gone so far, whether there is enough of the lyrical sense left in the reader to appreciate the right essay; whether the right essay would now be suffered; whether if any writer indulged its wilding nature, he would not be suspected of an inability to cultivate the growths that perceptibly nourish, not to say fatten, the intellect. We have forgotten, in this matter, that there are senses to which errant odors and flying flavors minister, as grosser succulences satisfy hunger. There is a lyrical sense, as well as a dramatic, an epical, an ethical sense, and it was that which the old-fashioned essay delighted.

"No Essays Please!"
by Joseph Wood Krutch

Every now and then someone regrets publicly the passing of the familiar essay. Perhaps such regretters are usually in possession of a recent rejection slip; in any event there are not enough of them to impress editors. The very word "essay" has fallen into such disfavor that it is avoided with horror and anything which is not fiction is usually called either an "article," a "story" or just "a piece." When *The Atlantic Monthly,* once the last refuge of a dying tradition, now finds it advisable to go in for such "articles" as its recent "What Night Playing Has Done to Baseball" it is obvious that not merely the genteel tradition but a whole literary form is dead.

I am sure that the books on how to become a writer in ten easy lessons have been stressing this fact for a long time now. If *I* were writing such a book I certainly should, and I think that I could give some very practical advice. To begin with I should say something like the following:

Suppose that you have drawn a subject out of your mental box and you find that it is "Fish." Now if you were living in the time of Henry Van Dyke and Thomas Bailey Aldrich your best lead would be: "Many of my friends are ardent disciples of Izaak Walton." That would have had the appropriate personal touch and the requisite, not too recondite literary allusion. But today of course no live-wire editor would read any further, not because this sounds like a dull familiar essay but simply because it sounds like a familiar essay. But "Fish" is still a perfectly usable subject provided you remember that salable non-fiction "pieces" almost in-

"No Essays Please!" first appeared in *The Saturday Review,* March 10, 1951; it is included in a volume of Mr. Krutch's collected essays called *If You Don't Mind My Saying So,* William Sloane Associates, 1964. Reprinted by permission of the author and *The Saturday Review.*

variably fall into one of three categories: the factual, the polemic, and what we now call—though I don't know why we have to deviate into French—*reportage*.

If you decide to be factual a good beginning would be: "Four million trout flies were manufactured last year by the three leading sports-supply houses." That is the sort of thing which makes almost any editor sit up and take notice. But it is no better than certain other possible beginnings. The polemic article ought to start: "Despite all the efforts of our department of wild life conservation, the number of game fish in American lakes and streams continues to decline steadily." Probably this kind of beginning to this kind of article is best of all because it sounds alarming and because nowadays (and for understandable reasons) whatever sounds alarming is generally taken to be true. However, if you want to go in for the trickier *reportage* start off with a sentence something like this: " 'Cap' Bill Hanks, a lean, silent, wryly humorous down-Easterner probably knows more about the strange habits of the American fisherman than any man alive."

Of course no one will ever inquire where you got your statistics about the trout flies, whether the fish population really is declining, or whether 'Cap' Bill Hanks really exists. In fact one of the best and lengthiest "Profiles" *The New Yorker* ever ran turned out to be about a "character" at the Fulton Fishmarket who didn't. Whatever looks like official fact or on-the-spot reporting is taken at face value and will be widely quoted. The important thing is that the editor first and the reader afterwards shall get the feeling that what he is being offered is not mere literature but the real lowdown on something or other—whether that something or other is or is not anything he cares much about.

Fling your facts around, never qualify anything (qualifications arouse distrust), and adopt an air of jolly omniscience. Remember that "essays" are written by introverts, "articles" by extroverts, and that the reader is going to resent anything which comes between him and that lowdown which it is your principal function to supply. "Personalities," the more eccentric the better, are fine subjects for *reportage*. Manufacture or get hold of a good one and you may be able to do a "profile." But no one wants any personality to show in the magazine writer, whose business it is to be all-knowing, shrewd, and detached almost to the point of nonexistence. This means of course that your style should have no quality which belongs to you, only the qualities appropriate to the magazine for which you are writing. The most successful of all the magazines functioning in America today seldom print anything which is not anonymous and apparently owe a considerable part of their success to that fact that nearly everything which appears in them achieves the manner of *Life, Time,* or *Fortune,* as the case may be, but never by any chance any characteristic which would enable the most sensitive analyst of style to discover who had written it.

The ideal is obviously a kind of writing which seems to have been produced not by a man but by some sort of electronic machine. Perhaps in time it will actually be produced that way, since such machines now solve differential equations and that is harder to do than to write the average magazine article. Probably if Vannevar Bush were to put his mind to the problem he could replace the whole interminable list of editors, assistant editors, and research assistants employed by the Luce publications with a contraption less elaborate than that now used to calculate the trajectory of a rocket. Meanwhile the general effect of mechanical impersonality can be achieved by a system of collaboration in the course of which such personalities as the individual collaborators may have are made to cancel one another out.

This system works best when these collaborators are divided into two groups called respectively "researchers" and "writers"—or, in other words, those who know something but don't write and those who don't know anything but do. This assures at the very outset that the actual writers shall have no dangerous interest in or even relation to what they write and that any individuality of approach which might tend to manifest itself in one of them will be canceled out by the others. If you then pass the end-result through the hands of one or more senior editors for further regularization you will obviously get finally something from which every trace of what might be called handwork has disappeared. One might suppose that the criticism of the arts would be a department in which some trace of individuality would still be considered desirable, but I am reliably informed that at least at one time (and for all I know still) it was the custom to send an "editor" along with the movie critic to see every film so that this editor could tell the critic whether or not the film should be reviewed. This disposed of the possibility that the review might in some way reflect the critic's taste.

Obviously, few publications can afford the elaborate machinery which the Luce organization has set up. However, a great many strive to achieve something of the same effect by simpler means and they expect their contributors to cooperate by recognizing the ideal and by coming as close to the realization of it as is possible for an individual to come. The circulations achieved by these publications seem to indicate how wise from one point of view their policy is. Those which still permit or even encourage a certain amount of individuality in their writers, even those which still offer a certain amount of non-fiction which is to some extent personal and reflective as opposed to the factual and the bleakly expository —must content themselves with relatively small circulations. Moreover, since they also print a good deal of the other sort of thing they create the suspicion that they survive in spite of rather than because of their limited hospitality to the man-made as opposed to the machine-made article.

No doubt the kind of essay which *The Atlantic* and the old *Century* once went in for died of anemia. It came to represent the genteel tradition at its feeblest. No one need be surprised that it did not survive. But what is significant is the fact that whereas the genteel novel was succeeded by novels of a different sort and genteel poetry by poetry in a different manner, the familiar essay died without issue so that what disappeared was a once important literary form for which changed times found no use. And the result is that there disappeared with it the best opportunity to consider in an effective way an area of human interest.

Because the "article" is impersonal it can deal only with subjects which exist in an impersonal realm. If its subject is not ominous, usually it must be desperately trivial; and just as the best-selling books are likely to have for title either something like "The World in Crisis" or "My Grandmother Did a Strip Tease," so the magazine articles which are not heavy are very likely to be inconsequential. I doubt that anyone was ever quite as eccentric as almost every subject of a *New Yorker* profile is made to seem; but if a topic cannot be made "devastating" the next best thing is to treat it as "fabulous."

Perhaps what disappeared with the familiar essay was not merely a form, not merely even an attitude but a whole subject matter. For the familiar essay affords what is probably the best method of discussing those subjects which are neither obviously momentous nor merely silly. And since no really good life is composed exclusively of problems and farce either the reading of most people today does not actually concern itself with some of the most important aspects of their lives or those lives are impoverished to a degree which the members of any really civilized society would find it difficult to understand. Just as genuine conversation—by which I mean something distinguishable from disputation, lamentation, and joke-telling —has tended to disappear from social gatherings, so anything comparable to it has tended to disappear from the printed page. By no means all of the Most-of-My-Friends essays caught it. But the best of them caught something which nowadays hardly gets into print at all.

Somehow we have got into the habit of assuming that even the

so-called "human problems" are best discussed in terms as inhuman as possible. Just how one can profitably consider dispas-
sionately so passionate a creature as man I do not know, but that
seems to be the enterprise to which we have committed ourselves.
The magazines are full of articles dealing statistically with, for example, the alleged failure or success of marriage. Lawyers discuss
the law, sociologists publish statistics, and psychologists discuss
case histories. Those are the methods by which we deal with the
behavior of animals since animals can't talk. But men can—or at
least once could—communicate, and one man's "familiar essay" on
love and marriage might get closer to some all important realities
than any number of "studies" could.

No one is, to take another example, naive enough to suppose
that all the current discussions of the welfare state are actually as
"objective" as most of them pretend to be. Personal tastes, even
simple self-interest, obviously influence most of them, but only
insofar as they introduce distortions between the lines. Everybody
who writes for or against the competitive society tries to write as
though he did not live in it, had had no personal experience of
what living in it is like, and was dealing only with a question in
which he had no personal interest. This is the way one talks about
how to keep bees or raise the Black Angus. It is not the way either
the bees or the Black Angus would discuss the good life as it affected them, and it is a singularly unrealistic way of considering
anything which would affect us. Even the objective studies would
be better and more objective if their authors permitted themselves
freely to express elsewhere their "familiar" reaction to conditions
and prospects, instead of working these feelings in disguised as
logical argument or scientific deduction.

All the sciences which deal with man have a tendency to de-
personalize him for the simple reason that they tend to disregard

everything which a particular science cannot deal with. Just as medicine confessedly deals with the physical man and economics confessedly deals not with Man but with the simplification officially designated as The Economic Man, so psychiatry deals with a fictitious man of whom there would be nothing more to be said if he were "normal," and one branch of psychology deals with what might be called the I.Q. man whose only significant aspect is his ability to solve puzzles.

Literature is the only thing which deals with the whole complex phenomenon at once, and if all literature were to cease to exist the result would probably be that in the end whatever is not considered by one or another of the sciences would no longer be taken into account at all and would perhaps almost cease to exist. Then Man would no longer be—or at least no longer be observed to be—anything different from the mechanical sum of the Economic man, the I.Q. man, and the other partial men with whom the various partial sciences deal. Faced with that prospect we may well look with dismay at the disappearance of any usable literary form and wonder whether or not we have now entered upon a stage during which man's lingering but still complex individuality finds itself more and more completely deprived of the opportunity not only to express itself in living but even to discover corresponding individualities revealing themselves in the spoken or the written word.

That the situation could be radically altered by the cultivation of the familiar essay I am hardly prepared to maintain. Its disappearance is only a minor symptom. Or perhaps it is just a little bit more than that. At least there are a number of subjects which might profitably be discussed by fewer experts and more human beings. They might achieve a different kind of understanding of certain problems and they might lead to more humanly acceptable conclusions. "Most of my friends seem to feel that . . ."

from "On the Reading of Essays" by Russell Nye

To define an essay precisely is extremely difficult. It is at once apparent that the essay is as distinctively and fundamentally literary, and as demanding of skill and creative power, as poetry, fiction, biography, or drama. Etymologically, the word *essay* indicates something tenuous, tentative, or unfinished, so that the indefiniteness of the thing itself is firmly fixed in its name. Its inherent vagueness has become more vague by the operation of a sort of historical natural law; among the strays of literature, those mavericks whose ownership and bloodlines are uncertain have been usually branded as essays. In effect, the frontier between the essay and other literary forms is, as Carl Van Doren said, as imperceptible as the Mason and Dixon line, yet as clear to anyone who crosses it.

But an essay, difficult as it is to define, is nevertheless marked by certain characteristics. To varying degrees, it is personal, establishing a more or less direct relationship between writer and reader. Its purpose is primarily to stimulate interest, thought, and attention for a relatively brief period of time; secondarily, it may amuse, instruct, prove, convince, narrate, or explain. The essay style is individualized and subjective, attempting to say in prose what it has to say in the best possible manner and the most personal way. Its scope is elastic, adjustable to the topic and its treatment; it need not be complete, usually treating one or more facets of a subject with some sense of finish, or perhaps only suggesting a treatment. Structurally the essay has no set form; its arrangement and emphasis are governed by the internal requirements of the subject matter and the logic of the topic itself. Its organization may vary from the formal on one extreme to the casual and accidental on the other. The essay may be loosely defined as a short prose form, dealing with its subject in a more or less limited manner from a more or less personal viewpoint, with considerable latitude as to style, method, organization, and scope. Or as one essayist remarked succinctly, "I doubt if anyone could define the essay, but I see no reason why anybody should be afraid to write one if he has anything to say worth essaying."

Among essays it is possible to distinguish really only two types—the formal and the informal. Within these categories there are doubtless subdivisions and subclassifications, depending upon the degree of formality or informality perceived by the reader. However, for our purposes, it is enough simply to note that some essays are more formal than others, both in subject matter and treatment. We need not concern ourselves with subclassifications or even with the almost impossible task of trying to identify an "average" or "median" standard.

The "formal" essay presumes a formal personal connection between reader and writer, a direct but complex intellectual relationship controlled by a respect for forms and conventions. The point of view and manner of presentation are likely to be serious, the structure consciously planned, the style tight, formal, soundly thought out. Its formality does not necessarily eliminate humor or lightness of touch, but it does ordinarily exclude the random, ephemeral, and unimportant.

The "informal" essay implies a familiar, relaxed, personal communication between writer and reader, a simple, emotional, direct relationship. It conforms to no obvious pattern, its structural unity being obtained by consistency of mood, tone, or point of view. In it the personal element rules; its style is ordinarily conversational, colloquial, unstudied, impromptu, casual. Its treatment of the topic may be tentative, possibly unconventional or unique. The informal essay is most of all an interpretation of a personal reaction, given in familiar terms.

In either case, the formality or informality of an essay is so tenuous a thing that it is not possible to label all essays accurately as one or the other, except within certain blurred limits. It is not wholly a matter of seriousness of intent, or lack of it, nor of subject, nor of structure, nor of style. It is fundamentally a matter of the personal approach, whether it be in the temper of the street corner conversation or the seminar room.

For essays, like other forms of literature, are written to be read rather than dissected; but to gain the most complete understanding of the essayist's manner of solving the literary problems raised by the form, it is often worth while to spend some time in analyzing them. Ideally every essay should be read at least twice—once for dominant theme and impression, a second time for an awareness of structure, style, and those subtleties of thought and expression that form part of the total picture. There are, of course, essays that withstand many more than two readings, just as there are novels and poems that bear repetition. A good essay, since it is an expression of an interesting mind, can become an old and valued acquaintance. However, two aspects of the essay are worth watching in any number of readings—structure and style.

The term structure means the method by which an author orders and integrates his thoughts to accomplish a maximum of effectiveness. It is, in the larger sense, the design of the whole work, as important to the essayist as a plan is to the painter, novelist, architect, or musician. Studying the structure of an essay reveals to the reader the methods by which the writer functions; he repeats the steps through which the author has passed, grasping first the germinal idea, then the whole design, then the method by which it is inspected, developed, its facets polished.

The structure of an essay is not traditionally fixed like the structure of a novel or an epic, but instead grows naturally from the idea or mood of the essay itself. In the so-called formal essay it is often possible to distinguish a beginning, middle, and end, and to

identify some of the rhetorical and logical devices used for ordering
and developing ideas—in other words, to locate an externally im-
posed structure. The informal essay, fragmentary and incidental as
it sometimes is, does not submit to analysis so readily. Occasionally
it is without any structure at all in a normal sense; it has, however,
a unity of effect that serves as structure—a central point of view
that operates as a cohesive factor in holding it together, not by iron
bands but rather by rubber ones.

Writers employ two types of devices to obtain structural pattern
in the essay—the mechanical and the inherent, or to phrase it differently, the external and internal. Under the first heading fall such
things as divisions into sections or paragraphs, where the structure
is indicated by numbering, indentation, or typographical arrangement. Introductions, summaries, and directional words such as
such as, therefore, since, next, again, another, are similar methods
of obtaining organization. These are obvious, conventional devices,
easily recognized and comparatively unimportant in structural
analysis.

But there is, in certain subjects, a sense of structure inherent in
the topic itself, an intrinsic internal organization. Some subjects
naturally ask for chronological treatment, divide normally into important and unimportant, conform to some innate pattern of logic,
display cause-effect-relationships, or form chains of stream-of-
consciousness association. Practically all events or ideas fall into
some sort of pattern, studied or casual, which orders their arrangement. In so fluid a form as the essay, this organization of materials
may be vitally necessary to their effective presentation, or it may be
relatively unimportant to it. The arrangement itself may vary according to the purpose of the essay. Two writers dealing with the
same subject, but with different ends in view, probably will order
their materials in quite different structural patterns. Structure in the
essay is purposeful, and an analysis of structure is valuable for
comprehending that purpose. In any case, it is the only manner by

which the reader may perceive the skeleton beneath the flesh of writing, the framework on which the prose hangs.

Good writing is the basic ingredient of the essay, the quality most necessary to its success. Yet "style" is as indefinable as the essay itself, incapable of being caught, pinned down, and identified. It is possible, of course, to analyze an author's style by counting syllables and words, or by calculating predominant sentence patterns and rhythmic periods, or by describing his vocabulary, but the result is never the thing itself. Style is not a technical process, to be taught or learned from rule and precept, like timing an engine or brewing beer. It is how a thing is said, qualified by what is said —an interaction between matter and manner—thought shaping expression and being shaped by it. With clarity of idea and purpose, and taste and conviction in expression, style comes of itself, the way an athlete, after long training, does the right thing at the right time without awkwardness or wasted effort. . . .

Index

Page numbers in *italic* after authors' names indicate quotations or discussions.